Stephen Clarke

Stephen is a full-time journalist who specializes in travel and music. He has also written comedy sketches for BBC radio, gags for a stand-up comedian, and comic-book stories for the legendary American illustrator Gilbert Shelton.

Beam Me Up is Stephen's first full-length novel, and was inspired by a long-held belief that the world would be a much safer place if its political leaders modelled themselves either on female punk-rock singers or Star Trek's Captain Kirk. Or preferably both.

enjoy !

[signature]

Beam Me Up

or
A Brief History
of the Future

Stephen Clarke

First published 2004.

Red Garage Books

Website: www.redgaragebooks.com

ISBN 2-9521638-0-4
Printed by FERRAGE PATRICK DELTA PAPIERS
166, bd de Stalingrad 94200 IVRY/SEINE France

Cover illustrations by SC © 2004
Cover design by Nic B

Why is it that whenever a new technological breakthrough is reported, someone always compares it to Star Trek?

"Police are developing a phaser-like stun gun", "Scientists are developing a Star Trek-style teleporter" ...

Is it just journalistic laziness? Is it an attempt to make boring technology sound sexier?

Or is there something bigger going on?

In 1997, a team of scientists in Austria announced that they had carried out the first successful attempt at teleportation.

They were, the media said, "boldly going where no man had gone before."

This novel aims to answer the fundamental question: why the hell did they bother?

1. Shore Leave

The sun was melting the tarmac on the pavement or sidewalk. The taxis growled through the traffic like parched dogs. The omnipresent police cars were emblazoned with the NYPD motto, "courtesy, professionalism, respect", but inside them the officers looked sweaty and dangerous.

The upshot was that Richie suddenly loved shopping.

"Hey, 25% off all shoes. Let's have a look," he told his surprised wife, Clara. Then, in the next street, "Oh, yeah, those skirts are cool. Go in and try some on."

It was only when he developed an interest in furniture – a purchase unlikely to fit into their suitcases – that Clara twigged.

They were standing just inside the entrance of a swish sofa shop. It smelt of chilled leather. Richie turned his face up into the jet of ice-cold air streaming down from an overhead ventilator.

"It's the air-conditioning, isn't it?" Clara said.

"Course not," he assured her, discreetly taking a step backward so that the draught hit his shirtfront and freeze-dried the sweat on his stomach. "We're in the shopping capital of the world for a long weekend. You've got to make the most of it."

"Liar. I wondered why you kept hanging round near the door. You've just been ventilator-hopping across the city!"

By the time Richie's laugh had faded she was gone, swallowed by the throng. He looked both ways along the street and finally caught sight of her, doing ten miles an hour and accelerating. He enjoyed one last second of ice-cool air and set off in pursuit.

It defied the laws of physics, he thought. She was a foot shorter than him, but she could walk fast enough to make him jog just to keep up. He still wasn't gaining on her. She was swerving through the shopping crowds as if it was mid-December and she needed brisk exercise to stay warm. Half a minute outside the air-conditioning, Richie was getting up a mean sweat.

Richie was not a heat man. He lived in Bournemouth, England, where May had been cool and blustery, about twenty degrees cooler than here – centigrade, that is. He was too big for heat – a heavily built six foot five, an inch less than usual since he'd shaved his hair off the day before. Clara had screamed when she'd seen him emerge from the bathroom, but this city was just too hot for hair.

As he jogged along, he was heartened by a woman who looked as if both buttocks were pregnant, and who had a miniature Colorado River running down her rear canyon. Then immediately demoralized by a bare-shouldered Black kid whose bone-dry muscles hardly rippled as he walked. Talk about a melting pot, Richie thought, I'm draining away.

At last Clara slowed down. She was looking in the window of a shoe shop. He caught up and tapped her on the shoulder.

"Hi, Clara, remember me?"

"This is where I tried on those orange trainers. I'm going to buy them," she informed him.

"But they were over two hundred dollars!"

"Yes well, the shop's got to pay its air-conditioning bill, hasn't it?"

From his vantage point under yet another arctic hairdryer, Richie observed Clara. She was trying on the orange trainers. They suited her, unfortunately. They went well with the slight reddish tint in her dark brown hair – a legacy of her mum's Scottish genes. They'd look good with a tan as well, dammit. The salesgirl was chirpy. Clara must have already said she'd take them.

How could she even think about getting *more* items of clothing in this heat? It was as if one of those force-fed foie-gras geese had decided to nip out for a bag of chips.

Clara came over with a large, bright plastic bag and an equally large, bright smile.

"Why don't we take a rest from shopping now?" Richie pleaded. "Just go and chill out for an hour? Literally chill out, I mean."

"Fine," Clara agreed, taking his arm and steering him towards a coffee bar. "I need to work out which other shops I want to go back to."

Richie's groan was drowned out by the honking of five or six cars at once. A yellow taxi had stalled, and its overheated engine was puffing out a slow cloud of steam into the shimmering, polluted air. The afternoon sun was reflecting off the stalled car's windscreen or shield right into Richie's eyes.

They turned away from the hooting and walked past a multimedia store. In its window was a large poster of William Shatner, circa 1968, advertising a box set of Star Trek episodes. Even Captain Kirk looked faintly worried by the atmosphere in 21st-century New York.

2. The Origins of Man

The stranger seemed to arrive from nowhere.

One minute it was a blue, empty morning, the next he was standing there by the roadside.

His car was a dark-grey Ford with an Iowa license plate. But it didn't look like a local car – not enough dents.

Riverside, Iowa had seen strangers before. They came in carloads, campervanloads, in Star Trek fanclub minibusloads, for the annual Trekfest. Because Riverside (population 850) was, or is, or will be, the birthplace of James Tiberius Kirk, Captain of the USS Enterprise. Little Jimmy will be born there, so the future historians or historical futurists say, on March 22 in the year 2233, with light brown hair and hazel eyes.

Mr Muller, the owner of the Kirk Birthplace (known locally as "the empty lot where the barber's shop used to be"), looked out of his window at the stranger, who stood almost as tall as the large model of the USS Riverside on its pyramidal plinth.

This was a seven-foot-high plastic spacecraft, a not-quite-exact likeness of the Starship Enterprise. Initially, Muller had wanted to mount a bronze statue of Kirk himself, but Paramount had demanded $40,000 for the rights. Then he'd asked permission to set up a model of the Enterprise. Permission refused. So USS Riverside it was, with just enough differences in the spaceship's design to avoid a lawsuit.

Muller was curious. People often stopped off on their way somewhere to look the place over, even outside of Trekfest times. But this stranger was different. He wasn't taking photos. And he wasn't wearing a Captain Kirk t-shirt, Mr Spock ears, a Klingon uniform or any of the other accoutrements that the more extreme Trekkies wore on their pilgrimages to Riverside. This one was dressed in an open-neck safari shirt and chinos. Casually military-looking. Short-cropped grey hair and tanned face. He was standing there staring at the spaceship, a faint smile on his lips, as if he was dreaming.

But he must have been paying attention to his surroundings because he suddenly turned towards the house and caught Muller's eye. The stranger smiled at Muller and nodded.

"Good morning," he said pleasantly when Muller went outside two minutes later. Educated accent, Muller thought. Very white smile. Expensive smile.

"Morning," Muller said, and shook the outstretched hand.

"My name's Max."

"Sam."

"Sam Muller, right, you own Kirk's birthplace?" The stranger nodded beyond the spaceship to the empty lawn that would supposedly be the exact site of the birthplace in 2233.

"Yeah," Muller admitted warily. It suddenly occurred to him that this might be a taxman. The car looked kind of federal in a dusty way. And Muller didn't *always* declare *every* penny of the cash payments for the Kirk Dirt (soil dug up from under the lawn) he sold for $3 a vial. "I don't charge people to visit, you know," he said.

"Well maybe you should. As things stand, I don't see this town producing a starship captain." The stranger jabbed a thumb over his shoulder at the sleepy rural backdrop. Well, more comatose than sleepy, he thought.

"Validated by Mr Roddenberry himself," Muller defended his income.

"So I heard. Smart move on your part – you convinced him, right?"

"Yeah. I read in his book that Kirk was born in 'a small town in Iowa' so I asked why not Riverside, and Mr Roddenberry said first come, first served."

"A brilliant piece of entrepreneurship," the stranger said. He smiled with warm approval at Muller. This brilliant entrepreneur looked like most of the other people Max had seen on his way into town – late middle age, stocky, with plenty of rural German blood in his veins. Only difference was, he was wearing plain urban pants and shirt instead of the regional uniform of overalls and an old baseball cap. The only blemish on this urban sophistication was that he seemed to have pyjamas for underwear.

"But I can't get over the paradox of Kirk being a fictional character," the stranger went on, a teasing glint in his eyes. Piercing eyes, kind of icy blue. "So how come anyone wants to visit a real birthplace?"

Muller had heard this one before. There were people, not many but they existed, who came just to mock this quasi-religious infatuation with a mere TV character. Star Wars fans, mostly. Or journalists.

"You a reporter?"

"Oh no. An interested visitor."

Ultimately, Muller didn't give a damn what the stranger thought about the Trekkies. The fact was that the Star Trek link had revitalized, or at least saved from immediate extinction, a town that had been dying of old age, its young people sucked away to nearby Iowa City or beyond.

"Well, anyway, Mr Roddenberry agreed that this is the place, and he's the man who should know," Muller said.

The stranger laughed. "True, true. And he's dead now so there's no going back. This is the place." He looked around at the small wood-and-brick houses with their low picket fences and their little statues of the Virgin Mary in the front yard. Above the trees on the skyline, he could see the steeple of the redbrick Church of the Assumption. A sleepy Catholic town that called itself a city. "You tried to get someone to change their name to Kirk, didn't you?" he asked.

"Yeah."

"Did it work?"

"Sure. You can go have a beer with James T Kirk's future ancestors at the Bar Trek on Main Street." Muller didn't say this with his usual tourist-industry enthusiasm. There was something about the stranger that prevented him. Something cynical, mocking.

"OK, so you've got the name, but the whole genetic problem remains." The stranger pointed almost accusingly at Muller. "James T Kirk has to have ancestors that will produce a fearless leader of men, an ambassador for the human race. Not, with all due respect, a barman."

Muller didn't take kindly to this literalism. "I don't get you. You criticize people for talking about him like he was a real person and then you start doing the same."

"Yeah, I see your point." The stranger relaxed, smiled. "I guess you could say that Kirk is fictional now, but he has until the 23rd century to get real."

"Sorry?"

"I mean, you have Kirks in Riverside now, so what's to stop a boy called James being born into their family in the 23rd century?"

Muller was beginning to wish he'd stayed indoors. All in all, he preferred the guys with the Mister Spock ears. "Listen, Mister," he replied, "I was more worried about making it into the 21st century. Can you imagine this place without the Trekkies? They're going to be our only source of income until the 23rd century."

The stranger nodded. "Yes. You're right. Your problems are right here, right now. Mine are more in the future," he said. "That's why I'd like to buy it."

"The spaceship?" People had tried to steal it before but not buy it. This guy looked normal but he talked crazy. "We got postcards of it, or posters. Or you can get models of the real thing. The official licensed merchandising, I mean."

"No, no, the actual birthplace. This." The stranger swept his arm around to embrace the whole lawn.

"Oh. No. Sorry but it's not for sale. I make a good living from it. Enough to pay my taxes anyway," he corrected himself.

The stranger examined Muller for a moment, and then he reached into the breast pocket of his shirt and brought out a long, slim piece of paper. He held it towards Muller. It was a cheque, already filled out.

Sam Muller leaned forward and squinted at the figures.

"My only conditions are that the transaction remains a secret and you continue to run the place," the stranger said. "You can keep the profits."

Muller took the cheque, turned it over, ran his finger along the stiff edges of the paper. He felt tempted to smell it, like a melon, to see if it contained everything its colour promised.

He was used to living on the fringes of fact and science fiction. He found it hard to believe this cheque was fact.

3. Burger to Go

The trip to the café wasn't as relaxing as Richie had hoped. The iced latte was good, the seats comfortable, the air temperature perfect. But no matter how much he complimented Clara on her new shoes, she was determined to check out more shops.

"Look, I'm not trying to be awkward," he explained. "It's like Gulf War Syndrome. Shopping Fatigue is now a recognized medical condition. It's all to do with testosterone levels."

"Ah, they're what causes men to become balding, homophobic, macho slobs, aren't they?" Clara asked.

"No, that's *excessive* testosterone. I'm talking about normal male levels. Most women have very low levels. That's why you're so shopping-tolerant and we men suffer if exposed to prolonged high doses."

Clara leant across the table to kiss him.

"Tell you what, we'll split up. We'll meet back here in, say, an hour. OK?" she offered.

"You don't mind?"

"No. You've told me which skirts you liked. All I need to do is pay for everything. You've done all the hard work for me."

Clara left to do some spending. After buying a multi-storeyed veggieburger to go, Richie was surprised to find that he was being drawn towards another shop, too. Perhaps it was some addictive shopping drug that Americans had invented. They'd put it in Manhattan's coffee supply to give the economy a boost.

This was a gift shop. He stood in front of the window display (it was on the shady side of the street) and wondered about presents to take home for the kids. George, his four-year-old, would love a model taxi or a police car. Ella (six) was more difficult. She'd want something flashy. A "gift". He went inside.

Richie's first impression was that everything was too expensive. The shelves were packed with highly tasteful Americana. And there was a large sign – "Thank you for NOT eating" – by the door. He slipped himself and his burger behind a display and looked around in the vague hope of finding something fun like an Oprah Winfrey Barbie or an inflatable Hillary Clinton.

He could hear the shop assistant talking to a customer.

"For only five dollars extra, we can transport the gift instantly to your giftee."

"By courier, you mean?"

"No, I've never heard of an *instant* courier," the salesgirl replied with a schoolma'am's exaggerated patience.

"How, then?" The customer, a woman of about 45, had a classy, intelligent voice that the assistant seemed to be mistaking for ditheriness.

"Let me explain."

Richie caught sight of some model cars a few yards away. A copmobile and some vintage-looking limousines. He went to check them out. He half-listened to the assistant's attempts to explain her delivery service as he surreptitiously munched his burger. They seemed to be discussing a "biscotti machine" or something similarly Italian. What could Italian rusks have to do with sending presents to England, he wondered idly. A Mafia plot to assassinate the President with a rusk? He stopped in mid-munch as it dawned on him what they'd actually said.

It was so improbable that he came out into the open, at risk of having his burger confiscated.

"Yes, that's it," the assistant was saying with some relief.

She and the customer walked over to a small machine. Richie moved closer, holding his burger behind his back and feigning interest in what appeared to be a real bison-skin miniature bison. "Guaranteed farm-raised", it said. Bonsai bison?

"Gosh, I never knew they existed," the customer said.

"Yes, the system's only just been put in place."

Richie was even more convinced that he had heard right. Involuntarily he tightened his grip on the bison. It mooed; he winced. The assistant shot him a disapproving glare but carried on with her sales pitch.

"It's exactly like Star Trek, Madam," the assistant explained. "You give us the address, we beam it there."

"Yes, but how does it work?"

This was what Richie wanted to know. He held his breath, put down the bison without a moo, and edged closer. He was still stuck somewhere in the Great Plains, feeling the smoothness of an Apache-made buckskin cellphone holder.

"I'm not exactly sure," the assistant said. "We've only had it a week. I guess it breaks the object down into molecules, then reassembles it."

The customer was frowning, trying to work out whether she wanted her expensive gift broken down into molecules.

"It's fully guaranteed, Madam. If your gift gets broken in transit or reassembles wrongly, you get a refund."

"But you don't know how it works?" the customer asked, frowning even more doubtfully.

"No, Madam. But I don't know how a TV works either, and the picture seems to travel OK."

"Yes, I suppose you're right. Isn't technology wonderful? To think that, in a few seconds, this could materialize in front of my sister's eyes a thousand miles away."

"So do you want to try it?"

"Oh, no, thanks, I'll take it with me on the plane. If you could gift-wrap it for me ..."

"Certainly." The assistant hid her irritation well. "How will you be paying?"

As the two women went off to discuss credit cards and wrapping paper, Richie homed in on the machine. He'd given up all pretence of being interested in authentic American knick-knacks. Half a tepid burger clutched in his fist, he looked down on the transporter machine, much as stone-age man would have gazed at the first chocolate eclair.

It was nothing like the open-plan teleporter on the Enterprise. It had clearly been modelled on, or cannibalized from, a microwave oven. A metal box with a door in the front, linked up to a normal-looking computer. You could only transport things of a certain size. A football just about. A basketball was out of the question. The door was open, and all he could see inside was bare metal plating.

"Please don't touch that, Sir."

He looked up to see the assistant smiling nervously over at him. People often smiled nervously at him since he shaved his head.

"No, sorry. I was just wondering ..."

"I'll be with you in one moment, Sir."

He turned back to the machine. The metal box had an American makers' name that he didn't recognize, IOA Instruments. The computer was a standard make of PC. It looked as if you typed in the coordinates on the PC – must be some incredible software – then put your object in the box and hit return, and whoosh. Or maybe not whoosh. Maybe several minutes of gradual disappearance as the molecules were dematerialized. Not that he knew anything about molecules beyond faint memories of school blackboards and floppy models made out of drinking straws. But yuk, just imagine watching yourself disintegrate. That was probably why he'd never heard of the machine. They couldn't have tested the principle on people yet.

Even so, it was amazing. A real teleporter. He worked with computers every day, but one touch of this keyboard, and –

"Sir, please ..." the assistant called out.

Richie started, and his finger hit return.

There was a faint whirring from the machine.

Richie lifted his hands in the surrender position, but it was too late. Something was happening in there. The door was shut. He must have shut it, but couldn't remember doing so.

"Excuse me, Madam." The assistant was on her way, looking anxious but determined, like some rookie cop who has to deal with her first gang fight.

"I'm sorry. I don't know how ..." Richie did his best to look inoffensive, but in his case it wasn't easy.

The whirring had stopped. The computer played a major chord to express its self-satisfaction at having achieved something.

"Can I just get a look at the screen, please, Sir?"

Richie stepped aside, his hands still held up. He shot an "oo-er" look across at the customer, who turned away, exactly as you would if you were stuck on a train platform with a madman.

The assistant had called up some figures on the screen.

"Did you put anything in the machine, Sir?"

"No, of course not. Oh." Richie looked around – at the counter where the machine was standing, at the floor behind him – knowing it was hopeless. "My burger. I must have ..."

"A hamburger." The girl twitched with forced calm.

"Veggieburger. I'm a vegetarian." He hoped it might make a difference.

4. Calvin Declines

The President would be pissed.

In the American sense of the word, that is.

Max Blender had had few direct dealings with his leader before, but he suspected that the head of state would be far from happy. Far like Iowa is far from Saturn.

It would not be a good time for Blender to request vast amounts of money and logistic support for his project. Which was a damn shame, because that's exactly what he was scheduled to do in a few hours' time.

When they weren't outright dictators, world leaders were invariably puppets, of course. You could almost see the ventriloquists' hands stuffed up the back of their shirts, controlling their mouths. At any one time the President of the USA had dozens of hands up his back (or his more intimate rear area). The military, the judiciary, tobacco, oil, guns and every other lobby, the farmers, the unions, Congress, the Senate, public opinion, and if he was lucky, a hot young intern or two, all trying to manipulate him to their advantage.

And now Blender wanted to get his own hand up there, preferably without getting it too dirty. A tricky manœuvre, even metaphorically.

So it was a shame that the President would be pissed, and therefore keeping his metaphorical buttocks tightly clenched.

It was all a journalist's fault. Blender had read an article in that morning's Washington Post saying that the President was impotent. In the non-sexual sense of the word, that is. Since the invention of Viagra, erectile dysfunction was one less worry for most middle-aged men.

Even so, it was a potent insult. And according to the article, the President wasn't only impotent – he was also boring. The headline was "Grey Man in the White House".

Blender's initial reaction was, so what? Maybe it wasn't a bad thing for him to be boring compared to some of his predecessors, who'd been bare-faced liars, bare-cheeked adulterers, or shot. Or more than one of those.

The writer went on to say that it was a relief to have a bore in the White House. It proved, he suggested, that real executive power was "in the hands of people who know how to use it", and confirmed the fact that modern presidents were little more than TV news anchormen, presenting other people's decisions to the world.

The President would almost certainly not see the article itself – rumour had it that he rarely read anything except golf magazines, Patricia Cornwell novels and the instructions on pretzel packets. But it would be picked up on the morning news, and apparently the President always watched that to see whether his previous day's soundbites had made the grade.

Getting laughed at on TV was bound to inflame the President's ego. He'd try to resist the twists of the ventriloquists' fingers. His advisors wouldn't let this situation last for very long, but even if it lasted for just one meeting – Blender's meeting – it could have dire consequences.

Sitting on the morning flight from Des Moines to Washington, Blender let the newspaper fall into his lap and stared angrily out over the vast Iowan flatness. Why had the journalist picked today to unleash his unhelpful opinions on the world? Couldn't he have chosen a weekend edition so that the President had time to forget the insults by Monday?

The article ended with a crushing quote from ex-President Calvin Coolidge: "It is a great advantage to a president, and a major source of safety to the country, for him to know that he is not a great man."

Not great? Shit, the President was going to be so pissed that it would ruin his after-lunch nap.

5. Evasive Action

The sales assistant opened the door of the machine, and bent down gingerly to look inside, as if scared of finding the container splattered with soya remains.

"Hmm." She didn't look disgusted, only perplexed.

Richie leaned forward to get a better view. "It's clean enough in there. No damage done, I hope." He doubted that his travel insurance covered wrecking a teleporter.

"Well, I don't know. It's not designed to transport burgers."

"What is it designed to transport?"

"Only certain types of gift. But you just transported your burger to ..." She clicked on a command and the screen showed an address. "A Mrs JP Gonzalez in Dade County, Florida."

"Wow. Do you think Mrs Gonzalez could send it back?"

Richie wasn't sure himself if he was joking or not, but the girl didn't laugh anyway.

"Sir, I don't think you realize. As a precaution, we always call first and warn the recipient that something is about to be transported. If I don't key in their permission, the machine won't send."

"What if they're out?"

"Sir, that's irrelevant in this case. I don't know how you managed to send your burger. We sent Mrs Gonzalez a crystal vase a few minutes ago. Maybe there's a bug in the system that lets you send two objects to the same address. I don't know." The girl's annoyance with him had started to turn into fear for her job.

Richie sympathized. "So presumably you called her earlier?" he asked.

"Yes."

"Is that her phone number there?" He pointed to the screen.
"Yes."

"Well, if you want to finish up with your customer, why don't I give her a call?" Richie pointed to the telephone by the computer.

The assistant was suspicious, but the customer had overheard, and made a gesture showing, in the politest possible fashion, that she was impatient to get the hell away from this lunatic. Richie gave an encouraging nod to the assistant, and she agreed.

"OK. Will you tell her it was your fault?" she asked.

"No problem," Richie smiled, using the phrase that Americans seemed to love best.

He dialled and waited for an answer. The two women were conducting a whispered conversation. A credit card was returned to the customer.

"Hello?" said a crackly voice with a Spanish accent.

"Hello, Mrs Gonzalez. I'm glad I caught you." Richie smiled over to the women, who were watching him intently. "I think I just teleported a veggieburger to you – … A veggieburger, you know – a hamburger without meat … Er, soya, I suppose … Genetically modified? I hadn't thought of that." Richie grimaced and turned away from the women. He was not handling this conversation well.

"Mrs Gonzalez? You just received a crystal vase, right? … A *vaahz* … Ah, I mean *vaice* …" (He was forgetting the American mispronunciation.) "Listen, Mrs Gonzalez. Just after you received the *vaice*, I accidentally teleported a veggieburger to you," he said. "Is it next to the *vaice*? Or in it? … Well could you have a look, please?" He waited as the woman pitter-patted across the room, then he heard a man's voice. She came back on the phone, and began to complain about black dust. "Black dust?" Richie said. "I don't know – … No, I didn't – … Look, all I know is that my burger seems to be lost somewhere between New York and Florida. If you find it, it's all yours."

He rang off and put his phone away. The customer was scuttling off towards the entrance. The assistant was staring at Richie.

"No burger," he said. "Where's it gone?"

"What was that about black dust?" the assistant asked. She began walking towards Richie and the machine, obviously convinced that he had screwed up her brand-new sales tool.

He was almost glad to get outside into the char-grilled street again.

Gene Roddenberry (1921-91), the creator of Star Trek, was a bomber pilot in the Second World War. He later joined the LAPD, where he wrote speeches for the police chief. As we've all seen in films like LA Confidential, the LAPD of the 50s was famous for its, let's say, unconventional morals. So it's not surprising that Roddenberry began to look for an outlet to express more idealistic views.

When he first had the idea for Star Trek in 1963, it was as a TV series about a multi-racial group of people in the 19th century visiting undiscovered cultures in a hot-air balloon. Luckily, his agent persuaded him to turn the balloon into a spaceship. Otherwise the teleportation machine would never have been invented.

A Brief History of the Future, chapter 1 (extract)

6. Fruitcake and Ketchup

The protocol was that the President considered a new idea and came to a carefully thought-out decision, but only after his policy advisors had told him what he was going to decide.

Today, though, the President wasn't sticking to protocol.

"So our boys get in a teleporter on their base and then five seconds later a division of US Army goulash materializes in the warzone? Forget it."

The nine other people in the room winced. Even those who agreed with him didn't want to hear him say it like that. The room was decorated for decorum, not gore. The long, oval table was crafted out of best American maple and polished so brilliantly that you could read the insignia on your gold buttons. The uniforms, the dark, expensive suits and the well-trimmed hair were all designed for civilized interchange. It was a Defense Committee but that didn't mean there had to be offence.

Each time Blender met the President, he was fascinated and horrified, rather like when he'd first seen the mandibles of a tarantula under a microscope. From a distance, or on TV, the President looked – well, like the President. An unchanging whole. The grey haircut that never seemed to grow to any different shape or length. The famous features. The suit or occasionally the golfwear. Yes, like Barbie's Ken, there was more than one model, but they were only models.

Now here was the President, looking all too human, just as the tarantula had turned out to have huge jaws and half a dozen eyes hidden away in its general furriness. He was looking even more human than usual – Blender could see the twinges of temper at the corner of the President's mouth and some tiny patches of hurriedly shaven cheek. He must have shaved after (or while) watching the news.

One of the older men in the room, a uniformed general called Colt, was looking especially earnest. Or trying to anyway – his cap had left a red welt across his forehead that made him look as if he'd just got out of electro-shock treatment.

"Sir, we must have permission to develop the transporter's military capacity. It has to be able to transport men," the general said, a faintly insane glow in his eyes.

"Well, I just don't think I can give you that permission," the President replied.

The general was instantly exasperated. "But it's vital for our country's stability and security, Sir."

The President ignored him. "How do these things work, anyway?" he asked.

A different general took over. A younger man called McNulty.

"Sir, if you look at page, uh ..." General McNulty opened his file, "nineteen of your dossier ..." He looked up, waiting for the President to follow suit. The President continued staring defiantly at the general. Partly to be obstructive, but mainly because he'd forgotten his bifocals. "Uh, it explains, Sir," the general went on, "that the technology is derived from experiments into the Einstein-Podolsky-Rosen paradox. The paradox states," he read, "that two particles may become 'entangled'. If this occurs, both particles are part of the same quantum system, and anything you do to one of them affects the other in identical fashion. It's therefore theoretically possible to transfer the properties of one particle to another particle, even if it's at the other end of the galaxy. In short –"

The President sighed. So did Blender, who understood the technology better than anyone but who also knew that there was absolutely no point trying to explain the details to a layman.

The general trailed off. There was an embarrassed silence in the room.

Blender leaned forward and placed his hand in the centre of the table. He faced the President and gave him a chance to make eye contact. He felt the head of state checking through the gallery of faces in his memory, thinking, where had they met? At the Pentagon, wasn't it? Yes, a scientist. Straight-talking kind of guy, though. Firm handshake.

Blender thought he saw a glimmer of approval on the presidential face, and spoke up.

"Basically, Sir," he said, "the machine analyses a particle, like an electron or an atom, at Point A, and transfers all its properties to another particle at Point B."

"Uh-huh." It was the most positive thing the President had said since the meeting began. "But have you actually tried transporting people yet?" he asked.

"Anything with a simple molecular structure – metals, artificial plastics, crystals such as silicon – is completely problem-free, Sir," Blender replied. "Machines, electrics ..."

"People?" the President repeated.

"No, Sir. But we're almost ready to begin."

The President shook his head. "This is too big. It's a global thing. A UN thing. And I know the UN won't back it being used for military purposes. I can hear them now, saying it would be just another tool for ethnic cleansing. You could feed entire populations through it and cleanse the hell out of a whole continent."

"But equally, Sir," General McNulty argued, "you could transport an army in to stop that kind of thing."

"Come on, general, you know the UN. They want us to send men in in blue trucks. It's got to be slow and laborious, otherwise they don't get any TV exposure."

The President's advisors winced again. Even in closed committees, American policy was not to knock the UN – it was to ignore it. Totally different.

"We could paint the men's helmets blue before we teleport them, Sir," General Colt said.

The collective groan around the table was almost audible.

At first sight, the 1935 Einstein-Podolsky-Rosen paradox seems to be a very dull paradox. So what if two particles can or can't become entangled?

You might suppose that Einstein himself thought it was dull, because he gave 66.6666% of the credit to two unknown young colleagues, Boris Podolsky and Nathan Rosen.

But in fact, it's not dull at all. Einstein and special guests were being provocative. They were saying that pairs of particles that became entangled shouldn't exist.

Because when the particles moved apart again, they remained part of the same quantum system. So theoretically, if you sent the two particles to opposite ends of the universe and started fiddling with one of them, you would instantaneously affect the other one. You would be transmitting information faster than the speed of light, which would contradict Einstein's theory of relativity. The old man wasn't too happy about that.

Ever since, scientists have been trying to overcome the scepticism embodied in Einstein's paradox. It's taken them 60 years to do it, too. He was a real shit-stirrer, that Einstein.

A Brief History of the Future, chapter 1 (extract)

7. A Brief History of the Future

All that evening, Richie was distracted. He was usually very attentive to Clara when they went out, even more so since they'd had the children, as if their time alone together had become doubly precious. But that night, as they sat in a crowded family restaurant in Little Italy, he was somewhere else. He chomped on slices of their tractor-wheel-sized "regular" pizza and stared into the middle distance.

"Don't worry, if you did burn out the machine, they'll never find you," Clara reassured him.

Richie didn't look reassured. He shifted uncomfortably in his chair, which creaked for mercy under his weight. Judging by the girth of the other diners in the restaurant (they ranged between Barry White and Shrek), the chairs got quite a bit of punishment.

"And even if it materialized somewhere dangerous," Clara went on, "in someone's brain or something, who's going to know where it came from? In any case, I doubt if attempted manslaughter by means of a teleported veggieburger is on the statute books yet, even in America."

"Thanks a bunch." They never had that problem in Star Trek. Richie tugged on a long string of mozzarella that was attempting to maintain a bridge between his mouth and the plate. "But I don't think I burned out the machine. I reckon the dust was the remnants of the burger. Must have burned up in transit. A crystal vase can survive higher temperatures than a burger." He popped the rolled-up cheese into his mouth. "Guess that limits the potential for human teleportation. And instant fast-food delivery."

"Talking of which, isn't this the best pizza you've ever had?" Clara wanted to steer him away from the thorny subject of teleportation.

"Yeah." But he was back in the middle distance again.

Clara refilled his wine glass with Californian Valpolicella. "Come on, Richie, what is it?" she asked him.

"It's that machine. I feel like –" He stopped and wiggled his fingers as if clutching for his words in the air.

"Like?"

He drank a big slug of the gullet-burning wine before answering. "I feel I've missed out. Like when you've seen a really beautiful girl, and you've maybe said a couple of words to her and then gone on your way, and you think, shit I ought to have got her phone number. You know?"

"No, I don't. And I would have hoped it was a feeling you didn't get that often either these days." Clara pretended to sulk.

"Well, I feel like that about the machine. I want it."

"What for?"

"Come on." Richie's face suddenly brightened. "It's real. I mean, it used to be science fiction and now it's *real*. You can actually teleport things. It's as big a jump as getting to the Moon."

Secretly, Clara agreed, but didn't admit it. "What do you need a machine for? It probably wouldn't even work in Europe."

"Yeah, but can you imagine Martin's face when I walk into –"

"Oh, now I get it." Clara threw her slice of pizza melodramatically down on the plate. "When will you stop trying to impress that bloody brother of yours?"

"I'm not –"

"Yes you bloody are. What has he ever done for you? He uses you –"

"He does not. He employs me."

"Employs? You call that employment?" Despite the ambient noise level of chat and Italian pop, other eaters looked across at Clara as she got into her rhythm. "He uses you as a bloody guard dog."

"That's not fair."

"No, it isn't, and I don't know why you put up with it. You sit about in that shop of his and then when it suits him, he takes you along to scare some poor sod into coughing up money." The other diners were intrigued but clearly confused. The subject matter was perfectly apt for Little Italy, they seemed to be thinking, but how come the British accents?

Richie held his hands up in defeat. He knew it wasn't worth arguing.

"What is it with you and that little brother of yours?" Clara was asking herself more than Richie.

He shook his head and emptied his glass. It was a question he couldn't answer, even though he'd been asking it himself for years.

For a start, his little brother was actually his big brother. Two years older although a good nine inches shorter. And Richie was using his brother as much as his brother was using him, which Clara knew very well.

Martin had set up a computer-game shop while Richie was away at college. When Richie had returned with his English degree but no idea what to do with it, Martin had given him a summer job helping out in the shop. That was seven summers ago, and now Richie was officially in charge of the shop's stock of new and second-hand games. But if he'd been the ambitious type, he would have considered himself a dismal failure, because the stock had dwindled to almost zero.

The shop was located on a steep hill just outside Bournemouth's town centre, and most of their potential customers rumbled past on buses or in cars. The shopfront was originally painted a lurid green, but this had now faded and dirtied to a dull puce, and Martin couldn't be bothered to repaint. Richie knew that the shop's sign would attract little passing trade – since it had lost a letter it looked like an illiterate ad for a British novelist: MARTIN'S AMES.

No, what income the shop earned came from Martin's side of the business, a sort of hack-u-like service.

In the far corner of the back room, Martin ran his cottage industry. Finding out for one of his carefully-filtered clients which online banking services were vulnerable. Helping to set up websites selling non-existent merchandise at such low prices that people couldn't resist offering up their credit-card numbers. Occasionally teaching a client how to plant porn in the deeper recesses of someone's hard disk prior to a bit of blackmail. All of this was billed as "computer training" or a phantom sale.

Martin never did the planting or defrauding himself, just provided the information. That wasn't a crime, Richie told himself, unsure whether he was right or not.

Richie worked at a desk in the shop. He was rarely disturbed by customers. He did a bit of research on the web for Martin, sold the (very) occasional game to some mug who didn't know he could get it cheaper on the web or in a megastore, and went along for the ride when Martin collected large cash payments. There was never any violence involved, because Martin worked for a small group of regular customers. He just wanted Richie along to stop anyone getting silly ideas. "Guard dog" wasn't a bad description, especially as his salary was only about enough to buy dog food.

However, Richie didn't complain, because in return he got plenty of time to do what he really wanted. He was, he informed his scornful mates, an almost full-time writer. He was getting paid for writing a book, a Brief History of the Future. "A what?" his friends asked, and then when he explained, "why?"

People's memories were so short, Richie thought. Who could remember a time before mobile phones or cash dispensers? This was what his book was about. The time when a computer the size of a London bus would be asked to calculate two plus two, telling its inventors three days later that the answer was a piece of perforated cardboard.

Richie had taken all the greatest works of sci-fi (plus a few of his favourite non-sci-fi works), and put them in a Top Twenty based on the accuracy of their predictions about the future and their influence on the global psyche – from Wells's Martian invasion, to Adams' paranoid android and Roddenberry's Star Trek.

The chapters were in reverse order, a countdown from twenty ending in the undisputed number one – Roddenberry.

Richie's central premise was not that these people were clairvoyant. It was that the best sci-fi inspired scientists to follow up their leads. That's why Star Trek was such a clear winner. Why else did we now have needle-less syringes and computerized beds capable of medical diagnosis? Electric sliding doors were only a dream when Roddenberry installed them on the Enterprise. A lot of mobile phone design was obviously copied from Star Trek communicators, and how come modems make that Star Trek whooshing-beeping noise when they're hooking up to the internet?

Of course Richie would have to rewrite his final chapter – when he'd started, he had no idea that the teleporter had really been invented. It must have been a closely-kept secret.

But the rest of the book was ready: two hundred pages, checked and re-checked, ready to print. A surefire hit aimed shamelessly at the pub quiz market – intelligent, but with a dash of alcohol poisoning. And a large chunk of the credit had to go to Martin, who'd given him the time to do it all.

So what was it between the two of them? Why the antagonism? And what bugged Richie most, and Clara even more, why did Richie still show a masochistic compulsion to impress his little big brother? He knew Martin was an unreliable, malicious bastard who missed no opportunity to drop Richie into the shit whenever he could. So why did he now want to spend a fortune (a teleportation machine was bound to cost a fortune) just to impress his brother?

Clara, as ever, was reading his mind.

"You don't have to buy one. You can look it up on the web and write about it. I mean, you didn't buy a lunar module, did you?"

"I know," Richie agreed.

"If you take one of those machines back, he'll steal it off you and sell it. Or take it to pieces. Or anything just to piss you off."

"I know," Richie said helplessly.

"Forget the bloody machine," Clara told him.

"I can't. I want to buy one. Not for Martin, for me. And not just to write about it."

"Why then?"

"I don't know. I can't explain it. It's like, could you explain why you have to have a pair of orange trainers?"

Clara brushed aside his irrelevant anti-shopping jibe. "Well we said we'd go to Coney Island tomorrow." She sounded pretty determined. "Who won this trip anyway?" she demanded.

"I did. If I remember rightly, your exact words were: 'oh no, you're not entering another hopeless newspaper competition.'"

"Exactly. You won it. I'm the guest. So I get to choose what we do." Clara stuffed the last bit of pizza into her mouth and sat back in her chair, replete. No way was she spending good money on what would turn out to be a present for Martin, even if it wasn't intended as such. She only tolerated the prat because she knew how important it was for Richie to finish his book. And now it was finished she wanted Richie out of his brother's clutches. One day, she knew, things would go wrong and the father of her kids would disappear for a couple of years in prison. If Richie could accidentally teleport a burger to Florida, she shuddered to think what bright ideas

Martin would come up with. He wouldn't get his own fingers dirty, of course. He'd want Richie to press return.

The American police have long been looking for a solution to the age-old problem of shooting unarmed suspects. One trigger-happy officer could provoke weeks of race riots.

First they conducted trials with a gun that fired a sort of Spiderman goo, which didn't prove too practical – unless you managed to goo a suspect's legs, he could still run away. All he'd have to do was wait until the goo hardened then ask a friend to chip it off with a chisel or power drill – easy.

So more recently, the police have been working with a company in California that has come up with a "freeze ray" which fires an electric current along a beam of ultraviolet light up to a range of 300 feet. It causes the target's muscles to contract, and induces short-term, total paralysis. The police are apparently very enthusiastic about the results. No mess, no escapes.

Basically, they can't wait to start firing Star Trek phasers.

A Brief History of the Future, chapter 1 (extract)

8. Eco-weapons

"Sir, just think. A hit squad could teleport into the bedroom of any dictator or terrorist you want to name. He'd tragically die in his sleep. No explosion, no murder weapon, no liberal outcry, nothing."

For the first time, the President thought he'd heard someone talking sense. Blender saw that he'd opened a breach and permitted himself the faintest of smiles.

"And if we start experimenting on mammals now, Sir," he said, "we can also begin work on a protective screen, to prevent certain terrorist powers beaming their people into the White House."

"Into the White House?" The President looked with faint alarm at the ancient, solid walls around him, made even more solid (he'd thought) by the robust golden-framed pictures of his predecessors hanging on them.

"It's a real danger, Sir. That's why we've got to stay ahead of the pack," Blender said. "No one has developed a more powerful version of these machines yet, but they're sure as hell going to try."

"So we make certain they don't get their hands on our technology," the President said.

"The small machines have gone on public sale, Sir, remember. There has been little or no publicity about the launch, but that doesn't mean it will have gone unnoticed. Our enemies may be dismantling one as we speak. I'm not saying the Chinese are our enemies, of course ..." Blender smiled diplomatically. "For the moment, trade between our countries is worth over $100 billion a year, mostly in their favour. And they're spending a sizeable chunk of the profits on technology of, uh, all sorts." He raised his eyebrows. People knew what he was implying – weapons. "We need to show the world, including China, that there are things beyond nuclear weapons technology. So if and when the Chinese economy reaches some kind of plateau, they're in no way tempted to take the military option."

The President was nodding to himself. Blender hoped the message was clear – basically, if he said no, one day soon a killer was going to beam in and slit his, or a successor's, throat.

"Well, there's nothing to stop us conducting preliminary tests, I suppose," the President conceded, involuntarily looking over his shoulder to ward off a materializing attacker.

"Thank you, Sir, a wise decision."

The advisors were doing their usual wincing thing, but the other faces around the table looked happy.

"I don't know how Congress will feel about military spending being given over to Star Trek instead of Star Wars, but I can live with that." The President got a laugh from the happy side of the table.

"We'll be conducting the tests in Iowa, Sir. A long way from Congress," Blender said.

"A long way from anywhere," the President said.

"Right," Blender said. "One other thing, Sir. We were hoping that you'd announce the testing when you go to England."

"Announce it?" The President was alarmed again.

"Yes. At the eco-summit in England."

"Announce military testing at an eco-summit? The press'll lynch me."

The advisors nodded in agreement for once.

"You could always announce that you'd be scaling down your nuclear capacity if all goes well," Blender suggested. "That's pretty ecological."

"What if all doesn't go well?"

"Sir, nothing controversial ever happens in Iowa," Blender said. "Nothing happens period. We aim to keep it that way for, oh, at least the next two hundred years."

9. Sex in the Morning

Clara waited for Richie to come back to bed. This was the best thing about being away from the kids – the long morning shag.

She'd felt him get up a minute ago. He never made love in the morning without having a pee first.

She thought it over – did she want a pee first? No, she was OK. She'd got up in the night. So now she could lie back and enjoy the feeling of sprawling naked under the single sheet in their deliciously air-conditioned room, with no worries about the kids bursting in and interrupting coitus. The bed squeaked a bit, but they'd take it slow. Then have a long shower and a lazy breakfast. Make the most of their last full day in New York.

She broke off her daydreaming.

"Richie?"

There was no reply from the bathroom, because Clara had dozed for almost half an hour between registering that Richie wasn't in bed and being awake enough to wonder why.

He got off the subway at West 4th Street station and walked a couple of streets over to the gift shop. He was banking everything on the shop being open and a different girl being on duty. If either one of these conditions wasn't met, he didn't know what the hell he'd do – give up or steal the machine, or anything in between.

It was the only way to do it. She'd never have agreed to come with him. Richie even hoped, unrealistically, that he'd be able to get back to the hotel with his prize before she woke up. That was why he hadn't bothered to leave a note.

A man's gotta do what a man's gotta do, he'd have said. Yeah, like fart in bed and scratch his scrotum, she'd have replied.

It was after nine and hot already, but Richie noticed the heat less acutely than before. Maybe it was his sense of purpose, he thought. He had something more important than his physical comfort to worry about.

The shop was open. Yes. One down, one to go.

He walked in, flinching at the electronic buzz as he stepped past the sensor. He knew there was probably a camera on him too, but tough. If the same assistant was on, he'd just walk out again. Or would he? Depends if she looks pissed off or not, he decided.

Beyond the shelves of gifts, he could see an older woman in a white blouse, forty maybe, Hispanic-looking. Kind, motherly face. It was a different assistant. Two conditions out of two. Yes.

What's more, he was the only customer. Three out of two.

He grabbed a bonsai bison from the miniature herd on display and marched towards the counter.

"Hi, I'd like to send this to the UK," he said. "What's the quickest way?"

"Fedex," the woman said.

"Fedex?"

"Yeah, Fedex," The woman answered nervously. The shaven-headed giant didn't look pleased with her answer.

"Don't you have –?" Richie gestured over towards the machine and almost dropped the bison.

The machine was gone. In its place was approximately half a cubic metre of nothing.

The woman's nervousness doubled. The customer looked like a blond version of that TV gangster guy. Soprano, the psycho who was all smiles until you crossed him, then he had his hands round your throat and was threatening to eat your babies. This one had a tourist's accent but a New Jersey head.

Richie stood with the bison in his outstretched arm.

"Didn't you have one of those teleportation machines?" he asked. "I came in yesterday and your colleague offered to, you know, *beam* stuff for me."

"Yeah. The machine's broken. Sorry."

"Broken?"

Again, he didn't look pleased with her reply. As if he didn't believe her. "Yeah, it – what they say? – overrode the send protocol or something. We had to get the OK every time we sent something, and it sent something without my co-worker typing in the OK."

"What did it send?"

"What did it send?"

"Yes. Without your co-worker giving the OK."

The woman looked embarrassed, as if he was going to think that her reply was stupid. "A hamburger," she said. "It's not supposed to send food."

But the giant smiled, not mockingly at all. He looked pleased.

"You don't know where they took it, do you?" he asked.

"No. Why?"

Richie hesitated. Should he own up to his guilty secret?

Clara's first-prize, all-expenses-paid, four-star last day in Manhattan was starting very badly. She tried to phone him, but couldn't get a signal. How the hell can they call it a mobile phone when you can only use it in one country, she thought. How "mobile" is that? The American name's better – cellphone. You can only get in touch with someone if you're sharing a cell with them.

She got hurriedly dressed and cursed the lift (or elevator) as it stopped on almost every floor between twenty and one (or zero).

Richie wasn't at any of the breakfast tables, which were occupied by a bizarre mixture of tourists in t-shirts, and businesspeople in strict suits that would turn into portable saunas as soon as they stepped outdoors.

Clara couldn't go and ask someone "have you seen my husband?". She was pretty sure where he'd gone anyway. The choice now was between a leisurely shower followed by a long, free breakfast or an immediate dash across town in the faint hope of catching up with Richie in time.

She went over to the buffet, took a bite out of a huge Danish, spluttered her room number and a hail of crumbs at a young waitress, and then ran past reception in a decidedly un-four-star fashion.

"You see, it's like a childhood dream come true," Richie said. "The idea that things can really be teleported. It's almost as if Captain Kirk and Mister Spock had come to life."

The shop assistant wasn't a Star Trek fan, but like all Americans she was moved by the sight of someone chasing a dream.

"We got the manual in back," she said. "There's an address on that."

"Brilliant."

"Wait here." She smiled at him. He had a cute accent. He might have Soprano's head but he was more like that English Star Wars guy, Ewan something. Only not so faggy-sounding.

She went into the office and returned with a small black-and-white printed manual and a pencil.

"Here," she said. She held up the manual, back page forwards, while Richie jotted the address down on one of the gift shop's cards.

"How do I get to Canal Street?" he asked.

She explained – it was just two subway stops away.

"I don't know how to thank you," Richie said as he backed towards the door, like a grateful subject not daring to turn his face away from the Queen.

"You can pay for that buffalo," the assistant said.

Approximately forty minutes later, Clara arrived in the neighbourhood. She made directly for the café in the Village where they'd decided to split up during their shopping trip.

She looked both ways down the narrow street. There was an Asian grocery store, a Brazilian club, her shoe shop. Nothing that might contain souvenirs and a teleportation machine. What should she do now? Start a grid search of the neighbourhood? Go back to the hotel? Grab the first man she saw and hit him for belonging to such a stupid gender?

She chose a direction and walked. She was almost certain that Richie had said the shop was right near the café. And he wouldn't have walked one step more than necessary in that heat.

She passed the Asian grocery store, another coffee shop, a tiny lunch bar that was just receiving its morning delivery of bagels, then, on the corner of the street, she found herself outside a taxi-yellow shopfront with a Warhol poster of the Mona Lisa on one side of the glass door and a Native-American rug on the other. Richie had mentioned Apache crafts. This could be it.

She mounted the single step to the door and pushed. It was locked.

Clara stared at the thick pane of glass in disbelief. The column of credit-card stickers above the wooden base of the door seemed to form an obscene middle-finger gesture at her.

"Bugger."

She grimaced at her reflection in the glass door and was surprised to see that she had grown a second head.

"I just went to get a cup of coffee." Pronounced caw-fee.

Clara turned and saw the paper cup before she saw the rest of the woman.

"That's OK," Clara said. "I'm just glad you're open."

"Hey, you're English," the woman said, fiddling with the doorkey. "There's a lot of you around this morning."

Canal Street was long and hot and busy, but it felt right. There were vans loading or unloading pallets of electrical goods in large boxes. There were shopfronts crammed with cameras, stereos and computers. And a man in a torn t-shirt and baseball cap puffing as he carried what looked like a microwave oven to his open car.

Richie checked the street numbers and set off towards his goal. He almost wanted to run. Best not to look too keen, though. From what he'd heard about this street, you had to bargain, and keen customers pay high prices. As he approached the address he'd been given, he slowed to an amble.

It was a small shop window, piled high with digital cameras, MP3 players and other shiny consumer durables, all labelled with handwritten cards that promised the best prices in town, as did every other shop Richie had passed.

He spent a symbolic moment looking in the window and then walked inside.

Like its window, the shop was full of boxes and labels, except for a tiny space in front of a low glass counter. Richie just had time to get used to the sudden shock of the air-conditioning before a young Asian girl emerged from a back room.

"Yeah?" she said, tucking a strand of bleached hair behind her ear. She too had obviously been told that being keen didn't get you a good deal.

"Hi," Richie said.

How did you say the next bit without seeming ridiculous? He looked quickly around the shop for a box marked "Teleporter – cheap price!" There didn't seem to be one. He became uncomfortably conscious that the girl was staring up at him.

"Have you got," he began. "I'm looking for, well, thinking about buying anyway," he gestured towards a camera. "A, er, teleportation machine."

"Agh!" the girl shouted, and turned away.

Richie was confused. She didn't looked shocked or in pain.

A young Asian guy in a stars and stripes t-shirt appeared from the back room. This, Richie decided, had to be Agh, or some similar name (in fact, the guy's name was An). He was muscular, his small but tight biceps stretching the sleeves of the t-shirt. The girl nodded towards Richie and said something, presumably in Chinese, that sounded mocking, but in a strangely neutral way. She disappeared out the back again.

"OK," Agh said to Richie, and bent forward to open a drawer beneath the cash register. "You know the price?" he asked.

"No," Richie said.

The guy told him. It was very high – $2,200 plus sales tax.

"Wow, that's very high," Richie said. "Will you knock off 10% if I pay part of it in cash?"

"No," Agh said, and closed the drawer.

"Ah," Richie said, expressing disappointment rather than trying to pronounce the guy's name.

Agh shrugged and made no move to continue the exchange.

"I didn't realize they were that expensive," Richie said.

"They are."

"I see."

"You want to buy one or not?"

"Well, yes. It's just that I didn't expect to pay that much."

"We're the only store in New York sells them. You think you can get one cheaper in LA or Boston, buy yourself a plane ticket."

It seemed that the old Soviet Union had sold its customer relations textbooks to Canal Street shopworkers.

"OK, yes, I want to buy one."

Agh opened the drawer again, and pulled out a sheaf of forms. He pushed the forms and a pen across the glass counter to Richie, who looked down and saw that the sheaf of forms was in fact one form, with three or four different-coloured pages in triplicate, glued together at the top.

"I have to fill in all this?" he asked.

"Yeah."

"What are they? Guarantee forms?" Richie asked.

Agh looked at him doubtfully. "You a store manager?"

"No," Richie said.

"You're not American, are you?" Agh asked.

"No."

"Don't write on those," Agh said, and went out into the back of the shop again, taking the pen with him to make sure Richie wouldn't disobey. The girl returned and stood there mutely, chewing on the ends of her hair.

Richie heard Agh talking in English. A one-sided conversation, on the phone presumably. Agh's voice sounded considerably more respectful than it had been towards Richie.

He took a look at the first page of the forms. It was marked "US Government" and was coloured a very official-looking dull grey-green. It looked worse than a passport application. He was going to have to write out his name and address, business address, social security number, and, it seemed, the name and address of a referee. Richie doubted that his old maths teacher's name would carry much weight in New York.

Agh returned. The girl left.

"OK," Agh said, and put the pen down again.

"You really need the name of a referee?" Richie asked.

"You want to buy one or not?"

"Yes."

"Well, you got to fill out the forms."

"But I don't know my social security number," Richie said. "We don't need them in Britain unless we get a new job or go to hospital."

Agh sighed, picked up the pen again, and left. The girl returned. Agh had another phone conversation while Richie stood there thinking that this was the most elaborate way of losing a customer that he'd ever seen.

Agh came back, the girl went.

"You got your passport?"

"Yes," Richie said.

"OK, fill out the forms except for the social security number and the local referee and print all your passport details in the box marked Comments." Agh put down the pen.

"Great."

"No, wait." Agh picked up the pen. "Give me your credit card. I want to check it's not stolen or over its limit."

Richie handed over the card and waited for the girl to arrive. He was getting quite attached to their short, silent rendez-vous.

"You come here often?" he asked her, giving her his best-behaved smile.

"I don't think he's gonna sell you one," she said. She sounded neither sympathetic nor malicious. "We never sold one to a foreigner before."

"Oh."

"You live in New York or you a tourist?"

"Tourist."

The girl shook her head as if it confirmed her worst suspicions.

The silence from the back room was ominous.

"Where exactly has your friend taken my credit card?" Richie asked.

Richie thought he must be telepathic. He'd seen the taxi coming towards him, and was just wondering whether to hail it, when it pulled over spontaneously.

He looked down at his arms to check that they hadn't got fed up of hanging around and tried to hail a taxi without their owner's permission. But no, they were still crossed in front of him, as annoyed and impatient as the rest of his body.

"Hi, Richie. Remember me?" So it wasn't telepathy. Clara was sitting in the back of the taxi. Richie didn't know what to answer.

"Are you getting in or am I getting out?" she asked.

"Uh, depends."

"On what?" Clara said. He was just standing there on the pavement, as if he'd been ordered to wait for the sun to rise above the rooftops and boil his head.

"On how expensive taxis are."

"Well, they're usually more expensive when you're in them than when you're not in them."

"Yeah." He looked around at the shop behind him, and glanced up and down the street. "Better pay him and get out, then."

"Have you bought what I think you've bought?" Clara asked when the taxi had pulled away.

"I'm not sure."

"Don't tell me you fell for the old 'pay us now and we promise we'll teleport it to your home' trick?"

Richie explained about the forms and the (temporarily) disappearing credit card, and, last of all, about the price.

"Holy shit," Clara said on receiving the news that all their prize spending money and half of their current account was no more.

She then pointed out the anomaly in all of this. "So where is it?"

"They told me to come and stand on the pavement and wait."

"You mean wait while they closed their fake shop and bolted out the back door?"

"No ..." Richie looked along the street again. "They said a van would bring it. They don't keep them in stock in the shop. They have to get them from a warehouse."

"Richie, I'm all in favour of a bit of retail therapy, but the idea is to get something in return for what you spend. Shopping without getting the shopping is called losing your money."

They stood and watched cars pass. They listened to a distant whooping siren and squinted upwards at the sound of an approaching helicopter. The water reservoirs on the rooftops looked like pots of soup put up there to simmer in the baking heat.

It wasn't just the price that was on Clara's mind. It was Richie. A machine won't beam all your troubles away, she thought. Or beam you away from your troubles. You've got to stand up to them, face to face. Disarm them. But now was the wrong time to go into all that.

"You sure they do after-sales service?" was all she said.

10. She's Got the Look

Blender hoped that he wasn't going to hear any sucking sounds. Or blowing for that matter.

It was always irritating when you heard recordings of people having sex. Either you listened and got frustrated trying to imagine what they were doing, or you had to scroll forward until the moaning, yodelling, whipping or (once, with a hooker and a pro-NRA senator) shooting stopped.

But this would be infinitely worse. Now that he'd got presidential approval for his project, he didn't want any Clinton-style White House scandals.

He'd received an email – scrambled, re-scrambled and then, just for good measure, converted into scramblese – from one of his people containing a conversation that took place in the White House shortly after the Defense Committee meeting.

The President was alone in a room with a young intern, a sexy-sounding girl with a slow Southern lilt. Blender hoped to God she was as ugly as her voice was enticing. Remember Clinton, stupid, he thought.

"Can you give me the basics, please, Shelle?" the President asked.

"I'd be happy to, Mr President," the girl said, in a slightly rasping soul-singer's voice. There was a rustle. Let it be papers turning and not underwear falling, Blender prayed. "Er, OK," she went on. "Name Maxwell Charles Blender, born in –"

Blender hit pause. Wo, he thought, the President's checking me out personally? This could be good or it could be bad. Does he distrust me or am I moving up in the world? Surely he doesn't want to set up a visit to Iowa? No one wants to visit Iowa. No one outside a Trekkie bus, that is. I hope. He pressed pause again. The intern went on.

"Minneapolis in October, nineteen –"

"No, wait, Shelle. I'm not going to do his horoscope. Tell me where he went to school, where he lives. Or tell me who his friends are. That's the way to really learn about someone."

"Wo, I never thought of that before, Sir," the girl said. Blender could imagine her flirtatious ooh-you're-so-wise look.

"Darling."

Blender flinched before realizing that it was a different voice. A door closed. Footsteps padded across a carpet.

"Have you finished here, honey?" The First Lady had come to the rescue. Blender smiled approvingly at this wifely defence of the nation's probity.

"Shelle was just about to read a file for me," the President said.

"Ah, well if it's not confidential, maybe I can oblige," the First Lady said. "I want to rest my legs for a while."

There was more rustling. Women getting up and sitting down. One of them moving, probably disappointed, to the door.

"Thank you, Shelle," the First Lady said.

"Yeah, thanks," the President said, more kindly than his wife.

"Hmm, cute," the First Lady said as soon as they were alone. There was a short silence, then she added. "No, not her, him. Who is he?"

Blender almost blushed. She'd almost certainly been looking at his official FBI-registered mugshot.

"He's a scientist," the President said. "Head of the team that's working on teleportation."

"Teleportation? He doesn't look like a wacko."

"Let's hope not. I've met him a couple of times. Seems OK. Thought I might invite him for a game of golf sometime. I asked for a list of the people he plays with. Is it in there?"

It sounded as if the First Lady was flicking through the pages.

"Wow," she finally said. Blender knew that, if complete, the list would be impressive. There would be lots of names she wouldn't recognize, but amongst those she would know there were politicians, very rich businessmen, and some Washington socialites whose only function in life was to host parties. "You say he's a scientist?" The First Lady asked.

"Yeah."

"Well if he is, he's a very *social* scientist."

11. Blow-up Mistress

Back in the hotel room, the only space big enough for Richie to put the box was on the beige velvet arms of the armchair. His new machine sat there like some huge symbol of marital discord. As if Richie had brought home a blow-up doll of his mistress and propped it up in the living room.

"If they made you fill out all those forms, it probably means they don't want you to take it out of the country. What will you do if they stop you at Customs? You won't have time to go back for a refund."

"I told them I was a tourist, and he rang to check."

"Yeah, well, anything to make a sale."

Clara collapsed on the bed and stretched herself full-length for a long sigh.

"I don't want to whinge, Richie, but you've just spent a shitload of money on something we can't really afford and that I'm almost sure you're going to lose one way or another. If it's not Customs, it'll be you-know-who."

Martin had always tried to steal or break every toy of Richie's. And when Richie had started getting girlfriends, Martin had done his best to scare them off or shag them. Once, Richie had been nobly wooing a girl called Jaqueline. Posh, she was, pronounced her name Jack-leen, lived over by the golf course. Richie, still a virgin, had spent weeks holding hands, rubbing her tits, being nice to her mum, genteel stuff. Only when Jaqueline dumped him without letting him pop his cherry did Richie find out that Martin had been regularly shagging her in her garage, in the back of her dad's Range Rover.

Richie sat on the end of the bed and looked fondly at his cardboard mistress.

"It's a chance I've got to take," he said.

12. Serious Handicap

Blender was pretty sure that there was nothing in his file that would scare the President off. He knew he'd been photographed outside his Washington home – that was normal for anyone who was due to have personal contact with the President. There were probably satellite photos of the base in Iowa in the file, too. He'd watched in real time as the photos appeared on a screen in his lab. His people had been watching the satellite watching them. That was OK – there was nothing on the base that would worry the FBI or the military. Well, nothing visible from the air anyway.

He knew what was said in the written appraisal of his character in the file. It had been drafted by an FBI man whom Blender knew. It gave his CV – doctorate in electronics at Stanford, assigned to the Pentagon 15 years ago – and talked about his refusal to take vacations. It said that he went on golfing, skiing and mountain-biking weekends. Apart from these he'd been working pretty well non-stop since 1997, when he'd got the go-ahead to recruit his new team. Almost literally non-stop, the report said, because he got by on only four hours sleep and two hours yoga per day. Better make that five hours sleep, Blender had suggested to the FBI man. Don't want to sound psychotic. It'd have all the stuff about his divorce. He'd given the FBI man a free hand with that. It was too painful to read about in a few cold sentences.

"Great eyes. Such a light blue. You know who he reminds me of?" he heard the First Lady ask. "Mr Robson," she answered herself.

"Who?" Blender and the President asked together, in their separate rooms.

"The Prime Minister's husband."

"Which Prime Minister?"

"Prime Minister Robson of England, of course. Her husband was at the British ambassador's garden party last week in aid of the George Harrison Foundation."

"What the hell's that?" the President asked. Blender smiled. Was that jealousy in the President's voice? Was the First Lady sounding too keen on these younger men?

"I honestly can't remember. Something to do with drug rehabilitation or endangered animals, I think."

"Save the dope-smoking whales?"

"Anyway, they played My Sweet Lord," she said.

"The whales did?"

Blender laughed out loud. He'd decided during the Defense Committee that he liked the President. When he shook off the ventriloquists' meddling hands, he was very witty in a kind of Ozzy Osbourne way.

"No, dear," the First Lady replied patiently. "The British ambassador and the Prime Minister's husband. He plays the piano beautifully. And he's so funny, too. He introduced himself as the First Lady of England. Don't you just love that Monty Python sense of humour the English have?"

"Monty Python? Aren't they those guys who dress up as women all the time? What's Blender's handicap?"

"Handicap?"

Blender could imagine the First Lady picturing false legs, deafness and the like instead of golfing ability.

"I'll look," the President said. "They have to give the guy's handicap in the file. If they don't, remind me to fire the head of the FBI."

That's a point, Blender thought to himself, if I'm going to be inducted into the country's most exclusive golfing fraternity, I ought to let the FBI know that I've improved my handicap. I wouldn't want to have an unfair advantage over the Leader of the Free World.

12A. Airport Coloscopy

Richie and Clara loaded their bags and the cardboard box on to the conveyor belt of the X-ray machine. Richie took his money out of his pocket, his belt off his trousers, and his shoes off his feet, and walked through the metal-detector gate without beeping. He passed the frisk test, unlike the woman just ahead of him, who beeped down at crotch level. They should put a notice at the entrance, Richie thought, "to avoid delays, please remove intimate piercings before boarding". His shoes were mechanically sniffed and found non-explosive, so he put them back on and went to stand by the out chute of the X-ray machine. He wasn't overly surprised that the box hadn't emerged. Two guards, a small mean White one with a limp grey fringe and a taller Black colleague with half-tinted glasses, were examining it on screen.

Richie held out his multicoloured customs forms, tapping with his forefinger on the US Government logo. "It has an exit visa," he told them.

The mean-looking guard took the papers and turned them over as if to check that they didn't have "THESE ARE FAKE!!!" stamped on the back. He and his colleague looked from the screen to the forms. Seeing "teleportation machine" written in official ink didn't seem to convince them that what they were seeing on the screen was real.

"You buy this in New York?" the mean one asked.

"Yes," Richie said. "I'm taking it back home to England."

"Never seen one of these before."

"Neither had I. We don't have them in England." Richie thought it would please the American to hear that his country was more advanced.

"Look at that," the mean one said to his colleague, pointing to the screen. Richie would have liked to see the circuits in X-ray, even if he couldn't interpret them.

"Should you really leave it in there for so long?" Richie asked. "It might damage it."

"No, it's perfectly safe," the mean one said.

"How do you know? You say you've never had one in there before." Richie tried his best to make the question sound apologetic, but the mean one looked at him meanly.

"We gotta check everything."

He gave a nod to the other guard, who spoke into a walkie-talkie, leaning away from Richie so that he couldn't hear.

The cardboard box finally rolled out of the machine, but the mean guard put a possessive hand on top of it and pushed it to the end of the out chute.

"Wait here a minute," he said and stood facing into Richie's midriff across the top of the box.

Clara resisted the temptation to serenade Richie with a few choruses of "told you so". She fetched a trolley and reached for the first of their suitcases which had also emerged from the X-ray machine.

"Just a moment." The younger guard stood up from his screen. "You got anything electrical in there?"

"No," Clara said.

"Yes, you do. Open it up."

"OK," Clara said, flicking at the combination lock, "but there's nothing electrical in there."

"Yes there is," Richie said. "I forgot to tell you. The buffalo can roam."

The security man performed a coloscopy on the bonsai bison and rummaged around in Clara's underwear before he let her close the suitcase and put it on the trolley. He threw the bison's battery into a bin that already contained batteries of all sizes, several Swiss penknives, a pack of Bic disposable razors and a large wooden fork. The security men were clearly determined to stop anyone tossing their own inflight salad.

Meanwhile a uniformed customs officer arrived and the mean guard beckoned him over to Richie's box. The customs man ambled the last few yards, obviously not happy to be beckoned at by a civilian. He was White – or pink anyway – with several chins and an overhanging belly. There was a ring of sweat above the waistband of his dark blue trousers. Without a word he took the forms from the guard, read the first few lines, and then tried to read the expression on Richie's face, which was one of patient innocence. The customs man was looking less patient, overworked.

"Where'd'you buy this, Sir?" he asked, scratching a chin.

"Canal Street," Richie said. "There's a stamp on the last page."

"Can I see your passport?"

Richie handed it over, and the man compared the number with that written on the form. He held on to both documents.

"You got an export licence?"

"Export licence? But aren't these forms –?"

The customs man held up his hand to interrupt, and turned away. He pulled the walkie-talkie off his belt and spoke into it. The mean-looking guard kept his hand on top of the box as if Richie might scoop it up and make a dash for the plane with a teleporter under his arm.

Richie gave Clara an "I don't understand what all the fuss is about" look. Her face was calm, but her eyes were bawling "this is another fine mess you've gotten us into."

"You have other luggage?" It was the customs man, back again.

"Yes," Richie said, holding his hand out towards Clara and her loaded trolley.

"Come with me," the customs man said. "Both of you."

"What about –?"

"Bring the box," the customs man said.

The three of them walked silently side by side as they criss-crossed through the airport, with Richie in the middle pushing the heaped luggage trolley. There were plenty of people with much more suspicious-looking packages than he had – slick businessmen with bulky leather bags that looked purpose-built for hidden compartments, and obvious targets like the Third-world residents with red, white and blue weaved-plastic sacks full of weird bulges. How come he was the only one to have an armed escort, Richie thought.

"Where are we going?" he asked the customs man.

"Customs," he answered.

"Right." Obvious, really. "What for exactly?"

"To make sure you're allowed to take that thing out of the country. Move aside, please, US Customs," he growled at a young family, threatening them with a wave of Richie's passport.

"It's ironic," Richie said to Clara as he narrowly avoided breaking the ankle of the lost-looking father who had been loitering in front of the trolley. "Kirk takes these things half way to infinity, and I can't even move mine around one measly planet."

Clara wasn't in the mood for sci-fi. "We better not miss our bloody flight," she said. "I'll get the sack."

Clara was reservations manager at the Prince of Wales Hotel in Bournemouth. This was the best hotel in town, a much-extended gothic building that was one of the first solid structures built on the clifftop when the resort was little more than a beach hut and a few sandcastles.

"If I lose my job, you'll have to get one. A real one, too, not dossing about writing fairy tales."

Richie didn't rise to the bait. "You won't get fired. You put in enough extra hours."

"And who's going to break the good news to my mum?" The kids were being looked after by their Gran, who loved them dearly but lacked the energy, negotiating skills and upper-body strength to look after them for more than a weekend.

They arrived in a long corridor and had to manoeuvre against the flow of oncoming trolleys until they reached a pair of glass doors engraved with a "US Customs" shield. They turned in beneath a stars and stripes that hung limp but proud.

Inside there was a wide entrance hall with glass-walled offices off it. At a table by the doorway sat two other customs officers, a small blond man with a Village People moustache and a muscular African-American made even bulkier by his bullet-proof vest.

"Wait here," Richie and Clara's escort ordered, and he took Richie's forms and passport into the nearest office. The grey-suited man inside looked at the forms and then stared for five full seconds at Richie's face. The man's eyes seemed to be filming him.

"We're going to miss our flight, I know it," Clara said.

The man in the suit made a short phone call then talked earnestly to the uniformed customs officer. The uniform listened, nodded, and came out.

"Come with me," he said again, just as gruffly as before.

"Where to?" Richie asked.

"Make sure you don't miss your flight." He inflated his already round cheeks and puffed tiredly at the prospect of his new mission.

Richie and Clara exchanged a bemused but happy smile and followed the customs man back out into the flood of trolleys. This time they went with the flow.

"What was that about?" Richie whispered to Clara.

"Let's not bother to find out, shall we?" she said.

The manual for the new machines tells you more about what you can't do with them than what you can do.

The section entitled "User Warnings" starts with the obvious: "This is not a waste disposal machine. Do not use it to dispose of garbage or unwanted items." Just putting ideas into people's heads if you ask me. What a great idea – you sit by the TV with your six-pack and every time you finish a can, you lean over and stick it in the teleporter. Whoosh – an end to those embarrassingly inaccurate lobs at the bin.

The section goes on with some equally obvious instructions: "Do not teleport any item before programming in its destination." Again, they're asking for trouble. Hey, let's beam Auntie Mabel's chihuahua to the South Pole. Hours of fun for all the family. Get rid of those unwanted Christmas presents by teleporting them to random destinations all over the world, or beyond. The first astronauts on Mars will discover piles of gaudy socks and chemistry sets.

But to be fair, the manual does warn you specifically against teleporting Auntie Mabel's chihuahua: "Under no circumstances is this machine to be used to teleport living creatures. Signature of the purchase form constitutes acceptance of this condition. Violations are tantamount to felony under federal law." In short, Auntie Mabel could have you extradited to the USA if her doggie goes missing and she finds its collar stuck in the door of your teleportation machine.

For those of you with really gruesome imaginations, the manual goes further: "Any attempt to teleport human body parts will result in the destruction of those parts and constitute illicit disposal of human remains, a violation of federal law. Do not insert your own body parts into the machine while in use. Users not following this instruction do so at their own risk. The manufacturers deny all responsibility for injuries caused to users or third parties while deliberately or accidentally inserting their own or a third party's body parts into the machine while transmitting or receiving."

The message is clear, kiddies – do not play the old "Auntie Mabel, can you just put your head in here for a second" trick unless you want to end up doing federal time.

The question remains: what can you teleport?

The answer: well, I'm still not 100% clear. There's no section entitled "hey, try this". There's no recipe book like you get with food mixers.

After wading through all the legal disclaimers, it seems that they're only willing to envisage allowing teleportation of items with a very simple molecular structure – New Age crystal users are going to have a field day, for example. As are diamond merchants, sellers of glassware, ironmongery and certain basic plastics plus anyone who wants to send their Auntie Mabel a few lumps of coal to keep her warm now that she's lost her live chihuahua muffler.

But all in all, the manual leaves you with one over-riding impression – disrespect. The makers of the machine (or their legal representatives, anyway) seem to have sat down and thought, now what are the stupidest things a stupid buyer could possibly do with a stupid teleportation machine? Is that any way to treat such an inspired piece of technology?

A Brief History of the Future, chapter 1 (extract)

14. Get on the Bus, Forget about Us

Blender was used to comfortable suspension and air-conditioning, and was not enjoying the sight of Central Park through the tinted window of a bouncing oven.

The Metropolitan Transportation Authority number-one bus was packed. The acrid sweat of the low-income, carless commuters hung in the air. Or lack of air.

But he was obliged to sit here at the back of the bus as it ground its way downtown through the early morning traffic because, as the IRA had proved so successfully in Britain in the 1970s, a crowded bus was one of the best places in a city to discuss secrets without being spied upon.

Blender didn't mind being seen with the woman whose damp thigh was now pressing against his – she was his employee. But he didn't want anyone overhearing their conversation.

"So what's new?" he asked above the growl of the engine.

His voice was pitched low, and was almost inaudible to the people on the seat in front of him.

His neighbour, a twenty-something nerdy woman in a blue Yankees t-shirt and combat shorts, turned towards Blender. When they met like this, much of their conversation went on via lip-reading because of the background noise.

"Someone from *England* has bought one," the girl said, mouthing the country's name with particular emphasis. She was quite excited by this news, but knew better than to show it. Blender, she had realized, was fascinated with his work to the point of obsession, but liked to play it cool.

"England?" Blender raised his eyebrows, interested.

"Place on the south coast near *London*. Called *Bornymouth*."

"How d'you spell that?"

The woman did so slowly from memory.

"That rings a bell," Blender said.

The woman nodded vigorously, and waited as the bus pulled away from a stop with a deep howl of acceleration. "There's going to be a *summit* there."

"Of course, yes. Any connection, you think?"

She shrugged, and told Blender that she would mail him all that she knew about Richard Fisher, which didn't go far beyond name, address, passport number and credit-card details. The information had been fed through from the sellers of the teleportation machine to the woman's office in Brooklyn. The office, set up by Blender and his associates at the Defense Department, was completely legitimate, its purpose to monitor the sales of this brand-new technology to the public. The licensed (and carefully vetted) sellers knew that the government wanted one verifiable purchaser name per machine. The only less-than-legitimate thing about the office was that a large segment of its budget did not show up on the Department's accounts, just as the allegiance of the office's three employees was to Blender rather than Washington. "He seems to be a British *tourist*. Only other large purchases here are *women's clothing*," the woman said.

"Hmm." Blender thought this development over. It hadn't occurred to him that foreign visitors might start buying the machines as souvenirs. They were conceived as bulky, unattractive work tools, like photocopiers, something you wouldn't expect to buy for personal use. "Maybe he has some kind of *import-export* business. Try and find out."

She nodded.

They bounced over a pothole, and Blender felt at least three months' worth of reflexology wrenched out of his spine. These buses broke your body down into molecules just as efficiently as a teleporter. They just didn't reassemble it.

"Christ. I have to get off this damn coffee grinder. You've given me an *idea*, though. I want to be at that *summit*. Maybe this English guy is a coincidence, but coincidences are there to be exploited. Make it your *priority* to send me anything you can find on him."

"Will do."

"See you."

The assistant nodded and smiled goodbye. But the smile lingered on her lips. She was pleased with herself – she'd given Blender an idea, and her boss was the type of guy who usually had his own ideas.

When the bus stopped, he stepped down onto the sidewalk and grunted with the realization that the outdoors was barely cooler or quieter than the inside of the bus.

Blender didn't look it, but he too was feeling pleased with himself. His machine was already heading across the Atlantic. He wanted to go and see how it would get on there.

15. Fisherman's Laugh

They arrived at Heathrow early in the afternoon. They didn't have enough bags to hide the machine on their baggage trolley, but Richie made sure that their one large suitcase got pole position.

"Don't look them in the eyes, don't look them in the eyes," he told himself as they rounded a corner and he looked straight into the eyes of a uniformed customs officer. The man gazed steadily back. Richie tried to empty his eyes of expression. This was a pine tree he was looking at, he told himself, in a forest of a million other pine trees. Boring as hell.

The man's mouth opened. Richie knew what he was going to say.

"Straight on through, please," the man said, proving Richie wrong. He nodded and walked as naturally as possible towards the exit.

"Oh hell," Clara whispered as the exit doors swung open.

Richie couldn't stop himself looking back guiltily towards the customs men.

"Look who's here." Clara was looking forward, not back. Richie did the same, and instantly saw the motionless figure waiting by a car-hire booth.

He was standing stock-still, feet slightly apart, hands joined in front of his groin as if protecting his manhood while meditating. His face was in repose, his dark moustache and chin-only beard devilishly symmetrical. His combat trousers were silvery grey, his t-shirt plain white and skin-tight. It was Martin, looking a bit rumpled but very cool. When they were both teenagers, Richie could never work out why only Martin had been born with natural cool. Now, Richie was almost sure it was rehearsed in front of a mirror. Almost sure.

"Did you give him the flight number?" Clara hissed.

"No," Richie said.

As Richie and Clara walked towards him, Martin nodded and smiled, but waited for them to join him.

"Bro!" Martin held out his hand. Richie grabbed it and shook it before Martin could try anything trendy like one of those fist-touching things that Black guys do. "Love the hair, or lack of it." Martin pointed to Richie's head.

"Great heads think alike." Richie stroked the top of Martin's shaven skull.

"Shops over there all empty now, Clara?" Martin asked, leaning forward to peck her on the cheek. The two of them were almost the same height. His beard rasped, but he didn't look as bad as usual, she thought. He often let his whole head, whiskers and hair, grow a uniform eighth-of-an-inch stubble. Velcro man. Today, close-shaven except for his satanic whiskers, he was just about acceptable.

"How did you know when we were coming?" she asked, deciding at the last moment not to opt for "what the hell are you doing here?"

"Your mum told me, so I thought I'd come and meet you." Martin smiled pleasantly, showing off his gold canine tooth. "Hey, bro, you got your credit card handy?"

"What for?" Richie asked.

"Well, I hired us a car but they need a credit-card number."

"What do you mean – you hired us a car?" Clara asked. "We booked a taxi."

"Yeah, your mum said. I cancelled it."

"You what?" Clara was aghast.

"Look, it's on me, OK?" Martin said. "I've got to drive back up here tomorrow. I'll drop the hire car off. We all win out."

"It's on you and I pay?" Richie scoffed. "No, ta. We'll get the train."

"Train?" It was Martin's turn to scoff. "You're in England, remember. Take fucking hours, if you ever get there, and cost you a fortune. Car's cheaper, believe me. And you should see the queue for taxis. Horror film." His face was a picture of pain at the idea of even thinking of getting a cab.

"Well we wouldn't need to queue if you –"

Richie interrupted Clara. He felt a long, vicious-circle argument starting. "Where's *your* credit card?" he asked Martin.

"I'll explain later," Martin said and fingered his double-pierced left ear, almost embarrassed for once. Richie knew better than to ask for details in public.

"OK, you give me half in cash now, I'll get out my credit card," Richie said.

"I'm almost out of cash," Martin replied. "I'll pay you back. Promise."

"OK, but I take your gold chain as security."

"Done," Martin agreed, and unclasped the thick chain from his neck.

"I'm going to give it to Clara to keep," Richie told him. "You know what that means."

"Sure. If I don't pay up, she'll melt it down to make herself a vibrator."

Clara weighed the chain in her hand. "Not much gold here, Martin. Only enough to make one your size, and that wouldn't keep a woman satisfied."

"Just rub it and see. Heh heh heh."

That was another thing she hated about Martin – his laugh. A series of sleazy growls, modelled on his hero, Sid James from the Carry On films.

Richie gave the chain to Clara. "If you two have finished scratching each other's eyes out," he said, "we can pay for the car and get going."

"And you're driving, Martin," Clara added. "Richie's too tired."

"No problem. I got us one of those new Beetles. Bright orange. Should be fun."

Richie was almost sure that Martin had done this just for the pleasure of driving a flash new car about for a day. Almost sure.

They had soon left the tangle of airport approach roads behind, and were heading in heavy traffic towards the south coast. Herds of trucks were stampeding down to the ports.

Richie was sitting in front with Martin. Clara was in the back.

"Did you get my present?" Martin asked.

"How could we forget you?" Richie assured him.

"Hand it over, then."

Richie pulled a CD from his shoulder bag and gave it to Martin.

"Cheers." Martin looked at the cover and nodded his satisfaction. "Whack it in, bro."

Richie whacked the disc, carefully, into the car CD player, and almost instantly a massive drumbeat kicked in.

"What's this, Led Zeppelin?" Clara asked mockingly.

Martin snorted as a minimalist bass line began to pound out, and a growling rapper threatened death and destruction to anyone who suggested he might be effeminate.

"Cool," Martin said. "Cheers, bro." He turned the volume up.

"Come on, Martin," Clara complained. "I've got a splitting headache and I'm totally jet-lagged. Can't you turn it off?"

"No. You mustn't fall asleep before your proper bedtime," Martin said. "Only make your jet-lag worse in the long run."

"You're so considerate."

Richie leaned forward and turned the sound down a notch, playing the mediator between the two of them, as he so often did.

On the motorway, traffic was flowing smoothly. Martin's shoulders rocked from side to side as he listened to the heavy beats, and, always keeping one hand on the wheel, he did the appropriate finger-splaying hand movements to punctuate the rapping.

Clara laughed. "Look at him. He really thinks he's a rapper, doesn't he? What do you know about the ghetto, Martin? You've never even been to New York."

Martin looked at her in the rear-view mirror, amusement in his eyes.

"Yeah, and, like, you often nip back to 19th-century Vienna for the weekend, right?" Clara was a Mozart fan. She ignored the century error.

"At least I don't pretend to *be* Mozart. You just wish so much that you'd been born in the Bronx, don't you? You're really pissed off because you're from Bournemouth. And instead of hangin' with your homies, you can only go down the pub and play snooker."

"Pool, lady. We play pool. None of us homies knows what snooker is. What kinda faggoty name is snookah?" Martin punctuated his rant with more rapper's hand jabs. "Snoo-kah? Sounds like some faggoty name for kissin' men. Come here, big boy, and gimme a snookah on my hairy butt."

Richie turned to Clara. "This is excessive testosterone," he told her. "Much more serious than Shopping Fatigue."

Clara almost always lost these verbal jousts with Martin. His skin wasn't just thick, it was a combination of elephant hide, lead and asbestos. Over a six-inch layer of reinforced concrete. Martin loved it when Clara came snapping after him. He bounced her off like a tiger playing with its cubs. But she couldn't help herself. He was so infuriatingly cocky, and she was certain that his cockiness was going to get Richie into deep shit one day.

"Buy anything good?" Martin asked Richie. He'd been intrigued when they put the microwave-sized package in the boot, but hadn't asked about it.

"Lots of shoes," Clara said before Richie could open his mouth.

"Big shoeboxes they have over there," Martin said.

"What were you doing up at Heathrow, anyway?" Richie asked, getting them off the subject of mysterious boxes.

"Ah. I got some business up there."

"Do we want to hear about this?" Clara asked.

"OK, maybe not," Martin said.

Richie turned the CD down another notch. "No, I'm interested," he said.

"Smartarse," Martin said. "OK, listen. Airports, key places, right? Biggest concentration of computers in one place in the world."

"What? More than at a computer company? Or a stockbroker's?" Richie asked.

Martin tutted impatiently. "OK, yeah, but I'm not talking about physical machines. I'm talking about servers. All those names."

"Names, you want names?" Clara asked, leaning forward between the two front seats. "Try the database at a chain of hotels."

"OK, so it may not be the absolute biggest concentration. Who gives a fuck." Martin was so disdainful of this nit-picking that he actually concentrated on the road for a few seconds. "I'm interested in all those names, often the same name returning regularly."

"Just like in a hotel."

"You obviously don't smack your bitch enough bro," Martin said. "She won't let a man get a word in."

"She's got a point," Richie teased. "Sounds just like a hotel to me."

"OK, OK, take a bonus point each," Martin conceded. "Remind me to return to that later. Could be interesting. Anyway, all these names, right, telling you about all these people who've spent hundreds, thousands on their tickets, and where they're going to be on a certain day." He looked across as if to ask whether Richie got his point.

Richie did. "So what's your scam, then?" he asked. There was always a scam.

"Block your ears up, Clara," Martin said, grinning at her in the mirror. "Just think. When you get back from a holiday or a business trip, are you sure you've got all your credit-card slips? Do you really think twice if you see a few quid charged to 'Smiths Restaurants, Inc' on your bill at the end of the month?"

Richie nodded. "So if you know someone's going to be in a certain city on a certain date, you can add a few bogus charges to his card without him suspecting a thing."

"Exactly," Martin congratulated him. "Without stealing his card or knowing his pin number. Very good, bro. You should go into the computer fraud business."

"Just one question, though," Richie said. "Do you actually need to go to Heathrow to check that out? What were you doing? Peering over the booking clerk's shoulders to see if you could suss out the password?"

"Smartarse," Martin said, and pulled out to overtake a few straggling cars.

"So what were you doing there?" Richie asked.

"Well, if you must know, I've been up in London for the last few days clubbing my brains out. Worse than Ibiza, that place."

"And you blew all your money?"

"Yeah. They were dishing out E's like sweets, man."

"Expensive sweets."

"Right, major dosh changing hands. Real growth industry."

"Stunt your growth industry, you mean."

"Ooh, hark at grannie." Martin cackled and slapped Richie on the knee.

Richie couldn't think of any witty comeback. It was true, he thought, when you became a dad, part of you turned into a grandmother.

Martin gunned the engine to pass a lorry full of potatoes.

"Anyway," he said when he'd got back into the centre lane. "About these databases at your hotel, Clara."

Clara just laughed. "You've got as much chance of getting near one of our computers as you have of shagging my Richie."

"Dunno. He's a sound sleeper."

"And since you're so interested," Clara went on, "yes we did have a good time in New York, thanks."

"Hey, I was forgetting." Martin looked at her in the mirror again. "What have you got in that box?"

"Presents for the kids," Clara said quickly.

"Great," said Martin. "I can't wait to see their faces when they open it up."

"Smartarse," Richie said.

Martin sniggered and turned his CD up again.

At number 17 is Anthony Burgess for A Clockwork Orange. Or rather, Anthony Burgess and Stanley Kubrick. The film deserves as much credit as the book.

Burgess did make one glaring mistake – he had the yobbos in Clockwork Orange use Russian slang because he took too much notice of all the American paranoia about Soviets trying to take over the free world.

But credit where credit's due – the film seems to have inspired the skinhead fashion for beating up tramps. As far as I can see from news archives, kicking the shit out of dossers was a lot less hip before 1971 than after. Sociologists might argue that this was because the whole world was getting more violent, but I'm not a sociologist.

Burgess's sociologists, who try to cure a yobbo by making him listen to Beethoven, really do seem to have made a lasting impression on the world.

In American shopping malls with a vandalism problem, it is common practice to play classical music over the loudspeakers. In Newcastle, England, the same policy was put into action on the city's metro system and vandalism and muggings fell by 40%. This wasn't, apparently, because classical music soothed the savage beast – kids just hate the stuff and prefer to vandalize elsewhere.

One Scandinavian head teacher tried to act out Burgess's suggestion to the letter: in 2001, at a school in the village of Ytterby, Sweden, kids found grafittiing school buildings were forced to stay in at breaktimes to listen to classical music on headphones.

The danger of this is obvious. Soon there may be a whole generation of Swedes who'll feel an irresistible urge to buy spray paint every time they hear Eine Kleine Nachtmusik.

A Brief History of the Future, chapter 17 (extract)

16. Fax or Fiction

The President didn't attend the next meeting of the Defense Committee. Most of the talk was self-congratulatory, but the younger general, George McNulty, who'd helped Blender persuade the President to allow military testing of teleportation, was looking troubled. As they left the committee room, McNulty sidled up to Blender.

"Max, maybe you can explain one thing that's been bothering me?"

"Yes?" Blender pulled the general ahead of the crowd, down one of the Pentagon's long, carpeted corridors. If they were going to discuss problems, he didn't want anyone overhearing.

"I mean, I support the project 100% of course. But I've been reading up about the first teleportation experiments in Innsbruck. And there's a fella called Braunstein –"

"Samuel Braunstein, yes."

"And he said that teleporters would be like 3-D fax machines, *duplicating* rather than actually *transporting* the original." The general looked up into Blender's impassive eyes. Blender just kept walking slowly down the corridor past the heavy office doors, unconcerned by the implications of what the general had said.

"And it is true, isn't it," the general went on, "that the publicly available teleporters duplicate objects, and destroy the original in a kind of high-speed microwave oven?"

"Yes." Still Blender was impassive. "When we released the technology, we didn't want to create inflation in, say, diamonds, so we added in the destructor. That's top secret, by the way, George."

"Of course. But doesn't that imply that if you transport people, either you take a chance and destroy the original, or you create a perfect replica? An instant clone?"

Blender smiled. They were approaching a small anteroom with two or three young interns sitting at desks. Blender walked a few strides past them in silence, then stopped and looked the general full in the face.

"Don't you ever get the feeling that reality isn't enough, George? That you want to get someplace *beyond* reality. Or at least start planning your trip there?"

The general didn't know how to take this. "Max, don't tell me you've turned Catholic?" he asked.

"Very funny, George, but I don't want to wait till I'm dead to get there. I'm talking about non-reality on *Earth*."

"Go to a games arcade. Or try watching afternoon TV."

The general didn't feel like treating Blender's hints with the seriousness he was obviously meant to. And anyway, he was irritated by scientists claiming to "reinvent" reality. In the general's experience, scientists spent most of their time arguing with each other about how to *describe* reality, or what minute parts of it they actually understood. And too often they seemed incapable of coming to terms with the most accessible part of reality – human life, human relationships. Some of the scientists the general had to work with in weapons development had the social skills of a dead whale, with the same taste in deodorant. Max wasn't like that – he was more of a political animal. So what was all this non-reality bullshit? Sure, everyone felt like getting away from it all now and then. That's what vacations were for. And what was with the superior smile now creasing Max's tan? The general knew that tan – it was the colour of men who had been testing very secret things in very remote places. Testing them outdoors, too, which meant large objects. Larger than diamonds, anyway. A month or two of testing was enough to detach any man from reality.

Blender took the general's elbow and steered him further down the corridor. "Do you have time for a drink, George?" he asked.

17. The Menagerie

The car pulled up outside the small, square Victorian brick house where Richie and Clara lived. Melodramatic though it was, Clara found herself feeling relieved that it hadn't been burnt down, vandalized or flooded while they were away. It wasn't a particularly beautiful house. It was typical of the dozen streets around it – reddish brick, small front and back gardens, crippling mortgage. The house was small, and too near the railway for her liking. But it was in a quiet side street, near a park, and a mile from the sea. Not a bad place for kids to grow up.

Richie got out of the car, stretched his origamied limbs and breathed in deeply. This was more like it. A breeze. You couldn't smell the sea, but you could feel its freshness.

As they unloaded the luggage, excited faces appeared at the window of their front room. Clara's parents had brought the kids straight here from school. The door and then the garden gate flew open.

"Mummy!" Ella launched herself at Clara, planting a wet kiss on her cheek.

"Hey there, Georgie boy!" Richie bent down to catch his son, and threw him up into the air.

Clara's mum waved from the open front door.

"Did you get me a present?" George asked when he landed in the crook of Richie's right arm.

"You sound just like Uncle Martin," Richie said.

"Well, did you?" George wanted to know.

"Of course, let's get inside first. Hello, pumpkin." Richie picked Ella up in his free arm.

"No, I want it now," George whinged.

"Hang on, you can have it when I've finished with it," Richie said, and made pantomime chewing motions. "I've been breaking in a piece of real American bubble gum for you."

"Err!" Both of his children laughed as Richie carried them indoors.

Even before the greetings had finished and the kettle had boiled, wrapping paper was being ripped off. Ella screamed with delight at her bonsai bison, and George was so excited when he saw the picture of his toy that he couldn't get the box open. It was a remote-control police car, with sounds: there was a whooping siren, and if you pressed a button, a voice yelled "come out with your hands up!" and "freeze or I'll shoot". Not surprisingly, Richie hadn't been able to find a toy that announced "courtesy, professionalism, respect".

He took George out into the garden to give the car a test run.

Their garden was narrow – the lawn was only about twice the width of the path – but fairly long, about thirty feet. At the bottom of the garden was an old creosoted shed which backed on to some bushes at the top of a high railway embankment.

The path was the perfect test site for a remote-control car. Richie showed George the basics, then stood back as the boy tried his skill.

"Try not to knock the fence down," Richie said, then felt a sudden heaviness in his chest.

From his position at the back corner of the house, he looked along the length of the fence to his left. Every time Richie came out here, he did the same. He'd only been away a few days, but he'd erased it from his mind.

He scanned the base of the fence for signs of digging. Looked along the slatted planks for a loose joint. It all seemed to be OK, but he was angry at himself for getting so obsessed with a stupid damn fence. Even angrier at his new neighbour. The fence was five feet high, the pitbull-staffordshire cross on the other side was usually either chained up or supervised, but how long would it be before the monster came flying over there to attack Richie's kids?

He looked over the fence. The neighbour's garden was dog-free, but bore the signs of canine inhabitation – a semi-circle of scuffed lawn at the limit of a chain, which was fastened to a fence post. The almost flowerless flowerbeds where the neighbour had been killing off plants by fertilizing them with dog turds.

What they needed, Richie thought, was an iron bar. Leave it permanently in the garden in case of an emergency. He was against violence between rational humans, but self-defence against a lethal, semi-legal dog was justifiable. Question was, would he be quick enough to intervene with the bar? Would one of his children already have sausage meat instead of a face? Or would a burglar use it to jemmy open the back door? Several of the houses in the street had been broken into recently. Shit, getting paranoid, Richie, he told himself, getting old. A grandma. Why didn't the neighbour just fuck off again and live somewhere else with his pitbull and his badly-tuned van that shattered the peace at six on weekday mornings?

"That's it, Georgie boy, you're doing great!" he called, and the boy turned, grinning with pure joy as the siren wailed across the adjoining gardens.

Richie left George playing and went back inside. Now it was Martin who was hopping about with delight. In fact, he was kneeling on the living-room floor, but was managing a sort of knee-hopping that Richie had never seen done before.

Ella was standing there, looking bemused, a long tatter of brown paper in her hand.

The machine lay on the carpet like the metallic core of a sunflower with wrapping-paper petals.

Richie looked questioningly across at Clara.

"He told Ella it was a present for her," she announced loudly. "He doesn't know how wrong it is to lie to kids."

Martin looked up, untouched by Clara's criticism. "This is fucking incredible!"

"Martin, don't use words like that in front of Ella," Richie told him. "And keep your fingers off, please. That's for me and I haven't had a chance to look at it properly yet."

Oblivious to everything except the metal cuboid in front of him, Martin ran his fingers across it as if stroking a cat. "Did you get the software?"

"Course I got the software."

"This is amazing." Martin sprang to his feet. "Let's get it down the shop and try it out."

"No way!" Richie laughed.

"What are you going to plug it into here? Your fridge?"

"No, the, er, *computer*?" Richie said in his most ironic voice.

"Your old crock? You wouldn't be able to transport half a lentil with that box of junk. You haven't even got bloody internet access." Martin tutted incredulously.

Richie did his best not to look at Clara. He knew what she'd be thinking: a mixture of "shouldn't you have thought of that before spending your money" and "why the hell do you never listen to me you dickhead".

"We're not moving it now. I'm too knack – tired. I'll take it down the shop tomorrow. You won't be there, though, will you?" Richie asked his brother.

"Yeah I will."

"What about the car?"

"Oh, yeah, no, think I'll drive it back now, save a day's hire fee. I'll drop the machine off at the shop as I go." Martin could be annoyingly organized when he wanted to.

"No, I'll keep it here."

"What, and carry it in on the bus tomorrow morning?"

"No, Clara'll give me a lift."

"I'm off at seven. You going to be ready?" Clara asked.

"OK, Martin, you take the machine," Richie heard himself saying, against his better judgement. "But I'm keeping the manual and the software here." Clara hit him right between the eyes with a lightning bolt of "told you so".

"And don't worry Ella, I'll get you a present." Martin was magnanimous in victory.

"Before her wedding day," Clara chipped in.

"But what sort of machine is it, Daddy?" Ella asked, slightly reassured by the promise of a replacement present.

Richie was stumped. How did you explain things like that to someone who's never seen Star Trek?

Richie carried his precious box out to the car again. He felt like a farmer's son delivering his pet calf to the slaughterhouse.

Martin opened the boot of the sleek, metallic-orange Beetle.

"You thinking of buying one of these or what?" Richie asked.

"Why?"

"It's taking you long enough to replace yours."

"Oh, right, yeah. Might. Nice drive."

Martin's own car lay rusting under a blue plastic sheet in the alley behind his shop. It had once been a silver Mazda sports car, but one night after closing time, Martin had tried to drive it on to the pier. He'd only got as far as a concrete pillar. The case was due to be heard in a couple of months' time, which would also be when his ex-girlfriend came out of her plaster cast.

Richie carefully placed the machine in the boot, and made sure it was stable.

"You don't try it out till I get there," he warned Martin.

"How can I? You've got all the stuff that makes it work."

Richie knew this was correct – he'd locked the software in his desk drawer – but as he watched Martin drive away, he wondered *how* correct.

18. Biting the Lemon

Blender took the general to a bar. It was a small place, but not the kind where a TV suspended from the ceiling is permanently tuned to a sports channel.

This was an old established Washington bar, with Chesterfield sofas, immaculately polished floorboards and subdued lighting. The kind of place where you imagined you were supposed to carry on high-powered political conversations.

Even though the general was used to carrying on high-powered conversations, they were usually in offices with guards standing outside the door, not in public sitting beside someone on a green leather sofa.

"Can we talk here?" he asked Blender after they'd received their drinks from a perfect waitress, probably sent here by her parents to get hitched to one of the tribe of rich Washington lawyers. Blender was on Perrier with a slice of lemon. The general needed a shot of Jack Daniels.

"We can talk, but not shout, if you get my meaning."

The general looked around. It was eightish. Most of the tables were taken up with men in ties and suspenders (in the American sense of the word – this was not a transvestite bar) and women with that Ally McBeal after-work chic look. The general was conscious of being the sole person in uniform. The only conversations he could hear were banalities. There were a couple of tables where people were leaning close, looking serious. You couldn't hear them at all.

"Well?" the general asked.

Blender leaned towards him and took up the subject of teleportation again. During the drive between the Pentagon and the bar they'd discussed the general's son and his chances of getting into Stanford. Not good, apparently, unless Blender, a graduate of the university, could put a word in for him.

"This is not the first time that we've talked to the President on this subject, you know. Or should I say this is not the first President we've discussed it with." Blender smiled to himself. Presidents come, presidents go, science carries on. "Clinton dismissed it out of hand at first. He said: 'No way can I justify spending billions of taxpayers' dollars on that kind of sci-fi bullshit.'" Blender did a good imitation of a Dixie drawl. "That's what I like about Presidents – when you get them away from the microphones, they're so down-to-earth." He took a sip of his Perrier, then bit into the slice of lemon.

"So how'd you get him to OK the first experiments?" the general asked.

"Well, we convinced him that it wasn't crackpot technology. We reminded him that before gunpowder, no one could have thought that mixing potassium nitrate, charcoal and sulphur could produce a massive explosion."

"And that convinced him?"

"Well, it started him thinking."

"There is a difference, though," the general said.

"What difference?"

"Well, unlike explosions, transportation isn't natural. Nothing solid disappears and reappears in nature. OK, you can make a few molecules jump about. You'll never be able to do it to whole people."

This time it was Blender who looked around to make sure they weren't being overheard. "Theoretically, if you can teleport an object, you can teleport a person. You just need to make an analysis of its molecular structure that is fast and detailed enough."

The general wondered whether to query the use of "its" when talking about people, but thought better of it.

"Right," he said, "and one of the documents I read said that the information required to analyse a person would fill enough CD-Roms to make a stack 1,000 kilometres high."

Blender took another sip of water and bite of lemon before replying. "And you know what Bill Gates once said about computers – 640k will be enough for anyone. Now the basic PC comes with – what? – ten thousand times that."

The general was about the same age as Blender but he suddenly felt older. Blender had managed to retain the arrogant certitude of youth. Perhaps that was what being a top scientist was about.

"What about the replica problem?" the general asked. "Are you going to replicate a man and destroy the original? Or does the teleported replica do the mission then get zapped? Who's going volunteer for that?"

Blender nodded. "We'd have to disable the destructor. But you're right. Human duplication is an ethical problem that will have to be looked into if and when it becomes feasible to transport people. It's not really a *scientific* problem. In any case, teleporting a living human being is not a practical option yet."

Not for the first time, the general felt that his arm of the project team, the military arm, was not getting all the facts. "What have you been doing on that base in Iowa? Testing the machine on corpses?"

Blender laughed. "No, no, we've just been looking into various concepts on a purely theoretical level."

The general was close to getting ruffled. "Hell, Max. I'm all for progress, but you guys have been watching too much Star Trek. You're trying to prove it's all founded on scientific fact. Next you'll be telling me you've discovered the gene that gives Vulcans pointy ears."

Blender's eyes were glinting humorously. "Funny you should say that, George," he said, and reached one hand up to his cheekbone, as if to pull off a mask.

They laughed together, but the general did not want to be distracted.

"Come on, Max, you don't really believe you'll ever be able to teleport people, do you?"

"I believe," Blender replied, "that we ought to go to my office. I need to show you some stuff."

The first basic experiments in teleportation were carried out in 1997 by a team of scientists in Innsbruck working on photons. "Photon" is a word that we all know very well (thanks to Star Trek's photon torpedoes) but I for one didn't have a clue what a photon really was.

Well, in fact it's a "bit" of light, the tiniest particle of light, an unimaginably small entity.

The Innsbruck scientists managed to transfer the polarization (the direction in which an electrical field vibrates) from one photon to another, making a perfect replica of the first photon appear three feet away.

They hit one major glitch – in effect, they hadn't really teleported anything in the Star Trek sense. They hadn't made something dematerialize and then rematerialize somewhere else. They had simply caused a photon with exactly the same characteristics to appear somewhere else. Duplication not teleportation.

At the end of their series of experiments they were pessimistic: they had achieved only a 25% success rate, and predicted that they might be able to repeat the experiment on molecules (which are a damn sight bigger than photons) in a decade or so.

In June 2002, an Australian team "teleported" a few photons (which they cleverly described as a laser beam to titillate the media). But they admitted that they had no idea how to extend the technology to solid materials.

So how come the sudden breakthrough to teleportation of solid objects? How come you can now buy a real teleporter in New York City?

Your guess is as good as mine – since those experiments in 1997, all the really cutting-edge activity in the field of teleportation seems to have been transferred to the USA under conditions of extreme secrecy. The Pentagon, it seems, has bought up the best scientists and their results, and has started working in its own corner.

A Brief History of the Future, chapter 1 (extract)

19. A Perfectly Ordinary Visit

The people at Blender's base in Iowa assumed that the big picture, the Whistler's Mother of all big pictures, was to teleport humans. When they were chatting together by their latte machine, they imagined that their ultimate goal was to beam back to their rented houses instead of having to drive their 4WD vehicles across Iowa's hypnotically dull landscape. But they were wrong.

Blender and a small circle of like-minded people had a much bigger picture than this. A picture as big as the future.

The members of the inner circle often had a specific objective of their own. This could range from collating information about progress in space travel, to buying the patent on an invention such as a Star Trek-like phaser, to investigating advances in photon-based technology. The one thing they all had in common was the desire not to let their shared, ultimate goal become known, even to their own teams of employees. They were all in charge of fairly large organizations.

They had no hierarchy, but Blender was high in the informal pecking order because he had a job with access to government funding.

When he wanted to communicate with one of the others, he had a simple method of doing so in private. It involved no hi-tech scrambling programs or messages written in urine between the lines of a shopping list.

He went to visit them.

He did this completely openly, because it was no secret that they knew each other. They never compromised each other's more immediate professional secrets. There were sixteen of them at this point, and they were pretty well Blender's only friends. He'd got bored with "friends" who only wanted to talk about family, baseball, their brainless bosses, or Viagra. He preferred to discuss something concrete – the future and his desire to shape it.

So when he arrived at the gates of a hundred-year-old mansion just outside Washington, he hit the intercom button and announced loudly, "Hey, Bill, it's Max."

He drove up the quarter-mile wooded drive to the house, got out to pet the Golden Retriever and shook hands with his friend. Bill was president of a political lobbying company. He was a young-looking 42 with curly black hair and a broad, frank smile. He was wearing only Ray-Bans, sandals and a pair of electric-blue swimming trunks.

Blender wandered through to the back of the house to admire the new pool and its retracting roof.

He changed into his swimming costume and then came to relax on a lounger sipping a mint julep alongside a similarly laid-back Bill. Bill's wife was working out in the basement gym and their kids were playing soccer on the lawn.

A completely normal country Sunday, except for the two men's conversation.

"You bought the birthplace?" Bill asked, awe-struck.

"Yup."

"With your own money?"

"Of course. My department owns several thousand square miles of Iowa already. Asking them to buy a few square yards more would be like getting a pig farmer to pay for hogshit."

Bill laughed. "Well, Max, I must say I'm envious as hell. It's a brilliant piece of strategy. How are you going to exploit it? Are there any Kirks living in town?"

"Well yes. But there are a few too many corn genes mixed in the blood down there. I really don't think they can be left to their own devices."

"I see your point."

"You should buy yourself a little house down there, Bill. Plenty for sale. Tractor included if you're lucky."

Bill laughed again and picked up his own mint julep from the earthen tiles surrounding the pool. He looked across the sunlit lawn towards his two sons, who were heading the ball to each other, three, four, five times without it hitting the ground.

"They're getting good," Blender said. "How old are they now?"

"Nine and eleven."

Blender nodded. "I met with the President last week," he said. That was enough of family talk.

"Yeah?" Bill put his drink down and turned back towards Blender.

"I said we wanted to test the teleporter on humans."

"Humans? Wow. I didn't know you were ready."

"Well ..." Blender looked pained.

"You're not ready?" Bill looked even more pained than his friend.

"Well, not exactly. I was a little ... premature."

Some men would have admired Blender's audacity – bluffing the President of the United States? But not Bill. He worked up on Capitol Hill and knew how the fusty old politicians reacted to anyone showing disrespect to the nation's institutions.

"You lied to the President?"

"Lied? No, I just strayed a little way beyond truth."

Bill didn't think this was funny. "Max. That's just plain dangerous. You could set things back years."

"But it was a condition for getting the OK to test things further. This is *teleportation* we're talking about, Bill. It's vital for the long-term development of the Project."

It was as if a Freemason had given the secret handshake to a cop who was about to arrest him for public nudity. The cop would have to pretend he'd seen underwear.

Bill nodded resignedly. "OK. What can I do?"

"I want to test the machine in England."

"What's England got to do with human testing?"

"Nothing directly, yet." Blender told his friend about the English tourist who'd bought a machine in New York.

Bill didn't look happy. Suddenly there were deep, creased shadows below his eyes which suggested that the blackness of his hair might not be totally natural. "But Max. You want to go messing around in the backyard of that crazy woman Prime Minister? What if something goes wrong? She'll have a televised hysteria attack."

Blender tried to look reassuring. "Bill. Leaving aside your sexism, 'going wrong' is how penicillin was discovered. Going wrong can be the best thing that happens to a scientist." He saw that Bill was about to object, and held up a hand. "But I don't anticipate anything going wrong in the bad sense of the term. I've taken all the necessary precautions."

Bill still didn't look 100% convinced. He was scratching irritatedly at the arm of his lounger.

"All I need from you, Bill, is to put me in touch with someone who can give me the OK. Preferably someone who sympathizes with us. I don't know anyone who works with the Secretary of State."

Bill got up and dived into the pool. Blender watched him do two sprinted lengths of crawl. Political lobbyists clearly had plenty of time to exercise, because Bill could swim faster now than Blender had been able to at 25.

After touching the rim of the pool at the deep end, Bill floated gently back towards Blender, getting his breath. Then, in one fluid movement, he pulled himself out of six feet of water and stood dripping on the tiles beside Blender's seat. The water swirled down his legs along the long black hairs and formed pools at his heels and the tips of his toes.

"OK, Max. I'll talk to the right people. Just tell me what you need."

"Thanks, Bill." Blender listed his basic dates, places and numbers. Bill repeated them back to him then lay down to dry off on his lounger.

"I'm sorry if this is difficult for you, Bill. But you know that it's worth taking chances," Blender said. "If humankind is to survive, it needs teleportation."

"Yeah." Bill nodded and, just for an instant, they were both looking two hundred years into the future.

20. Danger Mouse

It was almost ten when Richie got to the shop.

Martin was sitting at the counter drinking coffee.

"At bleeding last," he said.

"What's the rush?" There were, as usual, no customers. "Oh, you want to try out the machine, is that it?" Richie asked with crudely feigned naivety. "I've brought the software and the manual."

"No, I've got to go out," Martin replied, and hopped down off his stool. "I wanted you to mind the shop."

"Oh." Richie was disappointed. He'd been looking forward to his brother's impatience. "Hey, before you go, you got that cash you owe me?"

"No, sorry, bro." Martin touched his neck, where his chain

should have been. "Tomorrow. Promise." He picked up his phone and headed for the door.

"Clara will sell that chain, you know her."

"Tomorrow, OK?" Martin smiled chummily and left.

"Weird," Richie said to himself, and went out back to see if there was any coffee left in the percolator. "Holy shit."

In the back room of the shop, things had changed somewhat in the past few days. When Richie had left for his long weekend, there had been twenty or so new computers sealed in their boxes, stacked up against one wall. The long bench had had two broken PCs on it (camouflage – they were always there, always broken, because some of Martin's deals were put through as repairs) alongside two computers – one PC, one Mac – that Martin used for his work.

Now the stack of new computers had gone; the two broken PCs were lying on the floor, one with its screen apparently kicked in; and hooked up to Martin's PC was a gently whirring teleporter.

"The bastard." Richie examined his precious metal box. The door was closed, and the machine was making the same noise it had when he'd lost his burger. Richie looked at the computer screen. Back in New York, the machine had been connected to a dedicated computer, or at least one on which the whole screen was taken up with the teleportation software. Now, looking at Martin's screen, he couldn't immediately tell what was working. Surely the machine shouldn't be whirring continuously like that? It had only whirred for a few seconds when it had sent his burger. Not knowing what else to do, he rebooted. The whirring stopped.

He opened the door of the transporter, as gingerly as the sales assistant had done in the New York gift shop. This time, though, things were messier.

"Fucking hell," Richie groaned.

There was what seemed to be the skeleton of a mouse lying in there, dotted with flecks of black dust. He touched it and swore again. It was burning hot.

"I hope you were already dead, little fella ..."

Richie tried to call his brother, but Martin had wisely switched off his phone, so he swore and kicked walls for a while, then gave up and made himself a cup of coffee, which he took into the main part of the shop. There, undisturbed by passing trade, he went on to the net and looked up the official site of IOA Instruments, the people who made his teleporter. He made notes about the machine's capabilities and limitations and sketched out a new ending for his Star Trek chapter. His conclusion would be the same. He'd just be adding weight to it.

He stretched his arms contentedly, and did three slow neck-rotations – right, left, right. The satisfaction of getting something down on paper had, he realized, dissipated his anger.

Until he saw his brother walk in the door.

Martin was humming to himself, looking chirpy and carrying a brown paper bag.

"Here, want a croissant?"

Richie had prepared an opening line about lying, untrustworthy gits, but he was feeling peckish, and the sudden offer of a French pastry threw him a little. "Yeah."

Martin dropped the bag on Richie's desk and took off his jacket.

"A bit old-fashioned, though, isn't it?" Richie asked. "Hand delivery?"

Martin grinned. "Good one. So you saw?"

"Course I fucking saw. And I was rather wondering why you'd left half a rat in my machine."

"Half a rat?" If Martin was pretending to be surprised, he was a good actor.

"No, sorry, two-thirds of a mouse."

"What?" Martin dashed into the back room. Richie followed. "Why did it quit?" Martin asked, bending over the PC screen.

"I rebooted."

"Jesus!" Martin actually looked delighted. This infuriated Richie more than anything his brother had done that morning.

"Can you stop looking so pleased with yourself and explain why the fuck you tried to teleport a fucking mouse using my machine?"

Martin did a long burst of his wheezing Sid James laugh.

Richie took a deep breath and exhaled slowly, letting the urge to break his brother's nose pass peacefully. "What's so fucking funny?" he asked.

"Do you realize this is probably the first time anyone in the world has ever had this conversation? 'Why did you try to teleport a mouse using my transporter machine?'"

Again, Richie controlled himself. "I don't give a shit about how original my conversation gambits are. What the fuck were you up to? Do you think I bought the thing as some kind of pest-control unit?"

Being almost entirely free of a conscience, Martin was now having fun. "Hey, wouldn't be a bad idea," he said. "A mouse steps in there and pow! Any bits of it that don't get fried are transported to a cat sanctuary."

"Very humane."

"Well, I didn't kill the mouse."

"Bullshit."

"Didn't. Honest." Despite his devilish facial hair, Martin could look angelically innocent when he wanted.

"Explanation please?" Richie was used to his brother's bullshitting, but even he was finding it hard to keep up.

"It was receiving, not sending."

21. The Thighs Have It

Blender had seen London's ancient red buses. He'd seen the Queen's guards in their red jackets and hairy hats – damn useful in case of attack by an army of colourblind ticklish people.

But he knew that England did not cling blindly to all of its traditions. For example, he was waiting in a limo in an ancient-looking courtyard somewhere in the City to begin a meeting with Britain's first ex-punk Prime Minister. Ever since she'd been elected a couple of years before, the Opposition had never stopped harping on about her "youthful folly". He just hoped that she respected the ancient tradition of US-GB relations – America consults its closest ally, and then its closest ally does what America says.

If everything went to plan, he would outline his country's request to test the teleporter on an ex-RAF aerodrome in the South of England, near this town called Bornymouth or whatever. Then she and her Minister of Defence would say that they would study the proposal carefully. And Blender would immediately go down to the aerodrome to finalize his testing plans without waiting for their reply.

The only stumbling block Blender could foresee was the modern English tradition of not executing murderers. The Brits generally frowned upon his country's Old Testament justice, especially when applied to the insane, the under-age or the innocent. They'd disapprove of his recruiting human guinea pigs off death row. In exchange for being teleported, he'd told the men, we will get your sentences commuted to life. He'd had no problem recruiting volunteers.

The Prime Minister might be a bit squeamish about this, even though the men stood a far greater chance of dying if they stayed on death row. She had apparently been a real old-fashioned anarcho-pacifist in her student days.

It was the one point on which he would genuinely have to negotiate with the PM. It was lucky he'd managed to send General Colt off to the Embassy, he thought. On anything to do with human rights, the old fruitcake had the tact of a B-52 bomber.

The sun flashed off the brass hinges on a heavy blue door and she emerged into the courtyard. A small, black-haired woman accompanied by two very respectful older men in rumpled suits. In her wake, a male assistant carrying a fat black attaché case and her handbag. At least, Blender hoped it was *her* handbag.

She looked up at the men to say goodbye, shook hands formally, smiling her vote-winning smile, as he'd seen her do on TV so many times. Then she turned towards the limo and walked down the steps.

He knew she couldn't see him through the tinted windows of the limo, because he noticed that she seemed to click out of character almost as soon as she'd left her hosts behind her. She puffed out her cheeks in relief at her escape and blew her fringe girlishly out of her face.

She was dressed in character, of course, in a grey skirt suit, but Blender doubted whether that skirt was of traditional length. It was well above the knee. And her legs were bare. Unless she'd had top-notch training in getting into limos, he was almost sure to get a flash of prime ministerial thigh.

He shot a glance at his Palm Pilot. Yes, he was due to have a full hour's lunch with her. Thank God he'd got rid of the general. Politics was turning out to be much more fun than he'd expected.

22. He's My Brother

"You were beaming in a *mouse?*" Richie closed his eyes, hoping that everything would go away and leave him in peace, but when he opened them again, Martin was still there, and was clearly enjoying screwing his brother's head up, as he had been doing most of his life.

"Look, OK, so I promised not to touch it," Martin said *almost* apologetically, "but you know I'm naturally curious. So I went on line, downloaded the software and hacked around a bit on the company's home page, you know how it is, and then this morning there was a message from a guy saying, like, do you want to try out your machine? I was just waiting for a result when you came in."

"And you figured you'd better not hang around to watch me get mad at you?"

"That kind of thing." Martin grinned.

"Do you know who this guy is?"

"No, course not."

"What if he'd sent a bomb?"

Martin scoffed. "A bomb? Come on." But Richie's expression convinced him that maybe there had been a real danger of receiving something less innocuous than a mouse. "Fuck it, bro, if you didn't want this to happen, you should have listened to Clara. She told you not to buy the machine, and she warned you not to let me take it."

Richie bunched a large fist. "If you weren't my brother, I'd ..."

Martin didn't flinch. "If I wasn't your brother, you wouldn't even be working here. Talking of which, I'm going to have to make you redundant."

"What?"

"Yeah – here." Martin reached into his trouser pocket and pulled out a small roll of notes. "Take your pick. Either this is the cash I owe you for the car, or it's your redundancy money."

Richie, who thought he'd finally understood everything that was happening, was lost again. "What are you telling me?"

"Times are hard, bro, haven't you been reading the Financial Times? Those corporate bastards out there are getting too good at IT security for the likes of me. I think I'm going to have to shut up shop."

"What? So all that crap about the databases at the airport was –"

"Total crap, yeah. And I'm never going to buy one of them Beetles. My old car wasn't even insured."

Richie wondered why he ever bothered being surprised by Martin. Why did he not just assume the worst possible outcome for everything and work from there?

"Fucking hell. The judge is going to murder you. Drunk-driving, no insurance."

Martin looked martyr-like. "Yup. I'm pretty screwed. Unless, of course ..."

Richie interrupted. "Don't tell me. You want to beam yourself to another planet." He pointed at the machine and its skeletal contents. "Well I wouldn't recommend it."

"In a way, yeah. I've thought of a great way to transport us to a different financial planet using this baby."

"Oh, God." Richie could feel the machine slipping out of his grasp. It was hardly his any more.

"No, really. Can't fail. Listen –"

"OK, OK." Richie apologized mentally to Clara for not listening to her. He came to a decision. "Look. Tell you what. You write me an IOU for the price of this thing. I'm selling it to you."

Martin grinned. "Brilliant."

"Don't thank me. I'm only doing it to get you off my back. As soon as you make any dosh with it, you pay me, OK?"

"Yeah. I –"

"I don't want to know what you're planning to transport or where you're going to send it. Any shit you get into is your personal shit. OK?"

Martin nodded. "Fine."

Richie felt almost relieved. "I'm going to finish writing it up for my book, and then I don't give a toss what happens to it. I've had enough of teleportation. It's not what it's cracked up to be." He waved the machine away with his hand, and as he did so, a thought occurred to him. "Hang on, what about all those new computers that were in here – didn't you get some money for them?"

Martin grunted. "Oh, no, bit of bad luck there. Apparently they were stolen property."

"No way?" Richie's irony metre shot off the scale.

"Yeah, shocking. Anyway, the cops took them away all nice and quietly, in return for a bit of, you know, cooperation."

Richie knew all too well. "So the bloke who sold them to you is going to come and fire-bomb the shop, is that it?"

"No, he covered his tracks. The cops'll draw a blank. It's no sweat."

Richie was only half-convinced. But so what. Martin had made his bed of bullshit, let him lie on it. "How come the machine managed to transport bones?" Richie asked. "I thought it couldn't teleport organic matter?"

"Probably just transported the calcium. I expect they'll crumble to dust if you squeeze them."

"Well, cleaning the machine is not my problem. It's all yours." He held his hand out. Martin went to shake it. Richie

laughed. "No, the money, Martin, not your greasy palm."
Martin handed him the cash. That was one thing Clara would
be pleased about. "This is for the car, OK?" Richie said. "And
we'll go and write that IOU." He escorted his brother into the
main shop.

"How much was it?" Martin asked.

"To you, two thousand dollars."

"I'm not paying that – it's second hand!" Martin protested.

"Take it or leave it."

"Fuck it. What the hell." Martin wrote out an IOU for two
thousand dollars. Richie insisted that he date and sign it. And
mark it "US dollars". Otherwise, Martin would probably try to
pay him in Bolivian dollars, worth about one llama turd each.

"What about my chain?" Martin asked.

Richie laughed. "You'll have to ask Clara for that. Promise
you'll let me watch when you ask."

I can still remember what first got me interested in sci-fi.

*It was the sight of Mr Spock disabling his enemies by gripping
the pressure point on their neck. I was eight or nine, I'd just started
going to the gym to learn wrestling, and was spending most of my
Saturday afternoons being strangled by eleven-year-olds.*

*So this pointy-eared, skinny alien who always kept his cool, and who
could send the hugest hulk slithering to the floor with one touch of his
fingers, was a revelation. Plus he could do that neat salute by parting
his four held-up fingers into two. I could never do that.*

*My friends all wanted to be Kirk, the big-hearted hero who got to
chat up the girls, but I wanted to be Spock. Mr Cool.*

*So I was a bit disturbed when I was doing the research for this
book and found out that Gene Roddenberry had originally conceived
Spock as a woman. In fact, Roddenberry wanted half the crew,
including the officers, to be female, but this egalitarianism was
considered much too forward-looking for prime-time American TV.*

A Brief History of the Future, introduction (extract)

23. Warm Glow of Happiness

Despite the pleasant warmth of the evening, Clara was feeling grumpy as she walked the hundred yards or so from the car to the house. It had been a long, hard day at work – she'd done some extra hours to make up for her long weekend in New York – but that wasn't what was bugging her. She liked her job. Or the work at least.

It was her boss, Neil the hotel manager. He and his trousers were up to their tricks again. Nothing she could make an official complaint about, just lingering eyes, one or two innocent-seeming remarks about her character (what a tough businesswoman she was, how the warm weather in New York ought to have "loosened her up"). And, worst of all, the way he "absolutely had" to have lunch with her, just the two of them, so he could bring her up to speed on developments while she was away. And then he'd spent the whole lunchtime saying how work suppressed our real personalities, how hard it was to really get to know people, and all the associated blather that meant his trousers were after a bit of skirt on the side.

Either he was going through a rocky patch with his wife, or his mistress had dumped him, or both, but Clara didn't need this. He was a good boss when he set his mind to it. Knew the business inside out, didn't take any shit from the staff but treated them well, unlike some hotels.

His only flaw was that he occasionally picked on one of the women and started angling for a shag. In the three years Clara had worked there, one of the waitresses had got laid off because she wouldn't get laid, and one of the receptionists had given in but then left the hotel of her own accord when it became public knowledge. It never rebounded on Neil – he was good at selling rooms, and that was all the hotel's owners cared about.

Clara had been doing her best to ignore him, and it was a big effort. It was going to be an even bigger effort not to mention it to Richie. He'd only go down there and get himself arrested for assault.

Hence her grumpiness, which she now focussed on a new target, the neighbour. As usual, she hadn't been able to park in front of the house because the hairy twat's van was open and taking up two spaces. To make things worse, he was out there doing something in the van, and had ignored her when she drove slowly past trying to park.

As she walked nearer, she saw him emerge from his van with a small green-leaved tree. Its base was wrapped in a black bin liner.

"Not enough sunlight for it in the back there?" she asked.

The neighbour was about 25, a builder of some sort. He had unkempt blond hair, like a surfer, and always wore jeans and a denim jacket that were so old they looked bleached. He jumped down from the van carrying his tree.

"No. Going to plant it in the garden."

At some point in his building career, Clara thought, he must have received a brick on the head that had knocked out his piss-take detector.

"Rhododendron, isn't it?" she asked.

"Yeah," he said.

Clara hated rhododendrons. When she was at school, she'd been a volunteer on nearby Brownsea Island. Every Sunday, she used to go out there "rhodie-bashing", cutting down the shiny plants with saws, killing their roots with bitumen. Rhododendrons were choking the natural pine forest. On Brownsea, this meant that the small colony of red squirrels was losing its food source. In Bournemouth, the plants were invading every open space, turning the walkways from town to beach into dark jungles for muggers to hide in.

"You needn't have bought it," she told him. "If you wait a while, the rhododendrons will come marching across the neighbourhood on their own. They're taking over the whole town."

"Yeah? Can't wait that long, though. Need something thick and fast-growing for the end of the garden," the neighbour informed her.

"Thick and fast-growing, eh?" she asked. Like your dog, she thought, like your hair. Like you. She was pleased to notice that he was showing the first signs of pain at carrying the heavy plant.

"I've got four more in there." He nodded towards the van.

"Four? What do you want all them for?"

"Down the bottom of the garden. Stop the dog getting out on to the railway. He keeps digging under the fence."

"Oh, yes, we wouldn't want him to get squashed by a train, would we?"

"No." Again, not a flicker of awareness crossed the man's face.

"Where is the dog, by the way?" she asked.

"Out the back."

"Chained up I hope?"

"No."

"Christ."

Clara ran straight through the alleyway to her back garden.

"What's up?" Richie asked as Clara came in the back door and dumped her bag on the kitchen floor.

"That dog."

"What?" Richie turned away from the sink, where he was cutting an onion. He gripped the knife tightly. "Is it in our garden?"

"No, it's lying there next door like some big dirty black-and-white bean bag," Clara told him. "I just wish it was in a cage."

"Yeah." Richie returned to his cutting. His onion was now a dog testicle, and he sliced it extra-thin. "Pasta OK?"

"Yeah!" came a chorus from under the table. George and Ella were down there playing at schools or shops or something. The lino – white with green and orange squares – was the best present Richie and Clara had ever bought for the children. The squares became islands, plates, tortoises, anything. It kept them happy for hours.

"With sloppy sauce, Daddy," George said.

"Two sloppies coming up," Richie replied. Sloppy sauce – tomato puree with anything handy chucked in – was his speciality.

Clara bent down to peer under the table. Ella was copying

out some writing from a holiday brochure. George was blacking in the white squares on a newspaper crossword. "Don't I get a hello?" Clara asked.

"We're closed for lunch," Ella told her, smiling.

"I'll take my custom elsewhere, then," Clara said. She sat down and took a long draught from the bottle of beer on the table. "Get the money off your brother?" she asked Richie.

"Yup."

"Bloody hell."

"Naughty word, Mummy."

"Sorry." Clara was astonished. It was the first time that any business involving Martin, Richie and money had been resolved so quickly. Of course she didn't know about the sale of the machine, the IOU and the probable future absence of salary. Richie didn't think she needed to be told quite yet. He went on chopping and slopping.

"We had a visit from some security men at the hotel today," Clara said. "You know what that means."

"They've found out that you brought home two toilet rolls last week," Richie suggested.

Clara laughed. "Heavy-duty guys they were," she said. "Americans making sure we haven't taken on any Al Qaeda waiters."

"What, for that eco-conference?"

"Yeah. We're going to have some heads of state staying with us while they save the planet." She took another swallow of beer and burped, her severest form of political commentary.

"Mummy!" came a voice from under the table.

"Sorry. Pardon me. And don't tell your brother," Clara told Richie.

"Don't tell Uncle Martin what?" Ella asked from her floor-level eavesdropping post.

"That I burped, of course." This wasn't, of course, what she meant, and Richie knew it. What she meant was that she didn't want Martin knowing about the hotel's political guests before it was absolutely necessary. She thought back to the last party-political conference season, when she had forbidden Martin to come and hang around the hotel in the hope of getting some info that would be worth passing on to a blackmailer. He had taken to drinking in the bar with the full-time blackmailers, the reporters, and daring her to cause a stink by having him thrown out.

When Richie's onions were just softening, he poured his red mush, or slop, into the pan and it started to smell tangily appetizing.

"Hey, maybe you could get me some work there," he said.

"What, so you can snoop for him?"

"No, now that I've more or less finished the book, I thought I'd leave the shop. Might as well work a season in a hotel before looking for something decent."

"Well, thanks on behalf of my profession," Clara said. "No, it sounds much better than working for you-know-who. A definite change for the better. Hey, that reminds me. You'll never guess who's pregnant."

Richie stopped stirring. "Not you?"

"Chance'd be a fine thing," Clara gurgled. "No, go on. Guess who's pregnant."

"I don't know. Robbie Williams."

"Come on, really."

"Your mum?"

"For God's sake. I'll give you a clue. I phoned London today."

"What? Oh, not Angela?" Angela was Clara's sister. She was a hairdresser with a select group of mainly well-known customers and three children. "She's not having another one? She's like a roll-on, roll-off ferry, your sister."

"Charming. No, it's one of her clients." Clara was grinning ear to ear, bursting to tell.

"Not?"

"Yes."

"No. Are you sure?"

"Yes. Angie was there when she got the test results."

"Christ."

Richie's surprise was justified. The woman they were talking about was Angela's star client, Ann Robson, the Prime Minister.

"This is a national emergency," Richie said. "She'll be forced to stand down. Or lie down, anyway."

"Rubbish. She'll only have to take a week or two off."

"It'll be the first time anyone's been breast-fed during a Cabinet meeting."

"Don't you believe it. I bet Maggie used to make all her Ministers suckle."

Richie laughed and returned to his cooking. The pasta was almost done.

Clara described the scene as it had been breathily told to her just a few hours earlier on the phone. Angela had been styling the PM's hair, as she did every few days when the PM was in London, when a lacky had come in with an envelope. The PM had thanked him, and taken a deep breath before opening it. When she read it, she'd gasped and Angela had asked her if she was feeling OK. The PM had said, yes, she thought she was fine. She swore Angela to secrecy and confided in her. The letter contained her test results, which were positive.

Richie served up the pasta, slopped on the sauce and brought some steaming plates over to the table.

"She's crazy," he laughed. "Giving away secrets to her hairdresser."

"It's not something you can keep to yourself. She needed to tell someone, she said. She couldn't tell her colleagues, and she wouldn't be seeing her husband face-to-face for a couple of days. Oh, for Christ's sake don't tell you-know-who," Clara begged.

"Don't tell Uncle Martin what?" Ella asked, drawn out from under the table by the scent of secrets and food.

Clara burped again. "Don't tell him I keep burping, Ella. He'll think I'm such a pig."

The doorbell rang.

"I'll get it." Richie headed for the front door.

"If it's someone selling spare rhododendrons we don't want any," Clara called after him.

It was Martin.

"Hey bro."

"Smell the dinner, did you?" Richie said, standing aside to let him in.

"Dinner? Excellent. Anything except one of your veggie

mushes." Martin gave one of his laughs. "No, came to ask for my chain back, like you said."

"Can't it wait?" Richie didn't want to go into the precise details of their financial arrangements in front of Clara.

"You said you wanted to watch me grovel, now's your chance. It's bloody valuable, that chain." Martin strode into the kitchen. "Evening all."

"Uncle Martin!" George and Ella squealed.

"Hello, kiddies. May the warm glow of happiness light up your life."

"And up yours!" the kids chorussed.

"Don't tell me," Clara said, "Carry On Down the Toilet, 1935."

"Very nearly, dear sister-in-law," Martin smiled good-naturedly.

"You eating then?" Richie held up an empty plate.

"Mmm, smells of beef," Martin said. "I'll have a bit of bull's buttock." He grimaced at the children, who squealed again obediently.

Martin got down on his knees and tickled the children until they cried for mercy.

"Stop, stop, I'll tell you a secret," Ella wailed.

Martin let them go. "Oh yeah? What's that?"

"Ella ..." Richie warned, but it was too late.

"The Pry Minister's going to have a baby."

"Ella ..." moaned Clara.

"Is that true?" Martin screwed his face up in disbelief. At first he didn't grasp the importance of the news. Why would Richie and Clara want to keep it secret? "Was it on the teatime news or what?" he asked.

Clara moaned again, and gave a brief explanation of why complete discretion was needed.

"Wow," Martin concluded. "So no one else knows?"

"No."

"Your sister won't go blabbing it to anyone."

"No, she never discusses her clients with Brian or anyone." Brian was Angela's husband.

"And she reckons the Prime Minister wants to keep it a secret."

"Yes."

Martin stood there in the middle of the kitchen, oblivious to the eight eyes watching him. The steam was still rising from the plates on the table, filling the kitchen with droplets of herby odour. A train went by at the end of the garden, clunking slowly towards London 100 miles away. Ella and George were entranced, as if they expected Martin to pop like a balloon and disappear before their eyes.

"I'm going to have to raincheck that food," Martin finally said. "I've got to go and look at something on the web. Fancy a quick pint later, Richie?"

"Er, sure."

"You're not going to tell anyone, are you?" Clara asked Martin. She was genuinely fearful for her sister's job.

"No I am not," Martin said. "You think I'm nuts? And, you, Missy," he turned to Ella. "You tell anyone else our secret and you won't get that present I promised you."

Ella shook her head with relief at getting off so easily.

"OK, see you later," Martin said, and left.

Ninety minutes later, with the kids in bed and Clara snoozing in front of the TV, the two brothers set off on foot towards their local, The Huntsman. It was a warm, still evening, but the clouds were being whipped along by a high-altitude wind.

"So what have you got in mind?" Richie asked his brother.

"Making some money of course." Martin rubbed his forefinger and thumb together. "You're going to have to help me. You'll be needing some dosh yourself pretty soon."

The street was empty, the houses almost all lit up from within. The residents had come home from work, parked their cars along the pavement, and were sitting in their front rooms. It was a quiet, family kind of street. Lots of youngish couples saving up for bigger houses, a few old people hanging on. Richie looked in a front room that had no curtains. A blue light flickered on the wall as a young guy in a t-shirt watched TV in the dark.

"You looked up the Prime Minister on the web, didn't you?" Richie asked.

"Yeah. And there's no mention, on any site, of her being pregnant."

"So?"

"So we take bets on it." Martin grinned at his own genius.

Richie stopped dead. "No. We're not giving the secret away."

Martin puffed impatiently. "We won't give the secret away. No one'll believe a word of it. Not that cow. She's power mad. No way is she going to let a baby get in the way of her career. And she's nearly forty – she's probably on the hormone-replacement chewing gum already. Come on, I'm getting thirsty."

Martin tugged on Richie's arm.

It was like pulling on a lamp-post. Richie didn't move.

"Look, let's have a drink and see how things go, OK?" Martin reasoned. "My round. Pretty please?"

Richie started walking again, and Martin explained his strategy in more detail as they got on to the main road and within sight of the brightly-lit pub.

"We'll kick off by talking about your book. Then you start predicting the future – everyone knows that's your thing. You know, you do your 'in ten years time, everyone'll be cooking spaghetti in their mobile phone' bit." Richie smiled to himself. Had he really been that much of a futurist bore?

They arrived in the pub forecourt and stopped beneath the large painted sign depicting a jolly, red-coated huntsman. With a beard, he'd have been Father Christmas.

Martin finished his briefing in a low voice, scanning the horizon for eavesdroppers. "Then we'll lead the conversation round to the PM, OK? When we start talking about her, I'll get serious. Insult the silly cow a bit, call her a lesbian and stuff. You say, like fuck is she a lesbian, I bet she's pregnant."

"Lesbians do get pregnant, you know, Martin," Richie teased his undeconstructed brother.

"Fuck off, bro. This is a pub, not a fucking student union knitting club."

"I'm just thinking of our business prospects, Martin. There may be women gamblers in there. You don't want to scare them off."

"Yeah. Good thinking. No dyke jokes if there are women listening," Martin agreed.

"One thing, though," Richie wanted to know. "We're not going to make any money here tonight, are we? No one's going to pay up tonight on a bet about the future."

Martin shook his head. "Think long-term, bro. You've got to spend to earn."

Richie didn't like the sound of that.

Michael Crichton's Jurassic Park five places above Aldous Huxley's Brave New World?

Test-tube babies losing out to test-tube dinosaurs?

This might cause purists to whinge, but as far as I can see, Huxley has been far less influential on scientists than Crichton. It wasn't Huxley that inspired scientists to fertilize eggs in the test tube. He was warning us about them doing so.

But Jurassic Park set the whole world dreaming, and now scientists everywhere are getting funding for DNA-based campaigns to recreate endangered or extinct species.

If one day the US Open golf tournament is held up by a herd of grazing triceratops, it will be Crichton's fault.

A Brief History of the Future, chapter 4 (extract)

24. Alphabeti Securiti

The "heavy-duty" security guys that Clara saw were not the first FBI men to visit the Prince of Wales.

A preliminary team, who called themselves the "A Team", had come as soon as the eco-conference was planned.

The four members of the A Team flew into the UK for 48 hours and did the groundwork at all the venues the President was to visit in London and Bournemouth.

At the Prince of Wales, their main task was to get a full staff list, with photos and CVs, and to grill Neil the manager about past thefts and break-ins at the hotel. He was told that any employee with a police record or who tested positive for membership of any suspect political group would not be admitted on the premises during the presidential visit.

The A Team also took dozens of digital photos and more than an hour of video footage of the inside and outside of the hotel building, before returning to Washington to empty their overflowing cameras and laptops into the FBI's vast databanks.

There, the employee data was transferred to a dedicated mission file which would enable a computer equipped with CCTV to provide almost instantaneous identification of any staff member by matching the CCTV image with his or her scanned photo. In case this was not enough, staff passes were printed up so that workers would have to swipe their way through certain security checks. The photos and video of the hotel were turned into magnificent interactive 3-D graphics so that all the President's men would be able to memorize the layout of the hotel before leaving Washington.

The A Team's report stated that the mission had been a total success – the Brits were "kick-ass cooperative", as they had been since the 911 events.

The only real obstacle that the team reported was the language. In London, at places like Downing Street, the Houses of Parliament and Buckingham Palace, most people (or at least those who came into contact with the A Team) spoke clear, easy-to-understand English. Not so the Bournemouthians. The manager of the Prince of Wales Hotel was OK, but some of his staff were incomprehensible. The A Team therefore recommended that all US personnel be issued with the FBI's manual of British slang, called Britspeak. This should, they said, ensure that future teams encountered no linguistic obstacles.

Because, as mentioned above, this A Team was only the first group of agents to visit the hotel. A series of updates to the data were scheduled (on new employees, for example), and the "heavy-duty" men Clara saw were the second team. Their code name was A Team 2. After all, who wants to be called the B Team?

As we all know, the American military has a talent for choosing cute names for very uncute things. "Daisy cutters", for example, are devastatingly destructive incendiary bombs, and "friendly fire" is not friendly at all when it blows your head off.

The Americans are especially fond of choosing Hollywood names for their hardware. In chapter one I'll talk about how the space shuttle Enterprise got its name. And in chapter 12 we saw why the US called its missile defence system Star Wars (an apt title, because like the recent movie sequels of the same name, it was a hugely extravagant and ineffective way of spending preposterous amounts of money).

Jurassic Park has now joined this honourable list. The new F-22 stealth fighter aeroplane has been dubbed the Raptor, in honour of Michael Crichton's velociraptors. OK, so he didn't invent the species, but who'd heard of velociraptors before Jurassic Park? Full marks to Crichton for getting the name into our collective consciousness.

Even so, is it only me, or does it seem indecent to give a real killing machine the name of a Hollywood dinosaur? No – correction – the nickname *of a Hollywood dinosaur.*

A Brief History of the Future, chapter 4 (extract)

25. Mad Cows and Englishmen

Blender hadn't been to the UK for a few years, so before leaving the US he had logged on to the Pentagon library and done some background reading.

Unfortunately, it was all factual. Budget figures, GDP, recent laws, military capability, names of government ministers. OK, Blender conceded, some of the names might be useful, but what he wanted was real background, the stuff you get when you scratch the skin of a place and see what colour its blood is.

So he'd asked his Brooklyn girls to do some digging and write a quick report on the Brits as a race. Any themes that came up, he told them, let your minds roam free.

He got an email from them on his first day in London, a few hours after his lunch with the Prime Minister. A fascinating lady, he thought, with a quick mind and an ability to lead people without losing the human touch. Many politicians he had met made fools of themselves trying to achieve this – either they got too folksy and lost everyone's respect, or they tried the occasional outburst of chuminess before reverting to tyranny and lost everyone's trust. Mrs Robson didn't do that.

Blender downloaded the Brooklyn girls' collective musings about Britannia and read them on the drive towards the south coast. At least it meant he didn't have to make conversation with General Colt. Every sentence of Colt's seemed to end with someone getting killed or decorated for bravery. Right now the old fool was sitting there blankly, his hands resting on his attaché case, his age-freckled face set in a mask, as if he had been ordered to do nothing until he received further instructions, and he'd taken this to mean no thinking, blinking or breathing.

"Scientists," Blender read, "are usually wrong." He smiled to himself. The girl who wrote it was herself a brilliant scientist. "At least in the public's opinion they are. Example: the 2001 F&M outbreak. Brits blamed govt scientists for screwing up on the question of vaccination instead of the farmer who brought infected meat on to his farm and started the epidemic.

"Scientists are people who torture animals. The Body Shop began in Britain, and is largely responsible for convincing the British middle classes that 'scientists' are the type of folks who gain pleasure from dripping chemicals into rabbits' eyes." Blender didn't smile here – some of his recent experiments in Iowa had resulted in a fair number of flash-fried mammals.

"The Brits' attitude to animals is the most obvious symptom of their tendency to contradict themselves – their present wealth is founded on their great Victorian inventions but these days their inventors have to go abroad to get funding. The Brits despise the French but spend more money in France than any other nationality. They elect a Prime Minister with a landslide and then mock everything about her – her first gray hair, her choice of an apparently gay husband. Etc, etc."

Blender stopped reading here and gazed thoughtfully out the window at the cars driving down the wrong side of the highway.

"Back to animals: the Brits were collectively distressed by the culling of millions of animals in the campaign to wipe out F&M. Half a million adults say they became vegetarian as a result of this. But how many of those people would have thought the same if the animals had survived long enough to be slaughtered in an abattoir? Other example: a few years back, eaters of pork sausages all over the UK were warmed to their clogged arteries by the story of the 'Tamworth Two' – a pair of pigs who escaped from an abattoir and were subsequently saved by a national newspaper. Denial or what?

"Despite the Brits' reputation for reserve and cool-headedness, there's not a more emotional race that side of the Atlantic. Example: what they won't eat. They're the world champions of food scares – BSE, F&M, GM, salmonella, botulism – but only because they pay more attention to what's on their plate. Other countries simply make less of a fuss about a few dead meat-eaters. Even in scare-free times, the Brits are very picky. Their fellow Europeans are seen as heartless for eating veal and horsemeat, dirty for eating goat, eccentric for eating raw oysters, and downright disgusting for eating snails, frogs' legs and pigs' cheeks. Roasting baby lambs, though, seems to be OK, as does eating cockles and mussels alive alive-oh (quote from folk song). More contradictions. Having said which, these days the British middle classes will eat *anything* as long as it's recommended by a TV chef and marinated in balsamic vinegar."

All this talk of food was making Blender hungry – for a scientifically-certified organic, GM-free, grain-fed, smokeless-grilled steak. He tended to be as cautious as the Brits where food safety was concerned. He believed that the bulk of the American population would quite literally eat shit if it was stamped with the right logo and the portions were big enough.

He looked out the window again. The car was outside the city now, negotiating its way through an old town centre. A group of youths, dressed exactly like US teenagers, were gaping at the black limo with the small stars and stripes on the hood. They were standing in front of, and ignoring, a half-timbered Tudor house that would have most Americans gaping in wonder at its age. Mutual, incompatible envy, he thought.

He'd also asked for some info on Bournemouth. It had been, he read, a "seaside holiday resort" since Victorian times. "Average summer daytime temperature: 66.4 degrees (call that a summer???). Even today, articles in the British press often refer to it as the home of "the blue-rinse set", ie full of genteel retired ladies. But this cliché is contradicted (that word again) by reports in the same newspapers. The beach now has Baywatch-style lifeguards (presumably with centrally-heated wetsuits). Nearby Sandbanks is the most expensive square mile of real estate on the planet (yes, incl Hong kong, NYC, Bev Hills). Outside the summer season (which lasts approx three days in August), Bournemouth attracts mainly two sorts of visitor – nightclubbers and conference delegates, and it seems to cater efficiently for their two shared goals – getting intoxicated and getting laid."

Blender laughed to himself. The Brooklyn girls were getting very protective all of a sudden. Could it be that one of them was up for a spot of extra-curricular activities? Worth looking into next time he was in New York.

"What you laughing at, Max?" The general had apparently been given permission to breathe again.

"This report on the Brits. They're a weird bunch. What do you think of them, general? In one word?"

"In one word?" The general hmmmed and raised his eyebrows. He liked the question. He looked out of the tinted windows. Closed his eyes. Frowned. Smiled with satisfaction. "In one word?"

"Yes."

"Dunkirk."

26. Wanna Bet?

From the outside, The Huntsman looked like a large pebble-dashed house that had had its gardens tarmacked over and an ugly concrete toilet block built on one end.

Inside, it looked like a pub, as opposed to a "pub". It had been refurbished in the late 1970s to resemble a Victorian inn, with a long, dark wooden bar, brass fittings, flock wallpaper and deep red carpet, which twenty-odd years of smoke, knocks and spilt drinks had aged convincingly. What was left of the carpet really looked a hundred years old.

Being outside the trendy town centre, The Huntsman had escaped having its floor covered with sawdust, its woodwork scrubbed and its name changed to something "funny" like the Rat and Pipecleaner or The Lapdancer's Head. Did places like that have regulars, Richie wondered. What did they say? I'm just nipping down the Rat? Fancy a swift one up the Lapdancer?

The Huntsman didn't do food, but the beer was OK, there was satellite TV, the pool table wasn't ripped and the prices were reasonable. They had quiz nights and DJs, but since becoming a family man, Richie was usually too tired to indulge. These days, he only went there to watch a big match or if he needed to have a brotherly chat with Martin.

Tonight, the pub was crowded and smoky. Martin went to the bar and got in two pints of locally-brewed bitter. Richie nodded towards a table where three of their mates were sitting, and they went over to join them. The three guys were all in their late twenties, early thirties, like Martin and Richie. They were talking about the end of the football season, but broke off to greet Richie and ask him about his trip to New York. He gave them the painful story of the heat, and the even more painful story of the shopping.

"Richie reckons in ten years' time we're going to need air-conditioning units blowing cold air into the streets over here, what with global warming." Martin planted the first seeds of their plan.

"I bloody hope not," Richie disagreed. "I reckon we'll start creating massive zones with an artificial climate. Like, Oxford Street will be sealed in a huge dome with clean air and protection from extreme weather conditions. We'll turn whole city centres into malls with a perfect climate. And CCTV to keep the undesirables out, of course."

"Nah, cost too much," one of their mates said.

"Nearly happened in New York, you know," Richie said. "Back in the 60s a guy called Buckminster Fuller planned a geodesic dome for part of Manhattan. Reckoned it'd pay for itself with energy savings after ten years ..."

The night's work was starting in earnest.

A few pints later, Richie was feeling the strain, and they hadn't yet got any concrete results. He was still jet-lagged. A bit drunk, too. Martin had brought more people over to their table, some of whom Richie didn't know. Only one of them was a woman.

"How many lesbians does it take to change a light bulb?" Martin asked.

Richie looked at the woman to see if she'd react. But like the men, she was just trying to think of the answer.

"Two," Martin announced. "One to change the lightbulb. One to suck my dick."

Richie groaned but the woman laughed louder than any of the men.

"Tell you who's a lesbian," Martin snorted. "Annie dyke-drawers Robson."

Richie saw his cue, and reacted with only a microsecond's delay. "No way, she's married."

There were howls of incredulity. "What does that prove?"

Once again, Richie found himself apologizing telepathically to Clara. This pub game wouldn't lose Angela her job, and it might make us some precious money, he told himself as he took the plunge. "No, she's one sexy lady, our Prime Minister. I bet she never gives her hubbie a moment's rest. In fact, I bet ..."

American gays and lesbians were just one of the lobby groups focussing their attention on Star Trek. In 1991, Gene Roddenberry promised that there would be "gay crew members in day-to-day circumstances" on Star Trek. When Roddenberry died, the gay lobby was furious that the producers didn't honour his promise. They ran a mass email campaign demanding "an ongoing, positive, fully developed gay, lesbian or bisexual character" in the TV series. They stood little chance of getting Spock outed as a woman trapped in a man's body. (...)

But the Trekkies had more success with other campaigns: for example, the first US space shuttle was named "Enterprise" after NASA received 400,000 pleas from Star Trek fans.

And the Chamber of Commerce of the small farming community of Riverside, Iowa successfully campaigned to have the town recognized as the official future birthplace of Captain James T Kirk. When I did my research, Trekkies were urging the town to "invite Nobel Laureates and war heroes to move in and impregnate your women". It remains to be seen whether that *campaign will be successful.*

A Brief History of the Future, chapter 1 (extract)

27. Rush of Blood

Clara was happy to put Richie's name down for a summer job at the hotel. Not only would it earn them some money, it might convince Neil the manager to keep his lingering eyes to himself.

She went to see Neil in his tiny office overlooking the sea. He was drinking his early-morning tea, so strong it was almost orange. A taste he'd picked up in the army.

"Ah, Clara, what a pleasant surprise," he said, beaming his brightest smile. His eyes flickered down from her face to her body. His smile widened. What did he imagine she was here for, to ask if he'd like a shag to start the day?

She played it straight and told him what she wanted – a job

for her husband (you remember, she thought, the six-foot-five one with the large fists).

He swivelled his high-backed leather chair to face the staff roster, with its multi-coloured charts that showed him who would be where when.

"At the moment, our most urgent need is going to be for chambermaids. He doesn't look the chambermaid type, does he?" Neil laughed, or brayed. His laugh was as posh as his accent.

"No, he's never yet managed to make his own bed. I can't see him taking it up professionally," Clara said, instantly wishing that she hadn't mentioned the word bed in this context. "Is that all you've got?"

"Well, there's washing up, of course, but you wouldn't want him coming near you with hands like Brillo pads, would you?" Clara didn't react. "Hmm," he went on. "What about room service? Think you can trust him?"

"Trust him?"

"Yes, you know, going into the bedrooms of rich widows who want their pillows puffing up."

"I can trust him. We trust each other," she said, deadpan.

"Hm. How is he at serving customers?"

"Oh, he works in a computer shop, serves customers all the time." At least one a month, Clara thought.

"We'd need him to start well before the summer."

"No problem, I think he'll be available." The sooner the better, if it meant getting free of Martin.

"And it might mean working some nights. Can you handle that?"

"Yes, we can work out compatible timetables," she said. Room service wouldn't be bad, for a month or two at least. Good tips. They'd be able to save a few hundred and take an autumn break.

"OK, fine. I'll pencil him in." Neil did so, in light blue, then carried on studying his roster. "You think he'll be able to start in time for the conference? I'm beginning to get a bit worried about being understaffed. We only want one or two people off sick and the President will have to come and fetch his own breakfast." He swivelled back towards Clara.

"Yes, I'm sure he could start pretty well straight away."

"He'll need to be vetted. He hasn't got a murky criminal background, has he?" Neil brayed again.

Clara covered the violent rush of blood to her cheeks with an equally violent sneeze.

28. Zeropolis

There were two planes over Nova Scotia.

They'd taken off as soon as they got the word, and were now half-way to England. In the front plane was the cargo – machines, volunteers, low-grade military personnel. In the rear plane, enjoying the best luxury the US Air Force could offer outside the presidential jet (ie seats with armrests), sat some officers, lab technicians and ten of the nation's best scientists in the fields of molecular biology, quantum physics, electronics and the comparatively new discipline of teleportation. They were all under 50, and looking forward to getting down to some practical work after months of theoretical preparation.

General McNulty was not in the party. After some frank discussions with Max Blender, in a more private place than a bar, he'd decided that he didn't want to remain a member of the project team. There were too many levels of knowledge and secrecy. He knew that there were things he wasn't allowed to know. That was usual. But he also didn't know whether the things he did know were true. Or only half-true. Max Blender was juggling with people and information. But what if Blender himself was being juggled? It reminded the general too much of the Gulf War. Nowadays, he wasn't sure whether he'd helped to win a war, or had just taken part in a massive sales drive to get other Arab states to buy tanks.

He had told Max that he wouldn't be on the plane to England. Blender hadn't seemed disappointed.

Mark Johnson, age 47, a molecule man with dyed brown hair, abnormally hairy arms and an almost pathological desire for a Nobel Prize, was sitting between a small window and Jeb Hamlet, the teleportation expert. Jeb, age 36, had the stereotypical scientist's straggly beard, balding hippie haircut and badly-fitting trousers, but Mark Johnson did not view Jeb as a real scientist, despite his physics doctorate from MIT. To Johnson, Jeb was little more than a professional Trekkie. Still, if he was a stepping stone to a Nobel, so be it.

Hamlet had already been working on the project for a couple of years now, and Johnson was one of nine new recruits. But despite Hamlet's seniority, Johnson felt a certain superiority. It seemed to him that you only hired new experts if you realized the existing team wasn't up to the job.

"You been to the UK before?" Johnson asked Hamlet.

"Only once, to London when I was a kid. You?"

"Yeah, several times, lecturing at Cambridge."

"Cool. You know this Borny-mowth place?"

"I've heard of it," Johnson said, smiling to himself at the mispronunciation. He prided himself on being able to pronounce English towns. Wooster, Glosster, Nyu-carsel, Sluff (or was it Sludge?). "Full of retirees, apparently, like a rainy Florida."

"Sounds great. I really go for wrinkles and gums in a girl."

"I don't think we'll have much time for chasing after the local women," Johnson said, and turned to look out at the billowing clouds below. Honestly, he thought, this guy had no idea how much of a sprint race it was to land a Nobel. If you were lucky enough to get on a really innovative project, you had to work your butt off until you got a result. No letting up, or someone would be there before you.

"Shit," Jeb grunted. "The least we can do is go and check out some of these famous English pubs." He crunched his plastic juice beaker in his fist. He wanted a beer, and there was no alcohol allowed on the military plane. Johnson had him down as a natural fidgeter, but it wasn't that. Hamlet was nervous about how things were going to go in England. He was a scientist and Blender was trying to turn him into a spy.

Much of their teleportation research had been secret, of course. But when Blender had briefed Hamlet on what they were hoping to achieve in England, he had stressed that Johnson and the other new recruits were to be kept in the dark about their true objective.

It was the first time Hamlet had worked on a team where so few of the members knew what they were trying to do. He'd worked on teams where no one knew what they were doing, but that was different.

"Don't think the pubs will be that hot," Johnson said authoritatively. "It's a really quiet old place."

"Zeropolis, huh?"

"Zeropolis?"

"Yeah, you know, zero happening. Dead."

Johnson laughed. "Right. If they have pubs there, they'll probably be deader than one of these volunteers of ours after our first human teleportation experiment."

Hamlet was about to put him straight on that, but stopped himself just in time.

29. Chainsaw Massacre

Richie didn't exactly gain consciousness. It was more a case of suddenly being aware that he wasn't unconscious. Everything was black. There was no sound. But he knew he wasn't asleep, because he knew he wasn't asleep. If that was logical.

Then, a few moments after his mind awoke, his nerve endings must have got wind of it, because he suddenly felt pain. Fireworks in his skull. Needles in his sinuses. Someone inserted a handle into the top of his head and began twirling his brain on its axis. The plague of locusts in his stomach began hopping up his oesophagus and into his throat.

"Daddy, when you've finished being sick, are you going to take us to school?"

It was Ella, peering round the bathroom door. She was fully dressed. Richie was on his knees, as if deep in prayer to the toilet bowl.

He coughed, spat and swallowed. "Yes, pumpkin, don't worry."

"Whoa, Daddy's been sick. Blur!" George rushed in and tried to clamber on Richie's back. He was still wearing his Spiderman pyjamas.

"Don't, Georgie, please," Richie groaned.

"Yes, get off him, George, or you'll get covered in puke," Ella warned.

"Vomit," Richie corrected her. "Puke's a dirty word." As if to prove his point, he heaved again, sending a jet of thick liquid splattering into the toilet.

"Ah yuk." This was too much for Ella, and she left.

George, perhaps because he was worried about his Dad, stayed despite the smell.

"Daddy, do you remember when I puked in the car?" Richie was too ill to correct the boy. "I puked all over the seat, and all over the floor, and all over Ella."

"Yeah, yeah, Georgie."

"And then Mummy came to clean me up and I puked all down her front."

"Yeah, great."

"She was angry."

"Yeah, she would be."

Richie felt another wave of sickness.

But this wasn't physical. It was something else. Something that was going to make Clara very angry indeed.

"Oh God."

"Are you going to puke all down your front, Daddy?"

"Oh God."

"Are you going to puke down my front, Daddy?"

"Go and get dressed, Georgie, please."

Richie stood up, and went to splash water over his face at the sink. He looked at the deathly reflection in the shaving mirror and told himself, "You fucking idiot."

He wobbled as fast as his hungover limbs would let him back into the bedroom, and reached for the phone. He dialled a number, got an answerphone and hung up. Tried another number. Same thing. Another number. No luck.

"Fuck."

If his memory wasn't distorted by alcohol poisoning, he was in deep shit. He'd tried all three of Martin's numbers – home, mobile, shop – hoping to find out exactly how deep.

It felt weird to deal with the domestic necessities of life when all he wanted to do was charge down to Martin's place and yell: "What the fuck did I do last night?" But Richie made sure the kids were dressed, and had their bags and breaktime snacks. Clara had left a note on the kitchen table – two lines:

"If you're sick, clean it up.

No, I don't want to go on Who Wants to Be a Millionaire."

What did that mean, Richie wondered. How much had he told her?

Richie, George and Ella walked to school, more quietly than usual (except for Richie's occasional moans of pain), and they said goodbye at the school gate, as usual. The only real difference from their normal routine was that Ella didn't want her goodbye kiss – because of the nasty pong, she said – and George made Richie promise he wouldn't puke on Mummy. Overhearing this, the auxiliary teacher on gate duty gave Richie a strange look, but she often did that anyway.

It didn't help Richie's hangover to have someone try to slice his head off with a chainsaw just as he was approaching the shop. He swivelled round as far as his aching neck would let him, to see who would do such a thing, and then ducked instinctively as two enormous shadows came swooping out of the sky at him. The buzzsaw sound rose to a spine-shattering howl, and the USAF planes passed directly overhead to complete the last few miles of their flight.

"Fuck off!" Richie yelled, knowing that no one would be able to hear him above the engine noise. He couldn't even hear himself.

From its previous level of bearably painful, his thumping headache had now returned to its early-morning peak at just below suicidally blinding.

He staggered into the shop and was greeted by Martin, sitting at the counter with a newspaper and a mug of coffee.

Martin laughed. "In pain?"

"Yeah."

"Not surprised. You were really putting it away last night. Stage fright, was it?"

Richie collapsed in the chair by the desk.

"What was that racket?" Martin asked.

"Two fucking great US Air Force planes."

"US Air Force? What are they doing round here?"

"Dunno. Probably some terrorists hiding out underneath the pier."

"Shit. I hope they don't start dropping daisy cutters. I haven't paid the insurance."

Richie groaned. He would have welcomed a nice, clean bomb to put him out of his misery.

"Martin, tell me it isn't true."

"What? Oh, you're not still having your panic attacks? You were bad enough last night." Martin closed his newspaper and walked round the counter to the desk. "Listen, bro, don't worry, you've bet on a cert."

"Oh God." So it was true. Richie felt too sick to be sick.

Martin patted his brother sympathetically on the back. "You didn't bet on some old nag or a flip of a coin. You bet on something that has already happened. What can possibly go wrong?"

"What can possibly go wrong? That's your fucking theme tune, Martin." Martin cackled. "What about the money?" Richie went on. "I haven't got the money. I mean, I did bet ...?" He paused, hoping Martin would say, yes, five pounds, or ten pounds, twenty even. He could afford twenty pounds if he laid off beer for the rest of the week.

"Yeah, ten thousand quid at 100-1. You're going to be a millionaire."

Richie did not whoop with joy as you normally would when

told you're going to be a millionaire. He fought off the urge to vomit. "But if I lose, I'm going to have to sell my bloody house. If the bloke asks for the stake money, I'm going to have to sell my bloody house. Who was that bloke anyway?"

"Terry. He's a bookie. He'll pay up. I'll go and get you a coffee to celebrate."

"No, wait." Richie grabbed at the short sleeve of Martin's t-shirt and held him back. "What exactly is the bet?"

"You bet that old mother Robson will announce she's pregnant within three months. You've practically won already."

"But why did I bet so much?" Richie wanted to know. "I mean, ten ... thousand ... quid." He said the sum as if he didn't believe it could even exist.

Martin chuckled. "You're a right prannet when you're pissed. You started off OK, but after you'd had another pint, every time someone was like, 'no way, she'll never get pregnant,' you upped the stakes. Lucky I stopped you, or you would have gone up to a million."

"And this Terry took me seriously?"

"Oh, yeah, had no choice. You insisted on shaking on it."

Richie shivered. It was all too horrific. "But if he's a professional bookie, why did he take the bet? Does he know something I don't?"

"No, he just thinks you're a drunken idiot with a few quid to spare. At least, that's what I told him." Martin chuckled again.

"You what?"

"It was the chance of a lifetime, bro. A million quid!" Martin clapped Richie on the back, much harder this time, almost knocking him out of his chair.

"I'm going to puke." Richie clasped his head in his hands.

"No you're not, you're going to be a millionaire." Martin put a hand on each of Richie's cheeks and lifted his face up, gazing into his eyes as if trying to hypnotize him into a state of optimism. "It's perfect," Martin said, stepping away from Richie's morning-after breath, which was not up to its usual freshness, "because I was beginning to feel guilty about not paying your wages. But now you won't need my money."

Richie ignored the bullshit. "Did you have a bet as well?"

"Nah, never bet. It's a mug's game. Strictly for losers."

"What? You bastard." Richie grabbed for his brother, who darted out of the way, giggling.

While Martin was messing with the coffee machine, Richie wondered what the hell he was going to tell Clara. And what method she would use to castrate him.

His mood swung up and down from one second to the next, as a condemned man's must do.

It's going to be OK, I'm going to win.

Shit, I'm going to lose my money, my house and probably my wife.

Tell her, and we'll work something out.

Tell her and she'll cave my skull in with a garden shovel.

"Here, drink this."

Richie clutched at the hot cup and gulped down some sugared caffeine. "If I lose, can you bail me out?" he asked.

"No way. I've just handed my books over to an accountant. He's working out how big my fine's going to be for not paying tax. Christ knows how I'm going to pay him."

Martin chuckled. Richie wondered how Martin could shrug off all these financial problems. Maybe because he was single and childless. As well as being totally amoral.

"But don't worry, this time next week, we'll be millionaires," Martin said.

"We?" Richie asked.

"Well, I set the bet up for you. I deserve a share."

"But if I lose, you won't help me out?"

"You made the bet, not me."

Richie couldn't believe what he was hearing. "Martin. Have you never heard of logic?"

"Yeah, plays for Dynamo Belgrade, doesn't he? Slobodan Lojic." He gave a long, dirty Sid James laugh. "Anyway, you covered the bet with that IOU of mine, so in a way I should get all the winnings."

"Right, that clinches it. You have never heard of logic." Though Richie did find it strangely comforting to know that Martin would have to pay a sizeable chunk of the stake if he lost.

This, plus the buzz of the caffeine, lifted his mood a notch.

"OK," Richie said, "first thing is, we've got to go on the web and see if the PM's announced it yet. Then I'll have to get in touch with some publishers. If I do lose, I might be able to pay off my debts with an advance. Hey, maybe I can beam some kind of calling card to them in the teleporter? That would get me noticed."

"Now you're talking," Martin congratulated him.

Richie stood up, gently, to take his jacket off. "OK, to work."

"Right," Martin said. "First thing. I looked on the web and there's no news about the Prime Minister getting pregnant. Second thing, I've kind of hired out the machine."

Richie slumped back down again.

Clara was at the hotel, sitting in the ladies' loo talking softly into a phone.

"I'm really sorry, Angela. It was so stupid. You see, Martin dragged Richie down the pub –"

"Did he need dragging?"

"No, right. He was burbling drunk when he came home. I'm sure he spilled the beans."

"That's a polite way of putting it."

"What? Oh no, I mean –"

"It's OK, Clara, don't worry."

"But you could lose your best customer. Do you think she's told the news to anyone else yet?"

"No, it's really weird. She called me up last night and said they'd got her results mixed up. That wasn't her results they sent her. So she might not be pregnant, after all. She says she doesn't think she is. I don't know why she felt she had to tell me that, but there you are."

"They got the Prime Minister's results mixed up? I don't believe it."

"That's what she said. She thought it was hilarious – if there's one person in the country the Health Service would be careful not to get mixed up, it's her. But then she did the test anonymously, see."

"So she's sure she's not pregnant?"

"Yes."

"Oh, thank Christ for that. That's a weight off my mind. I thought we'd dropped you in it."

"No, it's OK. Listen, I've got to go now. My client's hair will turn orange if I don't go and rinse it."

As Clara emerged from the toilets, she met Jill, the hotel's deputy manager.

"Ooh, someone's looking pleased with their digestion this morning," Jill said.

Clara laughed happily.

30. A Clean Pair of Genes

Contrary to popular belief, there is room for emotion in pure science. Take the simple example of finding a cure for cancer. Even the most clinical of clinicians would be moved by the thought of all those lives saved. And all those royalties earned.

But this is a strong argument *against* a scientist with cancer, or whose family is afflicted by the disease, going into cancer research. Too much emotional involvement.

Which is exactly why Blender had not followed his heart and specialized in gene therapy. Soon after his son was born, the baby was diagnosed a haemophiliac, a surprise genetic throwback in Blender's wife's family. The condition was treatable, but it was harrowing, and the decision to have a second child was a difficult one.

Blender refused to admit that the genetic "impurity" had contributed to his divorce, but it had introduced guilt and conflict into the marriage. His line was that it was unfair to subject another child to a life of semi-inactivity and hospitalization for nothing more serious than a nosebleed.

But his wife had wanted a second child, and got one. A girl, a non-haemophiliac.

They'd held out for several years, but as soon as the kids hit adolescence, old issues had come to the surface and suffocated the marriage.

Ever since the divorce proceedings began, Blender had been disturbed to find himself thinking that this was his chance to find his genetic soulmate. A woman with his first wife's physical beauty and intelligence, plus the ability to produce a strain of perfect Blenders.

Now he had begun to calculate seriously. How many generations would there need to be?

31. Sea-Fi Sci-Fi

Richie's dad dropped dead at 41 – too much cholesterol, too many cigs, and one too many heart attacks. Martin was 17, Richie 15.

The worst thing for both brothers was that they had so few photos of their dad. They had only got the camera out on holiday. But their dad was hardly ever in the beach shots because he was the one who took the photos. When Richie looked at old photo albums, he always thought of himself smiling at a dead man.

Within six months of his father's death Martin had accumulated a large collection of stolen CDs, two cautions for joyriding, a four-week suspension from school and Richie's teethmarks across his knuckles.

If Martin had been American, he'd have gone to an analyst. As he was English, he went to the pub. But this only frustrated him more, because he kept getting thrown out. He was too small to pass for 18, even after he turned 18.

A psychiatrist would have said that he was punishing authority for deserting him, punishing himself for being the new man in the family, and trying to punish Richie for being the manliest. Richie did take on the paternal role in the family, but only because he was home more often than Martin. And unlike his brother, Richie came through it all pretty well intact thanks to the physical release of wrestling and his mental escapes into sci-fi.

Richie, of course, still took refuge in sci-fi to escape from his problems.

He spent most of his morning thinking about teleportation to avoid brooding about debt. And he'd even managed to dissipate the mist of his hangover by solving a puzzle that had troubled him since he spoke to Mrs Gonzalez of Dade County, Florida.

Not everyone knows the exact longitude, latitude and altitude of their office, do they? It's not written on the door: Fred Smith, Marketing Manager, 54 degrees West, 32 North, 212 feet above sea level, knock and enter.

So how did you teleport things to them?

He'd found the answer on the IOA Instruments website – a little gizmo called a locator that told you your exact longitude, latitude and altitude. Apparently, a locator had been sent to every address on the US electoral register. This was how people without their own transporter could receive things. Properly used, it eliminated the risk of veggieburger mishaps.

It was obvious when he thought about it – how else did they set up the delivery service in the USA? They didn't go round measuring the altitude of every house in the country, did they? They just dished out the locators.

He tacked these new facts on to the end of his final chapter (chapter one), and then, while a new copy of his manuscript was printing out, he hunted around for publishers. Within minutes, he had ten or more promising addresses. There was even one in Bournemouth. Sea-Fi Sci-Fi, it was called. Bloody awful name, but what the hell. He would give them a call, set up a meet.

"You coming, bro?"
"No, I told you, I'm not doing it."
Martin had explained that he wanted to go and see a man he knew about using the teleporter for profitably illicit purposes.

Richie had refused to accompany him, reminding his brother that the condition of selling him the machine was that he (Richie) didn't want to know what he (Martin) did with it. Martin had seemed to accept this argument, and had gone off on his own somewhere or other. Now he was back and had apparently forgotten their earlier conversation.

"I need you to come with me, bro."

"I don't feel like going anywhere except back to bed."

"Come with me now and I'll drop you off home after."

"Look, I'm busy."

"Busy on my computer, bro, in my shop."

"Busy not getting paid for it, as well."

"You won't ever get paid unless you come with me now."

Richie looked up from his list of publishers. Martin was standing there, twitching his shoulders, exploring his gold tooth with his tongue. Staring straight into Richie's eyes.

"No, Martin, sorry."

"Fucking hell, bro." Martin clamped his fingers to his forehead as if Richie had just missed an open goal.

"And stop calling me bro."

"What should I call you – Ricardo?"

"Or Richie."

"Yeah, or dick."

Richie grunted a laugh. "I don't know where you learned your negotiating tactics, but you should ask for a refund."

"Fuck it. I'm trying to be patient here." Martin walked over to the counter and slammed his fist down hard. A couple of disks jumped, and the shop's old, empty cash till sprung open with an expectant ring. Richie was put out by this emoting. Apart from the painful noise it caused, it was worrying – his brother rarely, if ever, admitted anything approaching defeat. "Richie, this is serious," Martin said.

Richie knew his publisher would have to wait. He sat back and folded his arms, in defensive listening mode. "Explanation, please?" he asked.

Martin leaned against the counter and explained. "This guy I'm going to see. His name's Biggs. Have I never talked about him before?"

"No."

"Everyone calls him Mr Big."

"Clever."

"It's not a subject I can joke about. He's a total psycho. I try to keep clear of him. He supplies bouncers to most of the clubs and pubs in town. And he buys debts, you see, and when those computers of mine went walkies" – Martin jerked his head towards the back room, where the computers had been stacked – "one of his bouncer boys came over and told me I owed him instead of the guy I bought them off."

"How much?"

"Oh, not much. I paid it off yesterday."

"So why do you have to see him now?"

"The interest, he calls it. Payment in kind. He wants to use your machine."

"Your machine. How did he find out about it?"

"I've been telling people, of course. Trying to drum up business. Advertising, it's called. And he wants me to do him some favours with it."

"Favours?" That didn't sound pleasant.

"Yeah. He says I'll get my cut of the profits. But I need you to come with me. He'll respect you."

"Meaning?"

"He likes wrestlers. All his boys are wrestlers, boxers and martial-arts guys. With him, everything comes down to a show of force."

"I don't do any more fighting, you know that." Richie hadn't wrestled since he was at school, and anyway, after last night's boozing he was even less inclined than usual to join in any activity that might involve receiving violent blows to the head or stomach.

"No fighting. Honest, bro. But you've got to come and protect me. Me and the machine." Martin looked sincere, or at least like someone who had done a lot of practice at looking sincere.

Richie knew he had to be strong. Just say no. His brother did nothing but throw himself into minefields, usually dragging Richie with him. Occasionally pushing Richie in front of him to see exactly where the mines were. But what kind of man lets his brother wander alone into a minefield?

"OK, I'll come along for the ride," Richie said. "But this is the last time."

Martin punched the air. "You're a lifesaver, bro."

"I want first option on any money you get, to pay back the IOU. Plus my salary."

"Redundancy."

"Whatever."

"Done." Martin was his old buoyant self again. Richie felt almost touched that the mere promise of his presence could cause such joy. Though it occurred him that there was one small blight on this moment of fraternal bonding.

"You paid this guy off yesterday?" Richie asked.

"Yeah."

"But you didn't pay me off?"

"I paid you for the car hire."

"Yeah, but not for the IOU."

"No, I didn't think you'd smash my shins with an iron bar if I kept you waiting."

Shit, thought Richie, this was one of the disadvantages of pacifism – you got paid last. "But where did you get the money? You said you were broke."

"You don't want to know, bro."

Was that a momentary flash of conscience in Martin's eyes? No, thought Richie, it couldn't be conscience. It was more likely to be the shockwave as an alien bacterial life form teleported into Martin's head and began setting up colonies on the dark, damp new planet.

"How come you never tell me the whole truth, Martin? It would make my life a damn sight easier."

"The truth, the whole truth and nothing but the truth, you mean? No such thing."

32. Who Wants to Be a Molecular Biologist?

Eleven of the world's most creative scientific minds were gathered in the wood-panelled briefing room of the borrowed English aerodrome. Through the wide, metal-framed windows they could see an expanse of English grass stretching away to a stand of ancient oaks and an immense sky full of clouds puffing north like the steam from invisible trains.

This was the first time Blender had seen all his new teleportation team under one roof. It was simultaneously encouraging and hopeless. Encouraging because they obviously didn't give a damn about anything as short-term as their appearance. Hopeless because surely anyone with an ounce of judgement – about science or more worldy things – should know when he looks like shit?

And not all of them had the excuse that they're ugly anyway so why bother. Didn't they know that these days technology allows humans to do more with their hair than just let it grow and comb it sideways across their heads? And that we have now invented scissors slender enough to penetrate into ears and nostrils?

Perhaps it was their age, Blender thought. The new generation of physicists, like his Brooklyn girls, mixed with computer geeks who had got rich and bought themselves a fashion sense (sort of a skateboarder style with a dash of autism). And the invention of rumple-free fabrics had helped the younger ones, too. Hamlet was the youngest of the team, and he only looked awful because of a general air of physical unawareness – no grace, no muscles, no razor.

The others were all 40-something, and belonged to the colour-blind-goat school of fashion.

One had on a blue-green striped shirt, the colour of the mould that grows on baked beans if you forget about them for a month. Into the stripe pattern he had worked an intricate sweat-ring motif. Another had a tweed jacket, presumably chosen to look English, which, to judge by its "shape", had spent the last 20 years being used as a fishing net.

Fortunately, when it came to work, Blender saw only the beauty of their minds.

He himself had always had a vain streak, because he'd realized early on that you could never have much influence over people if you looked like a dork. But as far as his scientists were concerned, he applied what his Stanford professor had taught him – don't worry about someone's appearance unless they're selling something for you or you want to fuck them.

"OK, gentlemen, you are here to solve three problems," Blender said. He didn't waste any time asking the scientists if their quarters were comfortable. He hadn't crossed the Atlantic to listen to complaints about lumpy mattresses.

Mark Johnson made a point of gazing at the ceiling. He hated it when people told him what he already knew just so that they could make it clear who was in charge.

In fact, it was quite an interesting ceiling. Low, panelled in what looked like real oak. Solid and classy. Probably dated back to when Air Forces were more like gentlemen's flying clubs.

"One, accuracy," Blender said. "Two, capacity. Three, human teleportation."

Ha, thought Johnson, I bet he tried for ages to find something ending in "y" for that last one.

"You are an elite, chosen to finalize a project of global importance. The results you achieve will set whole armies of wheels in motion. In short, you're a small team of whom we expect big things."

Whom, eh, Johnson thought. Someone's been reading his grammar book.

"We're pretty confident that we've brought all the necessary hardware and software with us. But your needs may change from day to day. Don't hesitate to update your wishlist, whatever the cost. Before you do anything else, check carefully through all your equipment, and if there's the slightest thing missing, we will get it flown over immediately."

"Oh no," Johnson ironized in his head, "I wasn't thinking of checking my equipment. I was going to leave it all in the crates."

"This is a priority mission. We have no fixed deadline, but we need results asap."

"God, why don't you let us get on with it, then?"

"What was that, Dr Johnson?"

Johnson jerked upright in his seat. Had he said that out loud? Everyone was looking at him – Blender, General Colt, his scientific colleagues. That hairy Hamlet guy was leering.

"I was just saying, Max," – he thought it best to use the all-guys-together first name – "that we're dying to get down to work. We haven't got long till the nominations for next year's Nobel Prize are due." He smiled as if to suggest he was joking.

Blender mirrored his smile. "I'm afraid you can stop brushing up on your Swedish right now, Dr Johnson. There's no Nobel Prize in this. If and when the tests succeed, their existence won't even be acknowledged. The Brits know basically what we're up to, but that doesn't mean we're going to share all our results with them, or anyone else for that matter. The prizes you will get are the nation's gratitude, a decent pension, and life tenure in your research post."

"Wo, over-generous!" one of the new recruits cheered.

"I already have life tenure," Mark Johnson said.

"After-life tenure, then," Blender answered, and got a laugh from everyone except Johnson. "Come on, guys, I've just been telling the Prime Minister of England what a great bunch of loyal Americans you are, even though the ink's only just dry on some of your naturalization papers. You're on a government mission. What do you think the government promises combat troops going into battle? Cash prizes? A washing machine?"

Precisely, thought Johnson, as the others in the room guffawed. Cash prizes. If my work doesn't earn me a Nobel Prize, I want a noble price.

Fortunately for the US government and the advancement of human knowledge, Dr Mark Johnson was a lot better at molecular biology than he was at puns.

Until the early 1990s, physicists (at least those who weren't Star Trek fans) dismissed the idea of teleportation.

They argued that the Heisenberg uncertainty principle of quantum mechanics forbade the accurate analysis of an object that would be necessary before you could teleport that object. The more accurately an object is analysed, the argument went, the more its state is disturbed by the analysis. You wouldn't be able to extract enough information from an object to make a duplicate before said object was so badly corrupted that it no longer existed in its original state. The result was total uncertainty about the true physical state of everything.

To give a crude example, imagine putting a British tennis player into a teleporter, which starts to analyse him prior to beaming him to, say, Melbourne. However, before the teleporter has gathered enough information to beam him, the analysis process turns him into an outsized chunk of camembert.

OK, the camembert might have more chance of winning the Australian Open, but that's not the point.

A Brief History of the Future, chapter 1 (extract)

33. The Agony and the MDMA

Martin and Richie were in a taxi, on their way to see Mr Big(gs).

Richie had refused to fetch his car from Clara's hotel, because he didn't want her asking any questions. And also because he didn't want to drive a car of his into such a shitty area. Why, he asked, did someone in charge of organized crime live out there on an old council estate?

"It was his dear old mum's house," Martin explained.

"Dear old mum?" Richie looked thoughtful.

"Don't even think it," Martin told him. "He grew up there, he likes the neighbourhood, and the police hardly ever dare to go in there. His fondness for his late mother is perfectly normal." He checked in the rear-view mirror to see if the taxi driver was listening. One of Biggs' sidelines was a minicabs. But the driver's eyes were fixed on the road.

Martin whispered. "There are photos of her all over his

living room, but you do not comment on them. Or on anything else strange that you might see in the house. Or the garden."

Richie tried to imagine what these things could be.

"You two have a lot in common," Martin said at normal volume. "He's a veggie, too."

"But you said he's a psycho."

"The two can go together." Martin put two fingers under his nose and did a cramped Nazi salute to remind Richie of the man who discredited the cause of vegetarianism in the 1930s and 40s. "In fact, lots of Nazis were kind to animals. Maybe the people-haters are the real vegetarians and you lot are just hobby veggies."

"Thank you, Sigmund," Richie retorted. "I get the message. Mr B is a psycho, but he'll be happy to swap soya sausage recipes."

The taxi threaded its way through a string of roundabouts, and turned into a street of cuboid terraced houses. They were circa 1960, made of beige brick which some municipal architect had tried to brighten up with a timber facade on the first floor. It was easy to see which houses had been bought by their tenants – the wood was varnished, or painted in bright colours. The facades that still belonged to the town were rotting gently in the afternoon sun.

There were groups of pre-teens hanging about on almost every street corner. They eyed the taxi like hyenas watching a limping zebra.

The taxi pulled up outside a cuboid with a facade that had been painted pale blue. Tasteful, Richie thought. This guy couldn't be all bad – a pastel kind of criminal.

The garden looked well tended, but strangely scuffed. And there was a large pile of dogshit in one corner of the lawn. Richie erased all questions from his mind as instructed, and went to unload the teleporter from the boot.

They rang the front door bell. A large silhouette appeared on the other side of the glass, and then Richie had the rare experience of facing someone as tall and broad as himself. Similar clothes, too. Black suit, white shirt. A bouncer. Richie and the bouncer eyed each other up, and Richie knew he was being assessed for fightability. He held the man's gaze until Martin interrupted.

"Mr Biggs is expecting us."

"You gentlemen carrying any weapons?" the bouncer asked.

"No," Martin replied.

"I'm going to have to ask you to stand back and let me check," the bouncer said, squaring up to block the doorway.

"You sure it's guns you're feeling for?" Richie asked, as the man frisked up his trouser legs.

"Richie," Martin warned.

"Well, Clara's the only one who gets that far up my thighs these days," Richie said. "Hey, now he's trying to feel my tits."

The bouncer kept an infuriating "seen it all before" look on his face as Martin stood passively and let himself be searched.

"OK, this way, gentlemen, please," the man said, and led them into the house.

The first thing that hit Richie was the smell. An earthy smell. He couldn't place it, but it wasn't at all a normal domestic odour.

The hall was narrow and badly lit, and Richie couldn't see anything until they turned into a lounge that ran the full length of the house. Here, the smell was explained.

"Hey, nice ass," Richie said.

Martin expressed his disapproval with a discreet groan.

But Richie was right – there was a cute young donkey standing in the middle of the room.

The donkey looked quite at home on the dark blue carpet and its grey coat went well with the pale blue wallpaper.

"His name's Rufus."

Martin and Richie turned to see an enormous man coming into the lounge from the back garden. He'd earned his nickname. He was as tall as Richie, and wider. He was about 55, and had a pot belly that looked as if it contained a sack of cement, but he'd still got a lot of muscle on his arms and shoulders. He was loosely, scruffily dressed in crumpled tracksuit trousers, a black t-shirt and an old grey Adidas top.

His hair was thinning and almost white, and he wore it long, with a straggly pony tail. He had a puffy face with large, lazy eyelids that made him look half asleep.

"Mr Biggs, this is Richie," Martin said in his politest voice.

"Better take him outside before he shits on the carpet."

Richie hoped Mr Big was talking about the donkey. His assumption was proved correct when the bouncer grabbed the donkey by the neck and started to tug it towards the door.

"Gently," Mr Big barked. He turned to Richie. "He treats animals as if they were people," he explained.

Shouldn't that be the other way round, Richie thought.

"This it?" Mr Big pointed to the machine. "Doesn't look anything special."

"Looks aren't everything, Mr Biggs," Martin said. "Let us show you what she can do."

"All right. Put it over there." Mr Big pointed to an oval dining-room table near the front window.

Richie walked over to put the machine down.

"Wait!" Mr Big ordered, and Richie stopped. "Here, put this down first." He handed a copy of the local newspaper to Martin. "Don't want to spoil that table. It was Mother's best."

Martin unfolded the newspaper reverentially on the cheap varnished table top, and Richie put the machine down.

As Martin wired up the computer, Richie looked around at the many photos on the walls. There were several portraits of a nondescript white-haired old lady. There was one of a huge teenager dwarfing his mother, and one of a black-haired, smiling woman in a straw hat. Portrait of the Mother as a Young Bride, presumably. No pictures of the father. A classic case of daddy denial, it seemed.

He stepped closer to a framed double portrait by the fireplace of a happy-looking Mr Big planting a kiss on his elderly mother's cheek.

"Arse Bandit," Richie said.

Martin nearly shat himself. He waited to see if Richie was about to get shot or bludgeoned, but Mr Big simply nodded. Martin wondered if he hadn't misheard.

"I knew I recognized you," Richie went on. "You were my hero."

Martin didn't understand what was going on, but then he'd never taken any interest in Richie's hobbies when they were both kids.

Now Richie was nodding too, as he remembered.

Ace Bandit had been one of the stars of the wrestling scene when Richie was a kid. He was the supreme baddie, a man so evil that old ladies would hit him with their handbags as he walked to the ring. He'd had jet-black rock-star hair, and would refuse to come out for each new round until his assistants had finished straightening his coiffe.

His assistants were two blonde babes in leather bikinis and fishnet tights who would give Ace's gullible opponents the come-on from ringside while Ace crept up from the rear. "Behind you!" the crowd would howl, but it was too late. The opponent was rabbit-punched, his last gesture before he collapsed a vain appeal to the bikini'd betrayers, who laughed as Bandit leapt on the semi-conscious fool and forced a submission.

Even as a kid, Richie had suspected that the handbag-wielding ladies were a plant, and that the opponents weren't quite as gullible as they looked, but when he himself took up wrestling he had learnt all Ace's moves – including the combing. And, behind the locked door of his bedroom, he'd occasionally propped up his naked Action Men to be his assistants. He had to imagine the leather bikinis.

Richie had represented the county at wrestling, but even when he was 14 and the proud owner of a cupboard full of cups and medals, watching the televised bouts on a Saturday afternoon was the highpoint of his week.

He was devastated when Ace suddenly disappeared from the TV forever. There were rumours, but no one ever gave a convincing explanation for Bandit's retirement. It wasn't long after that that Richie himself gave up the sport.

Despite Martin's warnings about excessive curiosity, Richie had to ask his question.

"Why did you retire?"

Mr Big gave Richie a brief paternal smile and then wagged a finger at him.

"I don't talk about that stuff, son, OK? I appreciate what you're saying, but I never talk about the past. Some very bad things happened. We're here to do a job of work. You finished yet?"

"Yeah, just turning it on," Martin replied.

"Oy, Michael!" Mr Big yelled, and the bouncer came jogging in from the garden. "Tie him up, will you?"

Richie thought this a bit extreme for asking one innocent question.

"All done, Mr Biggs." Again, it seemed that they'd been talking about the donkey.

"Right, you got that charlie?" Mr Big asked.

Michael the bouncer fished an envelope out of his jacket pocket.

"OK, this is your test," Mr Big said.

"Cocaine," Richie said.

"Yeah," Mr Big said. "I'm not asking you to snort it, just transport it, OK?"

Richie swore to himself. He'd always made Martin promise that he'd never get involved with class A drugs. Martin avoided eye contact. He must have known. The little shit.

"We're going to need this," Martin said. He took a padded envelope out of the machine's box and shook a small metallic cube into the palm of his hand. It was one of the locators that Richie had read about on the web.

"I had it couriered over from the States," Martin explained to Richie. "Mr Biggs advanced me the money."

"And this thing'll let you transport anything you can fit in the machine to anywhere you want?" Mr Big asked.

"Well, within limits. The locator is linked by a satellite phone connection to the machine. You just click to turn it on and it sends the coordinates."

"I don't give a toss how it does it," Mr Big said. "Show me. Here, try this first." He dug a packet of mints out of his cardigan pocket. "I'm sure Rufus won't mind if we borrow one of his sweets."

Richie took a sweet from Mr Big and handed it to Martin. "You sure this'll work?" he whispered.

Martin nodded. "Been testing it on sugar," he said.

"Only sugar?" Richie asked.

Martin put the sweet into the machine and closed the door.

"OK, one thing," he said. "The sugar will teleport, but if there's any gelatine in this, it probably won't work."

Mr Big erupted into instantaneous fury. "Course there's no fucking gelatine in there," he yelled. "I don't eat gelatine and neither does my donkey. You think I can't read the fucking labels?" A small pond of sweat formed in the folds under his eyes.

Martin didn't back down. "I'm just letting you know, Mr Biggs. We have problems teleporting animal matter."

"Just fucking show me what it can do. I'm not going to be teleporting salami fucking sandwiches."

"All right." Martin held the locator up between finger and thumb, like someone showing a toothpaste tube in a TV commercial, and walked around the room. He ran the locator over the tabletop, the mantlepiece, Richie's head, the bouncer's head, the windowsill, the top of the TV.

"What you doing? Mapping out the scenic route?" Mr Big demanded.

"No. I'm going to make it appear somewhere, and I want you to guess where."

"Bleeding hell. Thinks he's David Copperfield."

"Just want to make a tiny adjustment." Martin fiddled for a moment on the computer. "OK, poke your tongue out, Richie."

"Me?" Richie remembered the temperature of those mouse bones he'd touched. He didn't want a white-hot mint welding itself to his mouth.

"Richie." Martin gave his brother the look that he always used when he wanted to reassure Richie that whatever he wanted to do was actually safe, even if it seemed insane/expensive/lethal.

Richie did as he was asked. At least if he was in hospital with scalding of the tongue, he wouldn't have to be here when they started using the drugs.

"OK." With a magician-like flourish, Martin hit return and Richie braced himself for pain. He noticed the malicious glee on Mr Big's face.

There was a brief whirring, but no pain. Richie opened his eyes.

"Nothing," he said.

"Crap," Mr Big said.

"Garg," announced the bouncer.

All eyes turned to Michael as he poked out his tongue to reveal a small round mint.

It had worked. Mr Big laughed. "Give me that." He took the mint from Michael and examined it. He didn't complain about it being hot. Richie looked questioningly at Martin, who just grinned smugly.

"How'd you do that?" Mr Big asked. "You didn't click it in his mouth."

"No, I clicked in front of his face and compensated on the computer," Martin said. "You can shift the coordinates manually."

"How did you solve the, er, temperature question?" Richie asked Martin, not wanting to reveal to the bouncer that he'd almost had a circle branded on to his tongue.

"Increased the dematerialization speed," Martin said. "Seems to make the molecules less jumpy."

"OK. The charlie. You –" Mr Big pointed to Richie. "Go out there and get one of them kids from the corner. The tall one. Robbie, his name is."

Richie didn't move. "You're going to beam cocaine into the nose of a kid?" he asked.

Mr Big wasn't used to people questioning his orders. He thought for a second about taking punitive action before replying. "He might look like a kid to you, but that little shit has done more drugs and muggings and break-ins than, oh fuck it. Michael, get out there, will you? Tell Robbie to stand by the lamp-post on the other side of the road."

The bouncer left, and Mr Big grated his teeth at Richie. "You still wrestle, son?"

"No," Richie said.

"I might ask Michael there to try you out if you're not careful. OK?"

"OK. But I still don't see why you have to test this on a kid."

Mr Big's lazy eyelids stirred menacingly. "Just shut the fuck up, OK? Unless you're looking for a slap."

Richie saw his brother silently urging him to back down. In any case, he was getting nowhere. "OK."

"Right. I'll forgive you this once for Bandit's sake. Here, go and give this to Rufus."

Richie took the mint. It was cool to the touch. He went out into the garden, relieved to leave the old nutter behind.

Rufus was tied to a post in the corner of the garden, near the pile of what was clearly not dogshit after all. Richie didn't get it. Just because you were a veggie, you didn't have to keep a great stinking beast in your living room to prove you were kind to animals. Was Martin right? Was the donkey Mr Big's version of the Nazis' fondness for dogs and Schubert – proof to himself that he was human?

He held out the sweet on the palm of his hand and the donkey snuffled it up. Richie stroked the coarse hair on its neck and ran a finger and thumb along one of its long, twitching ears. "Can you bray any Schubert?" he asked it.

Inside the house, Martin was breaking some bad news to Mr Big.

"Er, you know, Mr Biggs, Richie's right," Martin said. "I'm not sure it's a good idea to try and beam coke."

"What? Don't *you* start." Mr Big was on the verge of another tantrum.

"I'm not sure how stable it is," Martin said. "So I brought some MDMA. Ecstasy."

"I know what fucking MDMA is. What fucking difference does it make?"

"Ah. Could make a big difference." Martin was talking fast, pitching his idea. "MDMA is a designer drug, right? Artificially created with a specific chemical formula: $C_{11}H_{15}NO_2$. Easy to make it pure. And therefore easy for a teleporter to analyse and transport."

"So the machine has to analyse stuff before it can send it?"

"Yeah."

Mr Big rubbed his chin. He was thinking hard. Probably, Martin thought, about all the impurities in his cocaine he didn't want anyone analysing.

"And you know that there are lots of other designer drugs with a similar formula," Martin went on. "There's DXM with a formula of $C18H25NO$. There's DMT, which is $D12H16N2$. You just change the numbers and you have a new drug. The law can't keep up. Half of these things are still legal, and they're ideal for teleporting." He felt as if he was selling a hoover, and Mr Big was beginning to look like the housewife in an old 50s ad, just getting her first glimpse of the way vacuum technology was about to change her life.

"So it's better to transport merchandise you know is pure," Mr Big said. "Home produce."

"Yeah."

"A niche market in teleporting pure designer drugs."

"Right."

"Or, designer drugs that you've cut with something you know you can transport," Mr Big said. "Like crushed mints?"

Martin had sold his hoover.

A tall kid, no more than sixteen, in a sports anorak came and stood on the pavement opposite. He grinned defiantly at Richie.

Michael ran into the house, and Martin jogged out. He went and explained something to the boy, gesturing for him to stand up straight. He then clicked the locator in the boy's mouth. Richie assumed he would compensate, so as to send the cocaine up into the nostril. Some more kids came wandering over, intrigued, but Martin shooed them away.

Richie called out across the road. "Christ, Martin."

"It's cool, bro," Martin said, unconvincingly. He jogged back into the house and Richie followed him. He didn't want to be nearest the scene if anything went wrong.

Martin made some final checks on the computer.

"Best thing to do if you want to beam something direct

into someone's nose or mouth," Martin said, "is choose a regular spot like this, and jiggle the coordinates according to the height of the customer."

"Yeah. You could mark off the feet and inches on the lamp-post," Richie added ironically.

"All right, Laurel and bleeding Hardy, just get on with it," Mr Big said.

"Mr Biggs." Michael pointed outside.

A small gang of kids were jostling the tall one for position in front of the lamp-post. The tall one was yelling and pushing them away.

"I'll sort them out," Michael said, and headed for the front door.

"You can't go ahead with this," Richie said. "If you're going to send anything, send a mint."

"Yeah, very lucrative," Mr Big said. "Individual fucking mint deliveries."

Michael started yelling threats as he crossed the road. Now the smaller kids were jumping about in front of the lamp-post, pogoing like punks in a moshpit. A middle-aged woman came out of her house and started shouting about bloody kids and hopeless parents and her husband calling the police. She and the bouncer waded into the scuffle almost simultaneously.

"Get ready," Mr Big told Martin, whose finger was hovering over the return key.

"Don't do it, Martin," Richie said.

Heartened by the arrival of reinforcements, the tall kid gave a couple of mighty shoves, and for one miraculous moment he stood alone and aloft in front of the lamp-post.

"Hit it!" Mr Big shouted, and Martin hit it.

The machine whirred, the knot of bodies tightened up again, and three men and a donkey watched nervously to see what would happen on the other side of the road.

Suddenly, the mini-riot came to a standstill, and everyone around the lamp-post stood back to leave room for the middle-aged woman to keel over. As she hit the ground, she was gaping like a beached carp.

"Get that fucking machine out of here," Mr Big hissed. "Michael'll drive you. I'll send word when I want to see your stupid bodies again." He took a phone out of his pocket and dialled 999.

Martin was already disconnecting wires.

The atmosphere in the car was rather fraught.

Richie, sitting in the front passenger seat, was dying to ask his brother questions that he couldn't really ask in front of Michael. Like how many years in prison did you get for supplying cocaine to a woman against her will? Richie didn't think that the judge would be mollified by the defence that the drugs were intended as a gift for a willing teenager.

"Think she'll be OK?" he asked.

"Silly cow," Martin said.

"Yeah, only got herself to blame," Richie agreed. Martin ignored the sarcasm.

"She'll be all right," Michael told them. "It was only about 40% pure." Like Richie, he didn't know that the drugs had been switched.

"What was it cut with?" Richie asked.

"Baking powder, icing sugar."

Great, thought Richie. So she wouldn't die of an overdose, she'd only suffocate on a plug of cake mix.

"That's a beautiful donkey," Richie said, and felt Martin jab him in the kidneys through the back of the seat.

Michael took his eyes off the road to examine Richie for any sign of sarcasm. Richie assumed his most innocent expression.

"What does it eat?" Richie asked, and was rewarded with another jab in the back.

"Why? You thinking of buying it a box of fucking chocolates?" Michael asked.

"No, I'm just thinking it must be difficult looking after a big animal like that in a house."

"Mr Biggs is patron of a donkey sanctuary," Martin said. He gripped Richie's shoulder with unnecessary force to stress that he should drop the subject. "It was his late mother's favourite charity, and Mr Biggs always keeps new arrivals at the sanctuary in his garden for a few days to make sure they're OK. Richie here's a vegetarian. Very fond of animals," Martin added, in case Michael felt like reporting the conversation back to his boss.

Richie's hunch was confirmed. Mrs Biggs' favourite charity? That clinched it. He and Martin had been recruited as drug traffickers by a man who thought that his dear old mum had been reincarnated as a mule.

34. Captain America

Jeb was lying on his bunk in the improvised dormitory, making notes on some new ideas he'd had. He knew he wouldn't be able to put them into practice yet, but that didn't matter. He was still very young in scientific terms, a whole generation younger than most of his colleagues on this English mission.

And, more importantly than that, he'd made the right contacts to ensure a brilliant future.

When Blender first came to see him, the older man had seemed genuinely intrigued by Jeb's theories on human teleportation. On their second meeting, Blender had made him the offer of a place on the government's research team – a team that included all the pioneers from the original Austrian teleportation experiments in the 90s. Hamlet couldn't believe his luck. And he'd genuinely enjoyed working with a project leader who encouraged his team to dream, and who came up with the money to let them try out their wildest ideas.

True, Jeb had been shocked when Blender had confided with him that their UK mission would involve a certain (ie large) amount of subterfuge. But he had a strong incentive to go along with the plan, because Blender had promised him that if it all went well, Hamlet would have some major funding for a long-term project of which he would be sole director.

He still remembered Blender's exact words: "It is time," he had said, "for an American to captain the ship again."

Jeb didn't care if his new colleagues weren't offered a job on the long-term project. Science is a dog-eat-Pavlov world.

He just prayed that the subterfuge didn't go any deeper than what Blender had told him. Well, not too much deeper, anyway. When he'd seen those prisoners being led off in chains to their hut, he got the chills. If any of them were put inside the large teleporter, they would be condemned to a horrible, and by no means instant, death. A bit like the electric chair, really, though slightly hotter.

Mark Johnson came in through the swing doors, made sure Hamlet was alone, and wandered over to the bed.

"Feel like checking out one of these pubs?" he asked his young colleague. Even if he was a bit of a dork, Hamlet was better company than the other scientists.

"I thought you didn't have time for such frivolous pastimes."

"Those lunkheads haven't finished unloading the equipment. We'll have to wait till tomorrow to start serious preparations."

Jeb scribbled a couple more words and put his pad down on his bedside table. His handwriting was totally illegible to anyone but himself so he didn't bother hiding his notes.

"OK, but if we go to the pub, we can't discuss what we're doing out here," he said.

"You think they'd understand if we did?" Johnson laughed. He reached into his pocket and pulled out a metal device. It looked like a small torch.

Jeb gasped. "You're not taking that with you?"

"Course not. Just don't want to forget to drop it off in the lab on the way out."

He pocketed the small device that would have solved all Mr Big's problems and sent Martin into orgasmic quivers of profit-related delight.

35. The Trouble with Neighbours

Richie thought it would look impolite to cross over, walk on the wrong side of the road for twenty yards, then cross back to go into his house. But he was tempted.

"Hi." It was the neighbour, range five yards and closing, taking his dog to add to the park's already rich collection of turds. The monster was trotting innocently along the pavement on its chain as if its muzzle was hiding nothing more sinister than a mouthful of marshmallows.

"Hi," Richie replied from four yards, not slowing down.

"What's that, a book?" asked the neighbour, pointing to the printout that Richie was holding.

Richie was still in the critical polite-smile-to-show-I'm-in-too-much-of-a-rush-to-stop zone. "Yeah."

"A book that you wrote?"

"Yeah."

Richie stopped beside the neighbour, but stayed facing his house. He made an apparently involuntary kicking movement with his foot, hoping that it would send the dog galloping off with its human cargo in tow. No luck, the dog stayed motionless, as cool as a shark.

"What's it about?" The neighbour was staring at the wad of pages.

"Sci-fi," Richie said. This was normally enough to turn people off.

"Oh, I'm obsessed with sci-fi," the neighbour said, as if repeating someone else's opinion of him. "Do you know Star Trek?"

"Heard of it," Richie said. He looked longingly towards his front door, even though when he got there he was going to have to face up to the dilemma of whether to tell Clara all about their exciting new debts.

"You seen the original series? With William Shatner?"

"Yeah, I think so."

"What's your favourite episode?"

"The one where a pitbull savages its master to death then

gets run over by a tank," Richie thought. But he said, "What's yours?"

The neighbour didn't hesitate for a millisecond. It was as if his reply was preprogrammed. "The Trouble with Tribbles. The one where all the little fluffy toys reproduce so fast they take the whole place over. If they hadn't found out how to stop them breeding, they'd have filled the whole Enterprise."

"Yeah, right." Richie was having serious doubts about the man's mental capacities. He was a human Tribble.

"I've got them all on video. The 29 episodes of the first season, the 26 episodes of the second season and the 24 episodes of the third season. The Trouble with Tribbles went out in December 1967. The 29th." He blushed slightly. "December the 29th, I mean, it wasn't the 29th episode. It was the 44th. I can bring you the video sometime."

"Yeah, great, anytime," Richie said rashly.

"Can I read your book?"

Richie looked down at the printout. Unpleasant as it was to admit it, this guy sounded like his core target readership. "Yeah, sure," he said. "I'll drop it off later on, OK?" He turned to go.

"No, I'll take it now," the neighbour said, and held out his free hand.

"But you're going over the park, aren't you?"

"Yeah, but then I'm going home again."

"Right." Sod it, Richie thought, the worst that can happen is that the pages will get blown across town and start up a word-of-mouth campaign to get me published. With any luck the dog will try to eat a chapter and choke itself.

He handed over the printout.

"I'll tell you what I think tomorrow," the neighbour said.

"Tomorrow?"

"Yeah, I'll read it tonight. I've got nothing better to do."

"OK. Fine."

"Bye." The neighbour's mouth froze in a quick smile and then he flicked the chain lead and set his dog in motion.

Richie watched them go. Just for an instant he wondered if the man wasn't an alien. But just for an instant, and not at all seriously. Martin would have known if there'd been aliens living in Bournemouth and made Richie bet on it.

I've written up the full history of all the sci-fi novels, TV series and films featured in this book.

The first episode of Star Trek, for example, aired on 8 September, 1966, and the show ran for three seasons, with a total of 79 episodes. By the time the 79th episode was shown on NBC on 3 June, 1969, a whole generation was hooked on this idealized version of the future, where humankind's fate depended on the superiority of its technology and the moral fibre of a good-looking, paternal captain.

At the same time in the real world, young Americans were being sent by spineless leaders to an alien world to get shafted by under-equipped underdogs.

A Brief History of the Future, introduction (extract)

36. England Expects Every Man to Do His Woman

The Prime Minister understood the way things worked. She'd gone through the motions of "negotiations" as if she knew perfectly well that they were all symbolic, and she'd shown no resentment at all. This was a British tradition that Blender especially approved of – being a good loser.

So he was astonished that she could be so incredibly indiscreet.

He had just received an email from Brooklyn containing a recording of a phone conversation she'd had with the British Embassy in Washington. It was made on a "secure" line, but surely she wasn't naive enough to believe that the US allowed the British Embassy to have a secure line?

"Darling, it's me ... your wife, fuck you."

My God, Blender thought, don't the media trainers purge that word from their Prime Minister's vocabulary?

"Are you having fun in America?" she asked.

"Oh, we're having a ball. I'm just so glad you're not here." His voice was smooth and masculine. His accent had the sort of English refinement that American snobs would die for. Kill for.

"Yes, well don't forget I'm going to snatch you away from the ball, Cinderella. Your country needs you," the Prime Minister said.

"Oh, God, not another royal funeral?"

"No, a conference."

"A conference? Ugh."

"Exactly. You've got to come and share my ugh. It's in your diary as you very well know."

"Yes, I've been drinking cocktails to forget. I might be a day or two late. I've got more clients to see."

There was a silence, as if the PM was trying to control herself. "OK, one day. I need you to come and do your duty." There was a vaguely threatening note in her voice.

"My duty? Not ...?"

"Yes, the time is right."

"Oh." He sounded offended. "I told you this would happen. You said all you needed was a successful husband who'd look good in the tabloids and get you elected. I've kept my nose clean, and now just because it suits your political ambitions, I'm supposed to ..." His voice trailed off.

"Can't you close your eyes and think of England?" she said, doing her best not to plead. "The England football team, that is. It's getting urgent."

Wo, Blender thought. A world leader with hormones. The President might be in for a tricky eco-summit.

And there was no way Blender could warn him – he couldn't let it be known that he had been bugging the Prime Minister's hormones.

37. Head Gorilla

Richie found Clara sitting on the sofa, reading the children a story. It was about a little boy who wouldn't say please. Yesterday, this would have been one of Richie's top priorities in life. Oh yes, kids, you've got to say please and thank you, he would have told them. Now he thought what the fuck.

He couldn't tell her anything. It would destroy the peacefulness of this moment. Two healthy kids sitting one either side of their loving mum.

Martin would have laughed at this reverence. He had never been married, and the longest any of his steady girlfriends lasted was a couple of months. He was upfront about it: he told Richie he just got bored shagging the same one. Sooner or later he always noticed something about them he couldn't stand any more. Gnawed fingernails, saggy tits, a stupid laugh (you can talk, Richie told him).

In his own twisted way, Martin was right, Richie thought. You know you've found the right person, because when you wake up in the morning you just want to look at them. A basic, simple pleasure. Same with your kids. You never tire of just looking at them.

He flopped down into an armchair and watched Clara concentrating on her book, hugging George and Ella, sighing and gasping at the ups and downs in the story. He enjoyed watching her. Her face was almost unchanged since age 21, except for the one or two care lines that are inevitable when you've got two kids on your mind every day. Her lips were sharply defined, slightly pouting, permanently kissable. Although she'd had two babies, overall her body was hanging in there. He still liked to watch her get up and dress her modestly rounded figure. Except when she put her bra on first. That made her look like a cow.

He tried to explain his domestic contentment to his brother one time.

"You don't know what happiness is till you've fed your own kid," he told Martin. "You know, given it food to help it live."

Martin was scornful. "That's evolution talking, bro. You just want them to grow up and start spreading your genes about. You're no better than bloody baboons."

Richie almost hit him.

Martin feigned terror. "Wo, easy, man. I was only pulling your leg."

Richie was genuinely surprised at the violence of his reaction. Someone had said a word against his family and his attack mechanism had clicked in. "That was weird," he said.

"See, I'm right, aren't I?" Martin said. "It's a tribal thing. You're like that big daddy gorilla in the Tarzan movie. You know, you're head of the what do you call it, flock?"

"A flock of gorillas?"

"I don't know, shoal or herd or whatever, and anyone criticizes your kids, they're attacking your herd. Don't forget I'm in the same herd, man. We've got the same genes."

That was one accident of birth that Richie could never forget.

Clara finished her story.

"Time for bed," she announced. The kids protested and tried to escape from her grasp. "Oh, by the way, I forgot," Clara told Richie. "I don't know what mysterious mischief you and Martin got up to last night, but it doesn't matter. I called Angela, and that news we got was wrong."

"What?" Richie asked. The kids were giggling loudly as Clara clung on to them. He hoped he hadn't heard right.

"She's not you-know-what. The PM," Clara said in a stage whisper. "Have you lost something?"

Richie had tried to get out of his armchair and had fallen forwards on to his knees. After his stint on the bathroom floor that morning, praying seemed to be his position du jour.

"I'm still a bit hungover," he said, with difficulty. His chest seemed to have shrunk 50% in volume. His ribs were going to squash his lungs at any moment.

"Whose fault's that?" Clara chided.

"Daddy was sick in the toilet this morning," Ella said.

"I know," Clara said. "But he cleaned it all up. Isn't he the perfect daddy?"

"Smelly Daddy!" George leapt on Richie's back, assuming that this was a good time to play horse.

"Do you happen to know," Richie asked with as much indifference as he could muster, "if she's actually trying for a baby and this was just a false alarm?"

"Uh?" Clara frowned, and Richie realized that he couldn't say much more without revealing that they'd just become penniless and were probably going to default on their mortgage very soon. He took George gently off his back, got up and patted his pocket to make sure his mobile was still in there.

"I'm just going down the garden for a fag," he said.

"But you don't smoke." Clara laughed uncertainly.

"Did I say fag? I meant fart. I'm going down the garden for a fart. It must be my hangover."

"I'm glad I'm a girl," Ella said. "Girls don't fart, do they, Mummy?"

"No, dear, they break wind," Clara told her. She was watching Richie very carefully.

"Dogs fart," George said.

"So do magicians," Ella said. "At Lucy's party she had a magician, and he kept farting. Her dad said he must be a useless magician if he can't even make his own farts disappear."

Richie stood facing the fence at the bottom of his garden, a bulky shadow against the pale light shining up from the floodlit railway. His left hand seemed to be slapping at midges, but in fact the slaps were aimed at his brother, three miles away at the other end of the phone link.

"Stay cool," Martin advised.

This was rather like telling Hiroshima to stay cool in the instants after the bomb hit.

"We'll work something out," Martin said.

As General Custer no doubt told his handful of surviving troops when the Sioux hordes closed in with their scalping knives.

"Martin, you sound like a bloody Samaritans training

video. What are we going to do?" Richie demanded of his fence.

"Easy. We'll just have to get the PM pregnant. Hey, you know, we could use the teleporter. Beam some sperm …"

Richie clutched at the fence for support. If he'd had a bit more money to spare, he would have hurled his mobile phone and, symbolically, his brother with it, down on to the electrified railway line.

38. Roadhogs

Pigs moving silently though the English night.

Silence, as any pig farmer will tell you, is something that pigs don't do very well. Unless they're sausages.

Which is why this silence was chemically assisted. And, to avoid suspicion, it was camouflaged by the characteristic snorting of other pigs.

The porkers were heading towards the new American airbase near Bournemouth, but this was not a raiding party of Orwellian animals on their way to sabotage human technological progress. Three English pigs were riding (and snorting) in an ordinary, steel-walled livestock lorry. To protect them during the trip, the floor of the lorry was partially covered with three large bales of hay.

Strictly speaking, the bales of hay were illegal immigrants, because they were made of American hay flown in that very night from the USA. And inside the bales, lying silently sedated, were three American pigs (or hogs), given the honorary rank of special agent by Max Blender in recognition of what they were about to do for their country.

All six of the pigs were Yorkshires. This is a white breed that has a long history of transatlantic cooperation. The first Yorkshires were imported to the USA from England in about 1830, and by the time an American pig research centre was set up at the end of that century (coincidentally, in Iowa), Yorkshires were beating all other breeds in speed of weight gain.

Their popularity on both sides of the Atlantic meant that they were the ideal animals for Blender's clandestine Anglo-American operations. Even after almost two centuries of separation, an Iowa Yorkshire is almost indistinguishable from a Yorkshire Yorkshire. Although a piggy expert would probably have noticed that, like their average human compatriot, the three American pigs were wider in the rump than their British counterparts, mainly because of a fat- and hormone-rich diet. But their guides on this night outing hoped that no piggy experts would see them.

The lorry had picked up the pigs from a nearby farm and then rendez-vous'd in a lay-by with an American truck carrying the hay-covered special agents. The transfer had been punctuated by English snorting and squealing, but fortunately no one in the few passing vehicles had heard the local pigs' attempt at treachery.

Now the livestock lorry left the last straggles of traffic behind and steered slowly through the leafy lanes of Hampshire. Out here, there was no one to observe them. The farmers were too exhausted from the day jobs they had to do to supplement their shrinking agricultural earnings. Most of the foxes had moved into town. And almost all the sharp-eyed owls had died out because of traps, poison and pesticides. The British countryside seemed to be tailor-made for covert US operations.

The lorry stopped at a guardpost at the entrance to the American base, then dimmed its lights and travelled at walking pace along a mile of service road.

It came to a halt outside an old fire-engine hangar that had been fitted out as an improvised pig pen.

The hangar doors were opened, and the lorry reversed inside. A soft electric light was turned on, to reveal a tennis-court-sized bed of straw and several troughs of fresh, cold pig swill. The rear ramp of the lorry was lowered and the English pigs came nervously out. They blinked for a few moments into the blaze of artificial light, and then one by one they went snuffling over to the troughs.

As soon as the English pigs were penned in, four Americans set about unloading the bales. This small pig task force was made up of three lab technicians and Jeb Hamlet.

As he shoved on a heavy bale, pricking his soft scientist's fingers on the stiff hay, he couldn't get one thought out of his mind: is this why I got my PhD?

The answer, he decided, was yes. It was fun. It was action. The hay smelt of summer camp and school outings to look at lambs and ducklings. And the only other times his work made him sweat was when the air-conditioning broke down or one of his projects came up for budget review.

The men opened the hidden doors in the hay crates, and heaved the American pigs out on to the floor. The crates had been well-designed, with straps wrapped behind the pigs' rumps so two men only had to pull steadily and the animals slid out.

Ten minutes later, three Iowan pigs were laid in a row on the straw, still fast asleep and dreaming of their ancestral home in Yorkshire.

39. A Road by Any Other Name

Blender couldn't get the terrorists out of his mind. Those British Asians who'd been accused of helping the 911 hijackers. Their houses had been shown on the TV news and they all looked like this one – a little brick box crammed next to another little brick box. Too ashamed to join up and make apartment buildings, too shy to spread out and become real houses, with real gardens instead of just a Kleenex-sized scrap of lawn and flower bed out front.

He was sitting in a car – a French one he'd borrowed so as not to look too conspicuous – just across the road from Richard

Fisher's house. It didn't look like the home of someone who'd be into teleportation. It was as low-tech as you get. But he had the file on his lap, and the address checked out.

It was one in the morning and no one was moving about in there. There seemed to be no movement in the whole street. No cars, no music, just suburban silence.

He toyed with the idea of breaking in, and might have done so if his file hadn't shown that the teleporter had never actually been used from this house. Fisher had to be keeping it somewhere else.

Blender was still a little in shock. In the past, he'd only really seen London, the universities at Oxford and Cambridge and the taxi route to Heathrow, during which he was usually reading or phoning. He'd never ventured out into the suburban hinterlands.

How, he wondered, did these Brits find their way around? He switched on a miniature torch and looked in wonder at his A to Z Guide to the town. He was trying to check out all the addresses where the machine had been used. But the roads, the roads. This town had them exploding out in all directions like some kind of random bacterial growth pattern. No, less random that that – there were pockets of organization in the street plan – the occasional grid or lattice, like a spider's web that's been broken and mended a thousand times by a thousand different species of spider.

And all the roads had *names*. The Brits must have devoted most of their centuries of history to naming their roads. Every ten yards they changed the name. There were probably more street names in Bournemouth that in the whole of the USA. No Main Streets or Third Streets, not even a simple Winston Churchill Street. In their place, these weird organic names like Wimborne Road. Wimborne? The Bourne was, he supposed, a river, but what the hell is a wim? And Holdenhurst Road? Holdenhurst sounded more like an Arthurian wizard than a run-down shopping street.

It had to be hell on wheels for bobbies. In an American car chase, the cops can radio in – "suspects are heading east on East Street", then "suspects turning north on North

Street." How the hell did the English cops do it? "Suspects are heading sort of northwest-ish on Wimborne Road, no, the road's just veered north, er, make that northeast, now he's turning kind of east into Holdenhurst Road, wait, he's turned again into, hold on, the road name's changing, he's now in … does that say crescent or gardens … Shit, why can't I just shoot the bastard?"

Then again, Blender liked to imagine his teleportation technology travelling along these tortuous avenues (and crescents, gardens, drives, etc). Not charging straight along a Main Street out into the prairie, but winding along Wims, fending off Holdenhursts, seeping into the corners of England like floodwater seeking out the channel of least resistance. There was something refreshingly chaotic about it.

A movement. The street was awake after all. A very blond man was coming out of the house next to Fisher's. He was carrying a thick wad of paper. Blender switched off his torch. The man was knocking at Fisher's door. Had to be a good friend, knocking at this time of night. It took Fisher a while to answer. Damn, from this angle, his face wasn't visible, just an arm that seemed to be saying go away. Not such a good friend after all. Ah no, Fisher was letting him inside. Interesting.

Or maybe not interesting at all. Who knew what these Brits got up to after dark.

Blender started up his engine, fought briefly with the gearstick (hadn't this country heard that you didn't need them any more?) and headed off to try and find the main road into town (which wasn't called Main Road, of course).

The next address on his list was a shop which, according to satellite photos he'd commissioned, belonged to someone called Martin S. Ames.

40. Don't Panic

The bit of the future that Richie was most looking forward to, he decided next morning, was the moment when his fingers would clutch Martin's throat.

The squeezing and throttling would be nice. But the moment when he first had that throat in his grasp would be exquisite. Worth, perhaps, letting go and grabbing hold again a few times to savour the feeling.

The rest of the future looked, on the whole, crap.

Which was sad, because Richie had spent years thinking about the future, and enjoying almost every minute of it. Apart from considering the technological innovations inspired by his favourite sci-fi, he'd also spent many a happy hour daydreaming about the moment when he'd walk into a publisher's office to discuss the sale of his book.

And now, here he was, standing in the entrance hall of a scruffy Victorian building in the town centre, looking for the Sea-Fi Sci-Fi plaque, and not enjoying it at all.

Instead of feeling excitement at the thought that the person he was about to meet might actually print his writing, Richie was simply praying that the guy would give him an advance. If he didn't get an advance, he was screwed.

Richie had become a media whore without ever being a media startlet.

He'd been surprised to get a meeting so soon. The publisher, James Bishop, had said he'd be "very excited" to meet a local writer. Most of his authors, he said, were in the US.

The premises weren't exactly the headquarters of a transatlantic media empire. The muddy beige wallpaper was damp and coming away from the plaster, as if several pizzas had been stuck on to the wall before it was applied. The wooden stairs were bare and creaky, and someone had been splashing large quantities of floor cleaner around to hide dubious odours. The staircase smelled like a bucket of old urine behind a fragrant pine tree.

The only door on the first-floor landing was painted glossy white. It was an elegant door with heavy panelling, its antique effect spoilt only by the cheap plastic of the Sea-Fi Sci-Fi plaque.

Richie was dead on time – ten o'clock – so he rang the bell and waited to be let in. He didn't have to wait long. About half a second after he pressed the button, the door was whipped open, and the young receptionist's first view of Richie was with his finger pointing at her and his mouth gaping in surprise. She stepped backwards.

"Mr Fisher?"

"Yes." Richie smiled, though he could see what she was thinking: this guy isn't a writer, he's come to collect the overdue rent.

"Come in." She scuttled away behind her beige metal desk. "Mr Bishop will see you in a moment. He's on the phone to New York."

"Wow. It's four in the morning over there," said Richie, whose body was still faintly conscious of the fact.

"Is it? You sci-fi authors obviously don't need much sleep." Again, she gave him an appraising look – is he one or isn't he? "Would you mind waiting just a minute?" She pointed to a tube-framed metal chair.

The office furniture seemed to have been bought as a job lot in a local-government clearout. The walls, though, were as white as the door, and decorated with promotional posters for Sea-Fi Sci-Fi books. There were five posters, each with at least ten book covers. Encouraging.

Richie sat with his printout on his lap. It was in a large, silky-smooth brown envelope. He'd emailed the synopsis and a sample chapter the previous day, and Mr Bishop had insisted he bring along the printout and a disk with the word-processed text. In normal circumstances, Richie would have been delighted. But it had all been spoilt for him by the urgent need for money. He drummed his fingers on his envelope.

The girl, who was about 20 and dressed in a distractingly tight t-shirt, was typing on a laptop. Sheets of headed notepaper began to emerge from her printer. They looked like invoices. Royalty statements, maybe? Richie, who'd put on a smart black jacket to go with his white shirt, felt a droplet of nervous sweat form between his shoulder blades.

"Mr Fisher?" A smiling man of about 40, with brushed-back auburn hair and a perfectly clipped beard, had opened the door to the adjoining office and was striding towards Richie.

Richie stood up and shook the outstretched hand. It was warm but dry.

"Richie," he said.

"James. My friends call me Archie."

"Thanks for seeing me, Archie. Oh, I get it. Archie Bishop, good one." He laughed politely.

"Yes, sorry, not my joke. Carol, can we have some coffee, please?"

There was a gleaming chrome espresso machine on a table by Bishop's office door.

"Of course. How do you like it, Mr Fisher?"

"Nescafé, please. With condensed milk, if you've got it," Richie said.

Carol squinted at him. Is he or isn't he joking? Then she relaxed and laughed.

"We haven't got any instant, I'm afraid. Will a cappuccino with Colombian arabica do?"

"Great," Richie said, and followed his potential publisher into his office.

Bishop's office looked like a real publisher's den. On top of his desk was a volcano of papers, with a crater just in front of the chair. Floor and tables were covered in manuscripts and cardboard boxes of books. Shelves were full of Sea-Fi Sci-fi hardbacks. Richie read a couple of the titles: "Monroe Shot JFK", "The Killer Warthogs of Iowa".

"I like your idea," Bishop said, still smiling. "Intriguing." From the lip of his volcano he took Richie's synopsis. "Is this true about the teleportation machine? Amazing."

"Yes, I brought one back from New York. Er, I hope you don't mind me asking, but you do do serious books, too?" Richie pointed towards the titles he'd seen.

Bishop swivelled. "Oh, those. I like to pander to my authors' whims. For every potential 'Star Wars' you get sent a thousand 'I Was an Alien Sex Slaves'." He leaned back in his chair and smiled some more.

"And you publish them." Richie didn't like to think of these losers competing with him for the world's paper resources.

"Well." Bishop leaned even further back in his chair. "We think of ourselves as a post-modern sci-fi publishing house."

"Post-modern?" Richie frowned. Post-modern sci-fi? That was like post-wet water. Or maybe Bishop was joking.

"You'd be surprised how well that Monroe-JFK book sells on the internet," Bishop said. "Anything to do with the JFK conspiracy theory will shift at least 1,000 copies. For Elvis with aliens, multiply by ten, if it's convincing. I pay people to go into the chatrooms and talk about these fantastic new books they've just read. Works every time."

"Wow." Richie nodded appreciatively.

"And we do publish some more respectable stuff, too, you know." Bishop reached to one side of his desk and pulled some comics from the bottom of a pile of papers. He handed them across to Richie. They were illustrated versions of Kurt Vonnegut stories by a top French comic-book artist. Richie nodded some more. The shabby entrance hall was forgotten already.

"And we're just about to publish the Hitch Hiker's Guide to the Galaxy."

"In comic-book form?"

"No straight text."

"What? A reprint?"

"No, a brand new text." Bishop was smiling mysteriously.

Richie knew he was missing something. "Sorry, I don't get it," he said.

"You're thinking of Douglas Adams' novel," Bishop said. "I'm talking about the guide itself. With 'don't panic' printed on the front and the entry describing the Earth as 'mostly harmless'."

"Did he write the actual guide? I haven't heard anything about it." Richie thought he was pretty familiar with the works, published and unpublished, of the big-name science-fiction authors, but this one had passed him by.

"No, he never wrote anything more than what's in the novels."

Again, Richie struggled to fill his yawning knowledge gap. "So you're publishing the extracts he wrote? The stuff describing Vogon poetry and how important it is to carry a towel with you when you hitch a ride with a spaceship?"

"Yes," Bishop said, but it was a long ye-es, meaning Richie hadn't quite got there yet.

"But doesn't he say that the guide is hundreds of thousands of pages long?"

"Exactly!" Bishop grinned. "That's the wonderful part. Before he died he gave us the rights to all the excerpts from the guide in the novels. And we're going to get the sci-fi public to write the rest. It'll be the biggest interactive on-line book in, well, in the universe as far as I know."

Bishop laughed at his joke, the sound of a man who knows he's going to be making large amounts of cash out of a simple idea.

Richie watched him, and the brilliance of the scheme slowly began to dawn on him, like champagne frothing up in a glass.

"You're going to get them to pay to be in the book?" Richie asked.

"Yes, you write your entry for, say, Pluto, you mail it in, pay ten dollars and you're in the Guide. You're an official contributor to the Hitch Hiker's Guide to the Galaxy."

"Fucking hell. Sorry."

The enormity of the universe, or more exactly of the profits to be made from the nerds who'd want to put their stamp on every piece of rock in the universe, loomed before him.

"No, you're right to swear. Potential earnings are, roughly speaking, the number of known planets, stars, comets and what have you, plus any that people might like to invent, multiplied by ten dollars. Fucking, as you say, hell."

Richie laughed. Here was a man who would never have any of the Fisher family's money worries.

Carol came in with a tray to find the two men in fine spirits. "I was just explaining the Guide to Mr Fisher," Bishop told her. She laughed too. Obviously on earnings-related pay, Richie decided.

He thanked her for his coffee and took a long swig. It was very good. Rich man's coffee.

"And before you rocket off to find yourself a luxury planet to retire to, you might want to publish my book?"

"Ah, yes." Bishop put down his espresso and sprang forward to clutch at the synopsis. He clearly didn't mind being dragged back down to Earth by Richie's personal concerns. "Of course it's not without its problems."

"Problems?"

"Yes. The chapter about Alien ..." he scanned down the page. "Don't provoke a single mum – she might bite your head off. It's a bit politically incorrect."

"No, it's ironic." For a guy who published "The Killer Warthogs of Iowa", Bishop seemed strangely lacking in humour. Or was he joking again? Richie began to wish he'd just said "yes please" when he was offered coffee.

"Ironic? Ho!" Bishop waved his hand dismissively across the desk. "Everything these days is ironic. Even irony's ironic. It's no excuse any more, particularly when you're talking about sexual politics." He must have seen Richie's look of irritation, because he held up his hands and added, "just a pointer if you want to sell in the US."

"I thought it was a pretty harmless joke," Richie said.

Bishop chuckled sagely. "Oh no, especially for American audiences, you're treading a very fine line drawn with a razor's edge in the shifting quicksands of people's sensibilities there."

Richie was now sure that the guy was taking the piss, and it was starting to piss him off. This man was apparently on the brink of immense wealth, and knew that Richie was here in the hope of earning just a small proportion of that wealth, and he seemed to be toying with him. Cut the crap, Richie wanted to say, just tell me yes or no and how much.

"I bet you ten Altairian dollars you can't repeat that exact sentence," Richie said.

Bishop seemed to get the message. "All I'm saying," he said, smiling, "is that you shouldn't get your hopes up about selling millions of copies."

"Oh, no. A few hundred thousand will do."

"Ha. Yes. I can't guarantee anything. I just want that to be clear."

"You do want to publish it, then?"

"Well, from what I've read so far, I think it's perfect for our catalogue. A clever way of using world-famous sci-fi brands without running into copyright problems."

"Well, that wasn't ..." Richie began, but it didn't seem the right time to deny his own cleverness.

"For a start," Bishop went on, "you've got all the Trekkies. They'll buy it, even if you do seem to be suggesting that they're a bunch of megalomaniacs. They'll probably be flattered. Half of them think they're Klingon warlords anyway." Bishop stopped speaking and stared at a point somewhere just in front of Richie. A thought had obviously occurred to him. "You're not implying they're some kind of global brotherhood trying to take over the world, are you?"

"Er no, I wouldn't go that far ..."

"Shame. Conspiracy theories sell. Anyway, what was I going to say? Ah yes, we do most of our selling via the web. Though now I suppose we could just put books on the floor here and people can beam them out of the office."

This time Richie laughed along with him. He couldn't believe it was all so easy. The first publisher he'd contacted was going to accept his book. After he'd put up with years of scorn and pessimism from his brother, his mates and, quite often, himself.

"I'd never heard of these Beam-Me-Up machines really existing," Bishop said. "Must be very new."

"Only been on public sale in the States for a few weeks, I think."

"Strange that there hasn't been more publicity about an invention like that."

"That's what I thought. It seems to have been very low-key. Marketed by some little company I never heard of. Perhaps they didn't have much of an advertising budget."

"Hm. Amazing. You mean someone could just beam out the contents of my safe?"

"I don't know." Richie looked over to the corner of the

room. Under a pile of books there was an old green metal safe, like something out of a cowboy film. He wondered if there was ten thousand pounds in there. That would wrap things up nicely. "As far as I know, the machine's capabilities haven't been fully tested yet."

"Yes, you said your conclusion wasn't exactly a conclusion, more a beginning. Clever."

"Thanks. I try to be."

There was a silence.

"So, about, you know ..." Richie didn't know how to phrase it. "You want to publish my book. I mean, under what conditions?"

"Ah, yes, the nitty gritty." Bishop was suddenly earnest. "You might not think so from all this lot" – he nodded towards one of his cartons of paperbacks – "but I'm a bit of a fan of e-books these days. The modern way to go. Quick, too. You give us the file and we can have you on line –"

Richie interrupted him. "What, you mean, no paper?" Richie had been looking forward to thrusting a few copies – autographed, of course – under his mates' sceptical noses.

Bishop knew all about this frustration. After all, Richie's wasn't exactly the first new author's face he'd seen.

"If the e-books sell well," he said, "then we'll consider printing on demand. But that only happens after a thousand or so e-books."

"A thousand? How long will that take?" Richie needed money now, not in ten years' time.

"Oh, it could take ..." Bishop searched the ceiling for a convincing number. "Anything from ..."

"What about an advance?" Richie asked. "How much do you –"

His question trailed off as Bishop snorted his surprise. "Advance? Sorry, Mr Fisher – Richie. I'm afraid, well, how shall I put it?" He consulted the ceiling again.

"Simply?" Richie suggested.

Bishop nodded and put his two palms together as if he was praying. "OK, here it is, Richie, straight. You give me two hundred pounds –"

"I." Richie couldn't say any more. Hopes, prayers and

illusions were tumbling around him like mangled corpses beneath the trampling hooves of an Iowa killer warthog.

Bishop saw that Richie was pumping out mental antibodies. He began his hard sell. "Hear me out, Richie. It's only the price of what? Ten CDs? You're paying to set up a stall in my market. That's all. I've got a market hall to run. Heating to pay for, a secretary," – he pointed through the door towards Carol – "posters to print. I pay my chatroom kids."

"No," Richie said, to himself more than Bishop.

"Then," Bishop went on quickly, "if your market stall starts to sell good quantities of second-hand clothes, or fish, or turnips or whatever, you get your outlay back and we both start to make profits. I can't afford to take risks. But I'll give you my full logistical backing to minimize *your* risk," Bishop said.

"No," Richie repeated. This time it was all to Bishop. He stood up, clutching his disk and his typescript. "Now I see what you mean by post-modern," he said. "You've dispensed with the ridiculous modern notion of paying authors. They pay you."

He walked out.

"You're right," he told Carol the secretary, "I don't look like a sci-fi writer. I'm a fucking turnip trader." He left, slamming the door behind him with an almost satisfying crash.

No, Carol thought, you're definitely weird enough to write sci-fi.

The worst thing was, if he hadn't been hit by his personal recession, he would have been tempted.

After all, he told himself, Bishop was providing a quick, easy service. It was the literary version of a wank. But the trouble with a wank was that you couldn't get it up for real sex afterwards.

If Gulliver's Travels was written today, it would probably be bought by a sci-fi publisher. It's too wacky to be satire and it's not gobliny enough for fantasy. Yes, it's sci-fi.

Apart from anything else, it contains an amazing piece of scientific prophecy.

Jonathan Swift describes astronomers on the island of Laputa observing that Mars's moons revolve around the planet in less time than the planet takes to make one rotation. This was in 1726. It wasn't until 1877 that the moons of Mars were actually discovered, and one of them does in fact orbit Mars three times for every rotation of the planet.

Only one explanation for this and the sheer misanthropy of the satire in Gulliver's Travels. Johnny Swift wasn't Irish at all – he was a Martian.

A Brief History of the Future, chapter 20 (extract)

41. Old-fashioned Marriage

Max Blender was softly singing his national anthem – or one of them, anyway. A young woman looked over the top of her large paper beaker at him, recognizing the tune but not the words. After all, she was English.

An American who overheard Blender might have thought that his nose was bunged up. But it wasn't.

"God Bless Arabica," he sang, "God Bless Arabica." He was feeling good, and all thanks to the simplest of things, a cup of espresso, courtesy of a chain of coffee shops that America has imported into the UK.

He felt good, he realized, because he felt at home. The soft rim of the paper cup on his lip, the staff uniforms, the familiar logo stamped on every available surface, it had all been imported direct and untainted from his native land.

Sure, the setting was still English. The coffee shop was in a row of quaint little brick buildings that must have been family stores in the olden days – a butcher's, a baker's, that kind of stuff. He'd just broken into a very similar one further down the hill and had managed to get in and out with absolutely no problem at all. The Brits' security was as quaint as their buildings.

The coffee shop was narrow, with a counter at the back and a row of stools along each wall, leaving only just enough space down the middle to wait in line. Blender was sitting nearest the window, and the traffic he saw going past was very English – a mix of Japanese, Korean and French cars, with just the occasional German-owned "British" make. Still, he thought, the people sitting on the ten or so other stools looked totally at home with the whole paper-cup/blueberry muffin culture. He'd expected the Brits to insist on China tea in china cups, and those crumpet things he'd had in Oxford one time, like a hot bathroom sponge with butter oozing out of the holes and on to your shirt front.

His only critique of the scene would have been that the kids working at the shop – a shaven-headed teenage boy and an older (ie just over 18), tired-looking woman, hadn't quite got the smile right. The counter staff at his usual branch in Washington managed a welcoming smile that was almost blindingly approving. But these Brits seemed to think that certain orders on the imported menu were inherently silly. A woman in line ahead of Blender had ordered a double latte with whipped cream and chocolate chips, and the young guy had repeated the order with a hint of italics – *double* latte? with *whipped* cream? and *chocolate chips*? – as if he thought that the woman should have ordered something more modest.

In the US, the woman could have ordered a triple latte with quadruple whipped elephant sperm and the order would have been confirmed as if it was the best idea ever, including the wheel, chilled champagne and oral sex.

It was like security and road naming. The Brits still had lots to learn about coffee.

But even so, overall, Blender was feeling good on the older side of the Atlantic.

He felt even better when his phone rang (ringtone: the theme of a certain classic TV sci-fi series) and it was one of the Brooklyn girls with news about Richard Fisher.

He listened for a few seconds then asked, "sorry, he put a bet on *what*?" The young woman who'd stared at him because of his singing turned to stare again, this time because of his accent. You didn't get many Americans in here.

Blender listened to the answer and thought for a moment.

"And that's – what – fifteen thousand dollars? Wow. Who is this guy?"

The woman stared again and grunted a soft "huh". Not just American, she seemed to be thinking, but talking loud and talking money. Typical.

Blender turned further towards the window, and saw a faint reflection of himself set against the English street, where a towering yellow bus was brushing past the low branches of a drooping pine tree.

The voice in Brooklyn explained. "Judging by his phone calls, he doesn't make a habit of gambling. He's freaking out in case he loses."

"So why did he bet so much?"

"He had inside information."

"So is she pregnant or isn't she?"

Again, Blender heard the soft "huh" behind him. What would the woman say, he thought, if she knew who they were talking about?

"We're not so sure. From what we hear in her calls, if she is pregnant, it must be a chance in a million. Her husband is totally open to her about his gay lover. Guy called Andrew, an attaché at the Embassy here in Washington."

"Really? So he and she don't ..."

"Not too often. When he's talking about Andrew, she says he's making her jealous, but she doesn't really object as such. More like, she's jealous of the fun he's having. Seems to be one of those old-fashioned bisexual open marriages."

"Hmm." Blender remembered the PM getting into the limo, pictured the flash of thigh. "You've given me an idea," he said. "Great work. Thanks."

"OK." The girl in Brooklyn was pleased to have given her boss yet another idea. And surprised that he'd been so full of praise. He set such high standards for himself that he often took his helpers' hard work for granted. He hadn't noticed that she'd been calling at what was for her the middle of the night, but maybe that was too much to ask.

42. Space Seed

"All you have to do is get the locator within an inch of her knickers and Bob's your uncle."

"What?"

"You get your sister-in-law to insert a microscopic version of the locator into a pair of the Prime Ministerial knickers, then we just beam the sperm into her."

"Martin, you are sick. Apart from anything else, don't you think she's going to notice if she's walking along and her knickers suddenly get all gooey?"

"Oh God. Gooey knickers. And you say I'm the sick one." Martin reeled back in his chair, shaking his head to get rid of the image.

Richie sat opposite him near the door of a town-centre pub (called, oh so humorously, The Ferret and Trouser Leg), wondering as usual how his brother pulled off this trick of his. Here they were discussing ways of saving Richie from the mire, and Martin, who was in serious mire himself, was treating it as an exercise in mental gymnastics, as if somebody had asked him how to drive from Southampton to Bournemouth without by-passing a single pub.

Richie took a long pull of his beer. The place was quiet except for the bustle of the aproned staff as they cleaned up after the lunchtime rush. The office workers had gobbled their bar meals and gone back to work. Only a couple of tourists and the Fisher brothers had stayed on. The bitter tasted bitter, much moreso than the beer at The Huntsman, but Richie thought that might be due to some residual bitterness inside his mouth. Life had got like that recently.

"Stop talking bollocks and concentrate," Richie said. "If you can't beam burgers or mice, you can't beam sperm, and you know it. The question is, can we beam gold?"

"Gold?"

"Yeah. You think we could beam some out of a jeweller's shop window into our machine?"

"My machine, you mean."

"Whatever."

Martin looked dubious.

"You think gold has too complex a chemical formula to beam in our machine?" Richie asked.

"Dunno," Martin said. "Maybe not. When it's pure, that is."

"You're right," Richie admitted. "It might not always be pure. Unlike –" he lowered his voice – "diamonds ..."

Martin gaped at him in disbelief. "What, Richie Fisher, who didn't want to know how I planned to make money with the machine in case it incriminated him, and who gave me an earful for transporting drugs? That same Richie Fisher wants to start dealing in stolen diamonds?" Martin was bouncing gleefully in his seat.

"Well, if I have to pay off my stake money and my family's on the line, yeah." Richie saw no option. At least teleportation crime ought to be clean. No charging in there with a shotgun, no unpleasant threats. You'd just beam the goodies away.

"Well, that is something I'd love to watch. I wouldn't even take my cut," Martin said. "Shame it's not feasible."

"Why not?"

"This isn't Star Trek, you know. Machines can't beam stuff in unless it's been sent from another machine. They can't just reach out and dematerialize things willy-nilly. Your target object has got to be enclosed in a teleporter and analysed by the software. How do you expect the machine to know exactly what to transport?"

"Shit."

Martin took a sip from his glass then seemed to have a lightbulb-over-the-head moment. "Hey, there is one possibility you haven't considered seriously yet."

"What's that?" Richie braced himself for the worst.

"Well, you're going to be working at the hotel, aren't you?"

"Yeah."

"Room service, right?"

"So Clara says, yeah."

"Well then. Make sure you wear a clean pair of underpants every day. What Prime Minister could resist a strapping lad like yurgh."

Martin's flow was cut off as approximately half a pint of bitter flowed into his groin.

43. Knock Knock Who's There

They arrived in two cars and a van. Twelve agents – nine men and three women – whose job was to finalize preparations for the President's arrival.

This was the third team to visit the Prince of Wales Hotel. Logically, therefore, they were A Team 3.

Theirs was in no way a secret mission. The vehicles, all models that were never usually seen in England, had been flown in from Washington on a military transport aircraft and driven in a convoy down to the south coast at a maximum of 55mph, the legal limit on most American roads, but an infuriatingly slow pace to your average speeding British driver. The convoy was identified and sworn at by every driver who overtook it. Secrecy was not on the menu.

Nine of the team were dressed in dark-blue suits and white shirts. They were the field agents. Three of them had on white sweatshirts, black combat-style trousers and leather jackets. These were the technicians. They all moved as if every gesture was rehearsed. Which it was.

The three vehicles pulled into the hotel car park in formation – car, car, van. They parked in a V-shape, the van at the point, flanked by the two cars. One passenger got out of each of the vehicles – three suited men – while the drivers kept the engines running.

The three passengers scanned the surroundings for potential threats. Each was responsible for a 120° section of the horizon. They noted respectively an expanse of tarmac leading to a small hedge and the road beyond – no snipers in the hedge; a row of visitors' cars (empty) in front of the white facade of the hotel – no snipers at any of the windows; and a low brick wall occupied by the hotel sign (five stars electrically lit) and one fat seagull – unarmed.

Inside the van, a female technician reported that no laser sights were being trained on them from the large hotel opposite. Engines were turned off.

One of the passengers tensed. "Incoming," he announced. A uniformed male had exited the hotel building and was jogging towards them. Three hands immediately went to three armpits.

The potential assailant's life was saved only by the almost instantaneous match-up between his facial bone structure as transmitted by digital camera to the computer in the van, and the staff identity photos provided by the hotel some weeks before.

A female voice came over the earphones: "It's the porter."

Hands emerged from armpits.

"Help you with your luggage, Sirs?" said Paul Taylor (19, Caucasian male, chestnut hair, blue eyes, small scar on left side of chin), unaware that he'd been one computer glitch away from a bullet wound.

"Please accompany us indoors," a blue-suited American replied. "We'd like to have a chinwag with the guvnor."

Neil emerged into the lobby, smiling broadly and holding out his hand.

"Welcome to the Prince of Wales," he said.

"Wotcha, mate," said the lead American.

He asked for an updated staff list, refused the offer of a cup of tea and set his team to work. The female technician stayed in the (bombproof) van, guarded by a field agent and a barrage of hidden cameras. The other agents carried three large black suitcases and several smaller bags into the hotel. These did not contain the presidential socks and pyjamas. They were full of the latest anti-bugging and anti-intruder equipment, plus the plans to the hotel and personnel files obtained by A Team 1.

The actual suite where the President was due to sleep was already empty, and being paid for by the US government.

The team began here with a full sweep for listening devices, cameras, and all the other conventional Cold-War espionage equipment. Because the world had entered a new era since the 911 events, the team was also obliged to do a biological weapons sweep with an adapted vacuum cleaner, and to instal a foot-level explosives detector in the doorway in case anyone tried to enter wearing booby-trapped shoes.

The hotel staff didn't see or hear anything from the team for two hours. Waiters, chambermaids and cooks came to the lobby to stare at the vehicles. Neil sat at his desk wondering when the Americans would get hungry or thirsty. But there was no sign of them until he got a phone call.

"We have an issue with your windows," an American woman said.

"An issue?" Neil said.

"We need to remove them."

"I'll be right up."

"Wait!" the voice called, to stop Neil ringing off. "Knock four times. One-two, one-two. Got that?"

"Yes, knock-knock knock-knocking on heaven's door," Neil said. The phone went dead.

"OK, stop me if you don't understand anything." One of the technicians, a thin Hispanic with a well-trimmed beard, was pointing towards a bedroom window. The other Americans were watching.

"Will do," Neil said. He was surprised to see that after two hours of meddling, the suite looked almost exactly the same, though it smelled of paint, electrics, perfume and sweat. There was a yellow plastic sheet on the floor, with a drill, rolls of wire and small pieces of electrical equipment laid out methodically across it.

"These windows are sealed shut," the technician said.

"No they're not," Neil said.

"They won't open," the technician said.

"Yes, they will," Neil said.

"We need to be able to open them in case of an evacuation situation," the technician said.

"I wouldn't advise that," Neil said. "It's a long way down."

"We have an inflatable escape chute," the technician said, pointing to a suitcase.

"Ah."

"But the windows are sealed shut," the technician said.

"No they're not. Let me try." Neil stepped forward.

"Wait!" The technician grabbed his arm. He gave a signal to the other technician, who stepped behind the curtain, then reappeared and nodded. Neil didn't dare ask what had been done. "Now go ahead," the Hispanic technician said.

Neil gripped the frame of the sash window at the top of the lower pane. He put one hand in either corner, and heaved upwards. Nothing. He shifted his weight a little to one side and heaved again. The window creaked and then shot open. The sea air wafted in.

"There," Neil said, rubbing flecks of paint off his fingers. "It's a knack. This is an old building, you know." He smiled, but inwardly he was cursing the generations of decorators who hadn't sanded down before repainting the windows.

The technicians were unimpressed. They exchanged a disapproving look with one of the men in suits. The man nodded.

"We need to replace these windows," the technician said.

Neil laughed. "I agree 100%, but you can't, I'm afraid. It's a listed building."

The Americans looked shocked. One of the suits, a woman, spoke up. "You mean it's structurally unsound?"

"No, not listing, *listed*. An historic monument. Can't replace a bloody lightbulb without consulting the British Museum." There was an old sepia photo of the hotel on the lobby wall. It fascinated the guests, but to Neil it was like being haunted by a ghost. He was in favour of ripping out every window in the place and putting in aluminium double-glazing – the energy savings would be enormous. But the council wouldn't let him.

"British Museum?" The female suit looked nervously at the floor and walls.

Neil suspected that a certain amount of excavation and carpet-ripping had gone on, though everything looked perfect. "No, no, sorry," he said. "That was an exaggeration. Bad habit of mine. It's just the facade. We can't change anything there.

Roof, brickwork and the like. Windows, as well, I'm afraid."

"Do you mind if we just sand all these windows down so that they open and shut properly?" the technician asked.

"Weh." Neil almost choked. He had never heard that sentence spoken in his whole career. It was as unbelievable as if a host of angels had come down from heaven and asked him if he'd like an eternal all-over warm-oil body massage.

"They'll be good as new by the end of the day," the technician said.

"Wuh." Neil shivered. The angels would be naked. "Be my guest," he said, mentally calculating how many weeks it would take his usual decorating firm to do the same job, and cock it up so that the windows would never open ever again.

"OK, issue solved," the chief suit said. He turned to Neil. "Ta, mate."

"Don't mention it, er, buddy," Neil replied.

No one saw anything more of A Team 3 until the early afternoon, when they began to fan out from the President's room. They were spotted pointing microphone-type things at walls and doors, and marking key points off on a set of 3-D plans.

They phoned to ask for some chairs.

"Chairs?" Neil asked.

"Yes. Apparently you have some metal-framed dining-room chairs, blue-cushioned, no armrests, weight approximately ten pounds." It was the Hispanic technician.

"Do we?"

"We need sixteen. Can we take them out of the dining room?"

"Certainly. Do you need any tables?"

"No, just chairs."

Afterwards, the A Team 3 was seen probing and listening to the chairs, and photographing them beside lift doors. Then the chairs disappeared.

Later, the Americans did a similar probing job on the car park and the lawns before climbing into the back of the van, which seemed to have a Tardis-like ability to make its interior bigger than its exterior.

The chief suit came to Neil's office just after six in the evening.

"We've finished. Please don't try to go into the President's suite. It's alarmed," the American said.

"Who wouldn't be."

"Sorry?"

"I mean, fine, OK, I understand."

"Thanks for your co-operation, Sir." The agent held out his hand. Neil shook it. "And tata for now," the American said.

"See y'all," Neil replied.

44. Carry On Losing

While Martin was up in his flat changing his trousers, he took the opportunity to do some surfing on his laptop.

His brother was a loser, he thought, but he did have some good ideas. And although this whole sci-fi thing had started out as a bit of a bore, it might just turn out quite profitable.

Martin called up a search engine, typed in "Hitch Hiker's Guide to the Galaxy" and waited to see what came up.

There were a couple of publisher's sites, the usual booksellers, some fans commiserating the death of Douglas Adams (including dickheads saying 'maybe he's just hitch-hiked to another planet'), and – there – what he was looking for.

"Shit," he said. "Too good to be true."

He clicked around on the site he'd found for a minute or so, then logged off and went downstairs to the shop to tell Richie the bad news.

"Forget your Sea-Fi Sci-Fi man," Martin told his brother.

Richie was sitting at a computer, emailing synopses and sample chapters to publishers.

"Why?" he asked. "Apart from the fact that he wants money that I don't have."

"That idea of his, to publish the real Hitch Hiker's Guide on line. Someone's already done it."

"What? You sure?"

"Yeah, saw it myself. It's free, too."

"But this would be the official one," Richie said.

"Big deal. If you see an established free site and a new pay site offering exactly the same service, which one are you going to choose? Forget him. He's a loser. Fuck it!"

Richie was touched. "Hey, it's OK, Martin. I wasn't planning to accept his offer anyway. But thanks for caring."

"What? I don't give a shit about him. We could have had our own fucking Hitch Hiker's Guide on line by the morning, start raking in some cash. Bollocks."

Martin let out a short primal yell of frustration and announced that he was going back to the pub to carry on the drinking session that Richie had interrupted.

Richie watched him striding angrily down the hill. OK, it was a trendy pub, but Richie wondered if they'd let Martin in without trousers.

45. Johnson's Ladder

Mr Big was successful not only because of his willingness to use extreme violence on anything that had less fur and ear-span than a donkey, but also because he had an excellent information network. His taxi-drivers all listened out for gossip and most of the pubs and clubs in town had his "boys" as bouncers and doormen. His boys weren't just there to keep out troublemakers, they were there to listen.

Richie had experienced this one Saturday night, when he'd been walking into a pub, talking about a friend who'd bought a duff car. Suddenly the bouncer's arm was barring Richie's way.

"Who did you say sold that car?" the bouncer asked.

Richie told him. He didn't know it, but the garage belonged to Mr Big.

"And you're saying they sell duff cars?" the bouncer asked.

Richie got the impression that "yes" was not the right answer.

"No, a mate of mine bought a car from there and he's been having trouble with it."

"Well I'm sure if he takes it back they'll sort it out for him. That's a good garage," the bouncer said.

"Great." Richie assumed the bouncer had a day job as a PR man for the motor trade, and forgot all about it.

Martin also had his network. He spent half his life hanging out in pubs, and could never have sat alone for a quiet drink while there was another human being to chew the fat with or chat up.

So when two Americans started to try out Bournemouth's pubs, and talk in alternately loud and suspiciously soft voices about computers and teleportation, they were bound to come to Martin's notice sooner or later.

Their first visit to a pub wasn't a success.

They chose one near the base, The Dog, a hostelry just outside of town known by locals for its unpleasant service and bad beer.

Professors Hamlet and Johnson strode up to the bar of the almost-deserted pub and interrupted the landlord's conversation about the upcoming friendly between England and Portugal to ask for "a beer, barman, please."

The landlord winked at his conversation partner and went to stand in front of his six beer pumps and his glass-fronted fridge full of beer bottles.

"A beer?" he asked.

"Yes." It was Johnson, as the more experienced traveller, who had ordered.

"Budweiser, Rolling Rock, Corona?" the landlord asked, having shrewdly guessed his new customers' nationality. He'd noticed the American forces' arrival, of course, as had everyone in their planes' flight path, and he'd already managed to rip off a few servicemen who were having trouble with the exchange rate.

"You have Bud?" Jeb said.

"No, we'd like some English ale," Johnson corrected him.

"English ale?" the landlord asked.

"Yes, some of that stuff your friend's drinking." Johnson gestured over towards the conversation partner's glass.

"That's Belgian lager," the landlord grinned.

"What about what you're drinking?" Johnson nodded towards the other glass on the bar.

"That's German lager."

"What about this pump?" Johnson asked, pointing to the Bass.

The landlord smiled. "Yeah, I suppose you could call that ale. You want a pint?"

"Yes, please," Johnson said. Provincial pubs weren't at all like the homely places he'd been to in Cambridge. This hick clearly hadn't heard that the words "service" and "industry" could go together.

"OK." The landlord turned to get a glass, and winked to his mate. The Bass barrel had just been put on. It wasn't ready to pour yet. He pulled on the handle and filled the pint glass with brown froth. "Mmm, lovely," he said, putting it down in front of a bemused American scientist. "Ten pounds please."

"Uh, I'll have a Bud," Jeb said, deciding to put off his investigation of the local culture till another time.

Not surprisingly, on their next outing the two scientists decided to go right into town in search of something more civilized. They'd had a word with the base's English commander (who had little idea what was going on there, as most areas were off limits to all but US personnel) and learnt a few essential phrases, such as "pint of bitter, please", and "got any ready salted?" They didn't know exactly what the phrases meant, but phonetically they were faultless.

The two scientists drove into town, arguing all the way about pigs. They had just done some tests transporting objects almost the size of a car. They had successfully teleported an engine, leaving it running while they sent it. It had cut out in transit, but started up again after a little tinkering.

They had beamed a dead chicken over a hundred metres. The teleported broiler had seemed molecularly perfect, no deader than before, and not even warmed up. Now, Johnson said, they were ready for a live trial on a pig.

What he didn't know was that Jeb Hamlet and Blender's lab technicians had faked the chicken test. The chicken that had "dematerialized" had in fact been burnt way beyond the capacity of the worst barbecue operator in the world. It was dust.

"Why not a pig?" Johnson argued, keen to use something as near human as possible.

"Why not a cockroach?" Jeb suggested. Blender had told him that important witnesses were to be invited to the pig test. It wasn't due to happen until the eco-summit was under way, and Jeb didn't have enough pigs to start zapping them beforehand.

"Cockroach? Why waste our new inventions on such a tiny, insignificant ... Holy shit!" Johnson hissed, momentarily letting go of the steering wheel.

"What is it?"

Johnson pulled a slim, metallic, torch-like object out of his jacket pocket. Their new invention.

"You dork! Why the hell do you keep that thing in your pocket?" Jeb demanded.

"You want me to turn back?" Johnson asked.

"No, we've come this far. Let's get a drink first. We'll stop at the first pub we see, OK?"

A couple of minutes later they saw a pub sign. The pub had a large car park. They pulled in.

"The Huntsman? At least it's one step up the evolutionary ladder from The Dog," Johnson the biologist noted.

They walked quietly into the pub hoping to look innocuous, and managing to blend in as well as a minibus load of Siberian maths students who had strayed into the Huntsman in 1979, apparently trying to prove that Soviet clothes factories could make bigger shirt collars than anyone in the decadent West.

Jeb was wearing two t-shirts – one dark blue (short sleeves) on top of another, chocolate brown (long sleeves), elastic-waist Gore-Tex trousers and a padded yellow waistcoat with bulging pockets full of pens and half-full chewing gum packets. The outfit was rounded off with beige socks inside thick orthopaedic sandals.

Under his all-purpose waterproof jacket, Mark was wearing what he always wore – a supposedly non-iron khaki shirt, one of a collection that his cleaning lady had been regularly boiling and then ironing at nuclear fission temperatures for years until almost all colour and shape had been washed out. His trousers were the kind a Rumanian airline would lend you if your luggage was lost.

As they entered, all heads turned. The head nearest to them belonged to a young guy at the bar who was grinning devilishly at them.

Jeb nodded and said hi.

"Hmm, you ain't from around these parts, are ya, boys?" Martin said. "What're you drinking?"

46. Richie Aid Week

Next morning Richie awoke with a jolt.

You're a genius, he thought.

Or you're an idiot for not thinking of it before.

It was before eight, but he rang Martin anyway.

"It's the middle of the night," Martin groaned.

"You're a shopkeeper. You should be up at the crack of dawn."

"Well, I've been up a crack, but her name wasn't Dawn."

Now it was Richie who was groaning, as Martin did his Carry On cackle.

"What's worrying you, then, bro?" Martin asked.

"Why do you think I'm worried?"

"Well, you wouldn't wake me up if something wasn't worrying you. Or have you just heard some good news on the radio?" Martin sounded hopeful.

"No, no news. I want you to come and make a collection with me."

"Role reversal, eh? What are you collecting for?"

"It's Richie Aid Week. I want you to help me talk Terry into calling off the bet."

Martin laughed. "No chance, bro."

"I'll give him a hundred compensation."

"He won't do it."

"I've got to try."

"He won't do it, I tell you."

Martin did his best to talk Richie out of it, but it was no use. In the end, he agreed to come and pick Richie up.

"Just give me an hour for my four S's, OK?"

"Four S's?" Richie asked.

"Yeah. Shit, shower, shave, shag. Might give the shave a miss, though. Dawn or whatever her name is is waking up."

Richie rang off with Martin's laugh echoing in his ears.

When Martin turned at Richie's house up two hours later, he was driving a silver BMW. Terry the bookie was in the passenger seat.

"Hop in, bro," Martin said, smiling at Richie's look of surprise.

Richie climbed in the back and Martin drove off as his two passengers shook hands in the gap between the front seats.

Richie only vaguely remembered Terry from the pub. His memories of most things that night were vague. Terry wasn't a regular at The Huntsman. He looked more of a golf-club sort – 40-something, suit and tie, suntan, longish but well-cut hair, like a faintly disreputable bank manager. Which was, Richie thought, what a bookie was, except that his customers rarely got to withdraw the money they deposited.

He wondered what the hell Terry was doing here. Did bookies make house calls?

"Martin's explained your problem," Terry said, in a hoarse smoker's voice.

"Problem?" Richie said, trying to catch Martin's eye in the mirror. But Martin was concentrating on steering them into the stream of traffic on the main road.

"Yeah. You want to scrub the bet, don't you?"

"Right. I was drunk, it was a mistake."

"Which means, I guess, that you can't afford to lose," Terry said.

"Well ..." Richie didn't know what to say. Put like that it did sound bad. What had Martin been saying to him?

"It is a very big bet. One of the biggest I've ever taken on," Terry said. "I should really have asked for the stake money up front."

Luckily, Terry did not have an stethoscope pressed to Richie's heart, because he would have heard a loud thump followed by a few seconds' total silence.

"It's only cos of Martin here that I didn't ask for it. He says you're good for it."

"Yeah," Richie said, trying to sound convincing. "But that's not why I want to call it off."

"You've got it but you don't want to lose it," Terry said.

"Er, yeah," Richie conceded. "But then, I'll get a million if I win. Are you good for that?"

"Ha!" Terry turned to look Richie in the eye. "Now you've hit the nail on the proverbial. You see, I *definitely* can't afford to lose. So I've laid some of it off. I can't cancel the bet now or I'm the one who'll be up to my balls in debt. You see, your problem is my problem. We're in this together." He turned to face the windscreen again. They were just coming up to a large roundabout. Martin took the exit that led into the town centre.

"After all," Terry went on. "What would you have said if I'd come to you the next day and asked you to cancel?"

Whoopee! Yes! Let's do it, Terry, baby! was the answer, but Richie simply shrugged.

"You'd have thought that I'd got cold feet, that I'd heard something that had convinced me I was going to lose. You haven't heard anything, have you, Richie?"

"No," Richie told him, "otherwise I'd be claiming my winnings."

Terry's good-natured laugh ended in a wheezing cough. "Well, you come and see me if you hear anything. And I'll come and see you if you don't." He laughed again. Winning and losing large sums of money was his daily bread, after all. Richie was more used to frittering away small change on the lottery and the Cup Final.

Martin pulled up outside a café, an American franchise with logos everywhere and high stools along each wall.

"This is where you want off, isn't it?" he asked Terry.

"Yup, best cappuccino in town," Terry said. "Just time for a quickie before I open up. Thanks, Martin. See you later, OK?"

"I'll be there," Martin promised, and shook his hand.

Terry and Richie got out of the car.

"Sorry, Richie mate," Terry said. "Out of my hands."

They shook hands and Terry went into the café.

Richie got into the front passenger seat.

"Shit," he said. "You his chauffeur or something?"

Martin's reply was a snorting laugh.

"No, come on," Richie said. "Why do I get the feeling that you two are too cosy for my good?"

Martin tutted disdainfully. "Stop whinging, bro. You're too paranoid. You should eat more meat."

"What the fuck's that got to do with anything?"

"You're not predatory any more. You've turned into a fucking gerbil."

"Martin. Stop playing Doctor fucking Doolittle and tell me why you and Terry are driving about together all of a sudden. And in such a swanky car, as well. You haven't just bought it, I hope?"

Martin shook his head and sighed. The innocent accused. "It's Terry's. He got done for drink-driving, so he needs people to drive him about," Martin said. "Thought if I offered to help him this morning he might go easy on you."

"Didn't work, then."

"What do you mean?" Martin squawked incredulously. "You ask to call off the bet, first thing he's going to do is claim his stake money, isn't he? Stands to reason. Lucky you called me instead of blundering in there on your own."

"Shame you helped me to blunder into the bet in the first place, you mean," Richie grumbled. "You sure it was me who suggested betting ten grand anyway? This isn't something you and him cooked up?"

Martin looked genuinely sad at Richie's lack of faith in him. "Ask anyone who was there," he said. "You think you're invincible when you're drunk. Remember all that money you used to lose at darts? They used to queue up to play you when you'd had a few. Sure to get a round out of it."

Richie cracked an involuntary smile as he remembered. The price of a round had seemed like a lot of money at the time.

"Talking of which," Martin said, "I met some interesting guys last night. Even worse at darts than you."

"Great. Think they'll play for ten grand a point?"

"Maybe." Martin did a paradiddle on the steering wheel. "You really ought to meet them. We got pissed and invented a brilliant new game. Teleportation darts. You locate on the bullseye and just beam your darts in. Can't lose."

"Can't lose? I've heard that one before."

Martin ignored his brother's grumpiness. "Where to then, bro?" he asked. "I don't have to drop the car off till this afternoon."

"Home, unless you've got some brilliant idea of where I can find ten grand."

"Home it is, then," Martin said, and U-turned back out of the town centre.

I have a theory about Marvin the paranoid android in Hitch Hiker's Guide to the Galaxy and his role in the British rock scene.

Marvin is always whinging that he's got a brain the size of a planet but that he gets given no-brainer things to do like opening doors.

Well, on Radiohead's third album, OK Computer (the title of which is a quote from chapter 12 of Douglas Adams' novel by the way), there is a song called "Paranoid Android".

What's more, around the time that OK Computer came out in 1997, Radiohead's singer Thom Yorke became a perma-whinger, always giving the impression in interviews that his brain was being wasted in communication with mere humans. The basic theme of the album is getting the hell off this fucked-up planet.

It seems to me that Marvin now has a human disciple, dedicated to sharing with us the android's message that humans are shit.

A Brief History of the Future, chapter 14 (extract)

47. Getting Itchy

Richie was sitting in the shop when he heard the door open. He was so used to being left alone that he ignored the intrusion, assuming that it was Martin.

"Excuse me."

Richie, who had been addressing some envelopes to publishers, looked up to see a 40-something guy in a linen suit and Lacoste polo shirt. A well-off, mature-looking adult. They didn't get many of those in the shop, even back in the days when they pretended more actively to be selling or repairing things.

"Yes?"

"I'm looking for one of those Beam-Me-Up-Scottie machines."

"What?" Richie examined the guy's face. Close-cropped grey hair, cold eyes.

"You know, a teleporter." The guy had a weird accent, with a sort of transatlantic twang.

"No such thing, is there?" Richie asked.

He wondered for a moment if it wasn't a trap of some kind. A cop investigating the cocaine-teleportation episode, maybe. Could even be US Customs wishing they hadn't let him export the machine.

"Yeah, there is. They were invented by the American

military. You can buy them in the States. Aren't they being imported yet?"

"Sorry, mate, I haven't heard anything about them." Richie smiled regretfully, hoping the guy would bugger off.

He didn't. "They're amazing, apparently. You get a small cabinet, and you hook it up to demolecularization software, and –"

"You tried Army Surplus?" Richie interrupted him. "They've got loads of American military stuff. Helmets, water bottles, latrine shovels. Maybe they've got a demolecularization machine." Richie smiled again, slightly less regretfully.

The guy looked at Richie as if he was memorizing his face. Disturbing. Then he relaxed, and gave a "no problem" smile. "OK. See you around," he said, and left.

48. The President's Pants

"Max, we've got to tell the others in the team what we're doing here."

"Why?" Blender turned away from the door of the old RAF hut he was inspecting and frowned at Jeb Hamlet.

"Either they'll work it out for themselves or there'll be a leak and then we'll have a civil war on our hands."

"Well, if there's a leak I'll know where to plug it, won't I?" Blender walked along the side wall of the hut, which seemed to be made of sheet asbestos. Not flaking too much, he hoped. "What's the distance between here and the control tower?" He looked over his shoulder at the whitewashed brick of the tower.

"Just over 100 metres," Hamlet said. He stood on the grass in the pale sunlight and weighed the arguments in his head – press his point and annoy his boss, or give in and endanger the project long-term. "I'm not going to leak anything, Max. Of course not. But now we're all working together on a daily basis, it seems –" he chose his next word carefully "– counterproductive for the whole team not to know about the tests. I mean, Christ, we've made some great advances. The new locator –"

Blender interrupted him. "Jeb, please. I thought we'd gone into the wider picture. Since Hiroshima, science has been as much a part of world politics as the strength of the dollar or the health of the President. In 1945 we had a paraplegic President but everything was fine. These days, if the President pisses his pants, the US economy goes through the floor. And believe me, Jeb, the President would piss his pants if he knew what was going on here."

"In that case, are we right to be doing it?" Jeb asked.

Blender gave what Hamlet interpreted as an arrogant laugh. "Jeb, you're talking like a man who's just got into a cold swimming pool."

"Uh?"

"Your balls have shrivelled." Blender took a step towards Hamlet, so that they were less than an arm's length apart. The older man looked into Jeb's eyes as if they would tell him his testicle size. "Human teleportation will be a far greater advance than splitting the atom, Jeb," he said, apparently trying to hypnotize him as he spoke. "It'll be bigger than getting a man on Mars. Hell, we could beam a whole damn baseball stadium up there, for the first ever World Series on another world. A president is elected for four years, eight if he's lucky with the economy or a war. How can you even think of endangering the future of scientific endeavour out of loyalty to someone who is no more than a fleck of fly shit on the human calendar?" Blender saw Hamlet's pupils constricting, and knew he'd gone too far. "As a political being, of course. As a man, I like the guy." He stepped back from Hamlet, who relaxed visibly. "So do, probably, the new members of the team. They haven't been with us long enough to trust. So let's just get on with the job of showing the world how fucking clever we are, shall we?" He jerked a thumb over to the main building, where the rest of the team were working, and where technicians were setting up a video link with the control tower. "So what if we're giving them a glimpse of the future instead of the present?"

Hamlet smiled his consent. Blender gave him a manly slap on the upper arm.

"And surely Jeb, you haven't forgotten the most important rule of science you learned in your university research days?"

"What's that?"

"The smaller the perceived distance between you and your objective, the greater your funding."

Blender laughed at his own joke and kicked the wall of the hut. A few flakes of toxic dust drifted slowly down to whiten the grass.

HG Wells – a giant, second only to the mighty Roddenberry. War of the Worlds, for instance, was not only one of the first alien monster stories ever, it was also a satire on British colonialism.

In this chapter, I'll be telling you how HG's book was inspired by the colonization of Tasmania – "a very frightful disaster for the native Tasmanians" he called it. This was in 1898, a year after the diamond jubilee of Queen Victoria, Empress of Britain and India and half the known universe, and 22 years after the Tasmanian Aborigenes had been literally hunted out of existence. Old HG was a bit ahead of his time. Australia didn't get around to agreeing with him till the mid-1970s.

The only thing I can fault Wells on is his grammar. He wrote a story called The First Men in the Moon. "In the Moon"? That's one bit of sci-fi that didn't catch on.

A Brief History of the Future, chapter 2 (extract)

49. Have I Got Gnus for You

Every Sunday morning, Richie went to buy a newspaper. On weekdays they always had the paper delivered, but they'd cancelled the Sundays long ago. Richie and Clara got tired of the paper boy treating their letterbox like a shredder. The size of the Sunday papers these days, you'd need a letterbox as big as a catflap.

He strolled down the hill towards the paper shop. It was another warm morning. A few clouds coming in off the sea, but they'd clear up. Richie hoped so, because the family was going on a picnic in the New Forest. Martin had rung up the day before to say that he'd got a loan of a Renault Espace, and insisted on taking his brother, sister-in-law, niece and nephew out for the day. He was even providing the food, and promised not to cook any of it himself.

Richie just had time to nip down to Dave's before Martin was due.

Dave was the local newsagent, the man who, more than any English teacher, had formed Richie's taste in literature, guiding him first from Beano to Shoot, then from NME on to more cerebral reading like Big Jugs.

Even now, Richie always asked Dave's advice before buying, as if Dave were the head waiter in charge of an ever-changing menu.

Except that since Richie's last visit two Sundays earlier, Dave's had gone. In its place was a snazzy shopfront with posters advertising glossy magazines and chocolate. It was definitely the right street corner, between the car parts shop and the mobile-phone shop, but now the old sign – the wonderfully explicit "Dave's" – had been replaced by an orange-and-purple logo, "Gnu's 4 News", with what looked like a bearded cow grinning at passers-by.

Richie went in. The door didn't ding like it used to. Instead, the mat triggered an electronic moo.

Dave was there.

"Dave."

"Richie."

Dave looked very different. In place of his customary Bournemouth football shirt, he was wearing a sort of orange tracksuit uniform, with the bearded cow on the chest. His balding rocker's quiff had been shaved off and he now sported a smart grey baldie cut. His shop looked very different, too. It was less cramped, with fewer shelves but bigger displays. In front of the counter there were bins with special offers on toffees and paperback books. The only special offers Dave used to have were things like "you want these crisps? They're past their sell-by."

"How was *Noo Yoik*?" Dave asked.

"Brilliant. Too bloody hot, though. Like a jungle without the nice green stuff."

"That why you shaved your head?"

"Yeah, what's your excuse?"

Dave explained. He had been bought up by a chain, and was now assistant manager of his own shop. He picked a badge up off the counter.

"I put this on when I see the boss's car pull up."

It was a plastic name tag, with Dave's portrait superimposed on a gnu's head. The badge said "David, Assistant Manager".

"Who's manager, then?" Richie asked.

"Some 21-year-old smoothie with a Mitsubishi 4WD. He manages all the stores in town, and he pops by every couple of days to 'review the point-of-sale'." Dave sneered.

"This is all very sudden isn't it?"

"No, I signed a couple of months back. I wasn't making much money, you know, despite your frequent visits to the lottery machine. Least this way I get a salary."

"Yeah, but now they could throw you out of your own shop."

"And my own flat." Dave lived above the shop with his wife.

"Bloody hell, Dave." Was everyone around here threatened with homelessness?

"Yeah, but now I've got a bit of cash to fall back on. And this way I don't give a toss about kids nicking sweets and fags. Not my sweets any more, are they?"

"Will you have to dress up as a gnu for Christmas, Dave? And say 'Happy Gnu Year' to your customers?"

"Fuck off, Richie. What paper do you want?"

The Sundays were all laid out on the counter like giants' wallets.

"What do you recommend?"

"There are some great fresh-fig recipes in the Sunday Times," Dave said, pointing to the thickest wedge of supplements. Richie occasionally had bouts of interest in cooking, as opposed to slopping.

"Right, with raw cocoa-bean sauce and minced kangaroo," said Richie.

"I think you'll find it's kangaroo coulis."

"No, come on Dave, what's on offer?"

"Win a Ferrari? Signed by Schuhmacher."

"No chance."

"Win a house in the Express."

"Coupons?"

"Yeah, one a day for four weeks then phone a hotline."

"Bloody hell, I could buy the house for that. OK, I'll take it. Nothing for cash?"

"Only the bingo."

"Bollocks to that. Nothing more, you know, imaginative?"

"NASA competition?"

"NASA competition?"

"Yeah. Win a trip for you and your family to Cape Canaveral. Interested?"

"Come on, Dave, you bastard. Where is it?"

"Independent."

Richie picked it up, started flicking through the pages.

"Page 4, Travel."

"Cheers." Richie read half a page of fairly complex questions about the space race. Good. The harder it was, the more chance he had of winning. There were too many competitions like "In what state is Houston, Texas? If you think you know, call 0898 bla bla bla. Calls cost £10,000 a minute." Mug's game.

Dave asked, "Any luck yesterday?"

"Nah."

"Want a ticket for next Saturday?"

Richie nodded.

"Usual numbers?"

"Uh? Yeah. Oh, and better do me one for Wednesday too, I'm desperate."

"How about a scratchcard, then?"

"I'm not that desperate. Oh, OK, bung it over."

While he waited for Dave to prepare the lottery tickets, Richie took a coin from his pocket and tried to look through the silver coating of plastic or whatever it was that was covering up the numbers on the scratchcard. Wouldn't it be hilarious, he thought, if he won £10,000? All his problems solved with one little coin, after so much fretting and lying. And of course he'd still have the bet on. If the PM really was pregnant, he'd have a million and ten thousand pounds. A little extra to buy Clara a hundred pairs of shoes.

As he scratched he felt light-headed. Perhaps the card-makers had managed to distill Essence of Hope out of the human heart, and inject it into the coating on the scratchcard. Richie sniffed, then scratched.

"I don't believe it."

Had he really got himself out of trouble with one scratch of a coin? Had he really won enough to pay off his debt to the bookie and save his marriage? Of course he hadn't.

"No luck?" Dave asked, in a very convincing imitation of surprise. It was his single most used phrase since he'd started selling scratchcards.

50. Small Is Beautiful

Something didn't add up, but Mark Johnson didn't want to go crawling to Hamlet or Blender for help.

He had spent the last three hours wading through the molecular analysis software on the computer that was hooked up to the largest transporter. It was Sunday morning and he was the only one working. Blender had given them all the day off.

But Johnson had come into the lab – the old briefing room where squadron leaders had given pep-talks during the Battle of Britain – because he was on to a scent and couldn't get it out of his head. It seemed to him that there was a whole slab of data missing. Either the software was a million times more efficient than it looked, or – or what?

If he was right, and he usually was, the teleporter shouldn't have worked on the chicken. And the test they'd planned for tomorrow was going to be a total washout. The software just wasn't powerful enough to analyse and store the molecular structure of a pig.

Even if you didn't try to measure the velocities of atoms in a living being, and just contented yourself with describing its atomic makeup, there wasn't nearly enough capacity in the software to process and transmit the information in the time allowed. It would take hours to teleport a pig, even a piglet.

Did Hamlet have access to some kind of booster, he wondered. Maybe that was why he always insisted on doing the final checks himself before a test.

"Shee-it!" He threw a shadow-punch at the screen, which refused to yield up its secrets. If there was one thing that Johnson hated more than anything, it was not understanding something. That, he told himself, was why he was a good scientist.

Something was going on. Something big. Maybe, Johnson mused, there was the chance of a Nobel Prize after all. Not for the work on teleportation as such. The only possible conclusion was that Blender or Hamlet or both had found out something new about molecular analysis. A new take on the Einstein-Podolsky-Rosen paradox, maybe.

Christ, updating Einstein? That was something every scientist dreamed of. But if they had discovered something, they obviously didn't intend to share the credit with anyone else, the bastards. Hadn't they heard of teamwork?

"Hey Mark."

Johnson froze, but had time to fix a smile on his face before he turned round. "Hey."

"Getting ready for tomorrow?" It was Hamlet.

"You know me, Jeb. Workaholic."

"Yeah, well don't overdo it. I'm going into town. Coming?"

"No, thanks. I, uh, want to go for a quiet drive. Do some thinking," Johnson said.

"OK. You got that laser locator?"

Johnson cleared his throat. "Yeah, in the dorm."

"I'd really prefer it if you kept it in the lab."

"Yeah, you're right. I'll put it back today. Promise."

Johnson wasn't religious, but he prayed silently to God that he would be able to keep his promise.

Since it was first published, the Einstein-Podolsky-Rosen paradox has inspired several new theories. Most of these were formulated long before anyone dreamed of actively trying teleportation. They were purely theoretical thought experiments.

In 1964, for example, an Irishman called John Bell put forward a theorem based on the socks of one of his colleagues, a certain Bertelsmann who never came to work wearing two socks of the same colour on any one day.

John Bell examined whether you could predict certain things about Bertelsmann's second sock if you'd only seen the first sock.

I presume Bell's theorem was more complex than this, but perhaps not. These were the Sixties, after all.

A Brief History of the Future, chapter 1 (extract)

51. If You Go down to the Woods Today

The drive out to the Forest was accompanied by the chink, chink of the extra bottles Richie had added to Martin's hamper. Given his acute financial worries, he thought he might be needing a little more wine than usual to send him off on his Sunday afternoon nap.

Richie sat up front, musing over his NASA competition. When was the first manned US space mission? Wow. 1961? Who was the first American to go on a space walk? Good one, that would need some research, too.

The kids were strapped up with Clara in the back. Ella was

singing a Madonna song she'd learnt in history at school. George was behind Martin, egging him on to drive faster. "Overtake! Overtake! Smash his bumper!"

"You're raving bonkers, you are, mate," Martin told the boy in his Sid James voice.

Clara leaned forward over Richie's shoulder. "Please don't win that one," she said. "Cape Canaveral's not my thing."

"OK, I'll win a house instead." Richie pulled the Express out on top of his pile.

Clara scoffed.

"Don't you worry, Clara," Martin said, "that machine Richie brought back is going to make us a few quid, I can promise you that."

"How?" Clara asked. "No, I don't want to know."

Martin winked at Richie and leered. Richie tried to place the expression. Yes, it was the look Martin had when he knew he'd scored. The look he gave as he walked out of the pub with the lucky lady. A strange expression to have on your way to a picnic, Richie thought.

Martin wasn't far out of town when he turned off the main road and bumped along a lane into some woods.

"What are we stopping here for?" Richie asked. "This isn't the Forest yet."

"Further on it'll be full of day trippers. We'll have this spot to ourselves. There are horses!" Martin shouted the last sentence over his shoulder and got a cheer from the juvenile chorus.

They were in a clearing by a paddock where four horses were grazing.

"You can still hear the main road," Clara said when she got out of the car. "Let's go on further into the Forest. It'll be quieter."

"You don't want to drive for an hour, do you? This is great. Besides, the New Forest is a swizz, isn't it kiddies? It's not new at all. It's been here for weeks!"

The children giggled at their silly Uncle Martin and bounded off to pick some grass for the horses.

Richie unloaded the food and drink. Martin had done a good job. He'd ordered it all from a restaurant in town, basket and all. There were salads, cheeses, cold meats, little cocktail sausages, plenty of fruit. He'd even brought a blanket and a corkscrew.

Martin said he'd set up while the others enjoyed themselves. Richie and Clara took the children to feed the horses, went looking for squirrels in the wood, had a game of frisbee.

Then they all came back to demolish the picnic. As they were eating, a small cargo plane marked "USAF" flew over, coming in to land somewhere nearby. Richie looked quizzically at Martin.

"Daddy," Ella said, chewing on a stick of celery and staring up into the sky, "why did they plant the Forest near an airport?"

"I don't think they did, pumpkin. I think they built the airport last."

"You mean they cut down the trees?" Ella asked, scandalized.

"Yes. England used to be almost covered in trees, you know."

"What even the houses?" George asked.

"No, not the houses. I said almost."

"What, even the beach?" George persisted.

Martin laughed. "Argue your way out of that one, David Attenborough."

"No, not the beaches. But all the hills and all the fields," Richie said. "Up until 500 years ago, Britain was almost all forest. Think how beautiful that must have been."

"That'd be horrible," George said. "You can't play football if there's trees in the way."

"It'd be easier to score a goal though – there'd be goalposts everywhere," Richie said, giving up on the history lesson.

They finished eating and stretched out in the sun for a snooze. Clara lay with her head on Richie's shoulder. They were just drifting off when Richie felt a nudge in his ribs. It was Martin.

"Come with me a minute," he whispered.

"What's up?" Clara asked, half-asleep.

"Nothing. Just going for a little stroll," Martin assured her. He beckoned to Richie.

"I want you to see something very exciting," Martin told his brother as they tramped through the woods. He upped the pace, and Richie was all too aware that he had almost a bottle of Sauvignon sloshing about in his stomach.

They came out on to another lane, and Martin looked at his watch.

"Five minutes," he said. "We'll wait here."

"For what?" Richie leaned against a tree and looked around. Nothing but more trees and an empty lane.

"For several thousand pounds, at the very least," Martin said.

"You keep promising money, but it never turns up."

"This time it will," Martin promised.

"For fuck's sake, Martin. Why will you never explain? You think I'll bugger off if you tell me?"

"You might. But you'd be better off staying because you need the money even more than I do."

A car was coming down the lane. Martin ducked back into the trees and pulled Richie out of sight. It was a white car, an estate, with one man in it. The man parked and got out, looking nervous. Martin scanned the trees around them and listened, as if checking that no more vehicles were on their way. Then, satisfied, he walked into view, beckoning Richie to follow.

The man saw them coming and looked even more nervous, especially at the sight of Richie.

"Hi," he said. An American accent.

"Hey, Mark," Martin said chummily. "How's it hanging?"

"Yeah, great," the man said, and wiped his brow with a hairy arm.

"This is Mark. I told you about him. We played darts together. He's a scientist," Martin told Richie.

Richie clicked automatically into his role as guard dog, staying totally impassive. He found that people were more intimidated that way. This time, his impassivity also covered up his complete ignorance about who he was intimidating.

"A molecular biologist, right?" Martin was still being excessively chummy.

"Yeah, right," Johnson said. "You got it with you?"

"You show me yours and I'll show you mine," Martin said.

Johnson pulled two folded pages out of his jacket pocket and handed them over. Martin unfolded them and frowned.

"This all?" he asked.

"It's enough. Those are the codes and instructions to get at the files where the actual plans are."

"Right, good," Martin nodded.

"Well, have you got it?" Johnson asked, a note of desperation in his voice.

"You joking?" Martin said. "These codes of yours might give me access to the plans for your outside toilet. I need to check."

"For fuck's sake. If you don't give it back, they'll find out and change all the codes anyway." Johnson looked nervously at Richie as he said this.

"Well I won't care because I'll have the prototype, won't I?"

"Shit. You stole it out of my pocket, remember. I'm being blackmailed here." Johnson was almost in physical pain. What the hell was it, Richie wondered, that Martin had taken off him?

"Don't worry, Mark. Tomorrow night, down The Huntsman, you'll get it back. If you have any bother, give me a ring and I'll leave it behind the bar. The landlord'll say it was left in there and he was waiting for someone to claim it. We're so thick us Brits, aren't we? We wouldn't know what the fuck it was anyway. What do we know about teleportation?" Martin gave Johnson a mean, ironic glare. "Now bye bye, Markie, see you tomorrow night. My round."

At this, Martin turned and walked off into the woods. Richie stayed to watch the expression of panic spread across Johnson's face. So this nervous wreck was a teleportation expert? Shit. Alone in the woods with a teleportation expert – it seemed the perfect opportunity to ask some questions.

But judging by Johnson's staring eyes, the scientist felt as if he had shared way too many secrets here already. Richie followed Martin. They were ten yards into the woods when they heard the car drive off. Richie grabbed his brother's arm.

"Explanation, please."

Martin punched the air with delight. "We did it, bro!"

"I want to know what we did exactly, Martin."

Martin pulled a small torch-like object from his pocket.

"This," he said, "hasn't even been talked about on the web yet." He pressed a button and a red point of light appeared on a nearby tree. "It's a laser locator. Based on the ones that the Special Forces used to guide in the bombers in Afghanistan. Hook this up to the transporter and you can teleport things with pinpoint accuracy without going anywhere near your target zone. And look." He hit another button and the beam disappeared.

"Great," Richie said. "It has an off switch."

"No. Ultraviolet locator beam. Amazing, isn't it?"

Richie had to admit it was.

"And," Martin went on, "there are only three in existence. Two on that airbase over there, and one in my hand. And thanks to my careless drinking pal Mark, I can now go into production." He held up the folded pages.

"Until they catch you," Richie said.

"If that's how you look at life, you'll never get anywhere," Martin said, and headed off back towards the sleeping picnickers.

52. The Pig Has Landed

"You seem in an indecent haste to try the machine out on those prisoners," Jeb told Johnson. It was Monday. The day of rest was over.

"Why do you say that?" Johnson snapped at his colleague.

They were connecting up a computer to the enlarged version of the teleporter, which looked like a portable one-car garage standing on the tarmac of the aerodrome.

The plan (at least the plan that Blender had announced to the team) was to beam a pig about one hundred metres into a small hut by aiming the laser locator from the first floor of the control tower. Jeb and Johnson were in the control tower while their colleagues were down below at teleporter level. Blender was in the main aerodrome building, drinking coffee with the VIP guests.

"Well," Jeb said, "I can only think that if the pig experiment goes to plan, then you'll want to try it out on a human."

"Yeah, well, let's just wait and see, shall we?" Maybe that was it, Johnson thought. They hadn't updated Einstein at all – Hamlet had weakened the molecular analysis software so that the pig experiment would go wrong and he could avoid the responsibility of trying to teleport the first human. Cowards don't make good scientists.

"But even if the pig materializes alive," Jeb said, "we won't know what the consequences are for quite a while. What if it develops a degenerative disease? Or organ malfunctions? Those prisoners are living human beings, for Christ's sakes."

"Only in the strictly legal sense of the term."

Jeb thought that this was probably meant to be a joke, but it was said with too much malice to be humorous.

He wasn't looking forward to pressing the button in a few minutes' time. If everything went to plan, he half-suspected Blender of being willing to OK an experiment on one of the prisoners, just to take the symbolic step and force his project ahead.

If he did so, Jeb would be faced with a dilemma – refuse to do the test and lose the chance to direct his own project, or do the test and be sure of killing a man. The fact that the man was a self-confessed murderer and a volunteer didn't really change things.

"OK, all set," Johnson said.

"Right, you got the laser locator?"

Johnson blushed. "I'll go and get one."

He ran downstairs, and Jeb looked through the binoculars at their target, the old white hut. They were going to fire a laser beam through the window on to the floor of the hut, which was visible from their higher vantage point, and teleport the pig on to that exact spot. Theoretically, what the distant observers would see on their closed-circuit TV screen was the animal, materializing in front of their eyes. Theoretically.

Johnson returned with a laser locator, one of the two that hadn't been entrusted to Martin.

In the aerodrome's oak-ceilinged main hall, a huddle of 20 or so people were watching a jittery still life on the bank of video screens. A tethered American pig was standing in the gloom of the teleporter, its head and limbs twitching occasionally as its sluggish mind tried to pull its body free of the effects of sedation.

The observers were a fifty-fifty split of Americans and non-Americans, and they included British, Chinese and Russian military men and the British Prime Minister, who'd insisted on coming down to observe the experiment she'd been forced to accept on her territory.

She spent most of her time "in character", being the technocrat, talking gravely with soldiers. Blender knew that she'd got a roasting in the media about military spending cuts, and even if this meant that paltry British spending had gone down from one peanut to half a peanut, her chances of re-election depended partly on convincing the public that she wasn't going to hand the defence of the islands over to a commune of anarcho-pacifist hippies.

But she had clicked out of character long enough for one brief exchange with Blender.

"Poor pig," she said. "I hope it'll be all right." They were standing slightly apart from the crowd, drinking black coffee from dainty little porcelain cups.

"A volunteer," Blender replied. "British, too. A symbol of your national courage."

"I'll have to recommend it for a knighthood."

"A knighthog, you mean, Prime Minister."

The PM laughed politely. "Oh dear, Dr Blender, you seem a bit too relaxed about all this." She nodded towards some foreign uniforms who were being briefed by Blender's team via translators. "Are you sure it's going to work?"

"Quietly confident," Blender said.

"Hmm, that about sums you up, doesn't it, Dr Blender?"

She took a minute sip of coffee and looked up at him over the cup. "As a nation, I mean." She planted her cup and saucer in Blender's free hand and walked away.

Blender watched her backside appraisingly as it travelled across the room in its black skirt. It stopped in front of a Chinese uniform and turned so that Blender was able to admire it in profile. He memorized the curvature and then looked down at the cup in his hand. He wondered if it contained saliva.

Jeb called up Blender and got the go-ahead to begin the test. He received confirmation that the video camera was rolling, and then Johnson took his binoculars and pointed the locator beam across the tarmac. He watched the red point of light flicker over the wall of the hut until it homed in on the window. Now the red dot was jiggling on the floor inside, and Johnson put down the binoculars in order to steady his grip – they'd have to attach the locator to some kind of sniper rifle, he thought. He couldn't hold the beam and observe what was happening inside the hut at the same time. Despite his scepticism about the experiment he could feel his heart thumping excitedly. "Wait for it," he told Jeb, who was at the keyboard. "Three, two, one, now!"

He wished he had dared to say "energize", but somehow it would have seemed too flippant.

Jeb hit the button. The computer screen showed a green contour plan of the tethered pig. The dots began to fade. Johnson waited for Hamlet to feign disappointment and abort the test.

One, two seconds passed with Johnson holding the beam firmly in place, three seconds, then a pinkish object began to materialize in the hut. Another second and it took shape. To Johnson's astonishment it was quite definitely a pig. A moment later there was a loud squeal and the newly materialized pig disappeared from sight. From inside the hut came the unmistakeable sound of an enraged sow butting a lab technician.

"We did it." Johnson couldn't resist the temptation to do a high-five with Hamlet. He didn't know how they'd done it, but he could see the proof with his own eyes. For once he didn't care about not understanding.

Human cries started to emanate from the hut as three more lab technicians ran over. Before they got there, the door was flung open, and a man in a white coat flew out, buttocks first. He was quickly followed by the pig, which was slavering and kicking like a rodeo horse.

Walter Nusbaum, a physicist from Houston, came bounding up the stairs to get a better view. "Shit," he said, "it's gone crazy. Is there anywhere we can do a brain scan on that thing?"

"Sure," said Jeb, relieved that things hadn't gone 100% to Blender's plan. "We'll just put some pants on him and take him to the local hospital, shall we?"

Perhaps the Beam-Me-Up machine only seems weird in real life because it has entered civilian life.

In the early Star Trek episodes it was first and foremost a military tool. For all Captain Kirk's humanism, the first three series were the futuristic equivalent of a US Navy aircraft carrier touring the world and telling the natives to behave like good, democratic Americans.

In this sense, you shouldn't view Kirk's crew as real human beings. Because if they'd been anything like real American sailors, they would have left a trail of massage parlours and sexually transmitted Earth diseases right across the galaxy.

A Brief History of the Future, chapter 1 (extract)

53. Crabs and Beetles

Richie was having a dream.

There was this beautiful girl who really wanted to have sex with him. She was lying on a bed waiting for it. He kept on walking towards the bed, but pulling back at the last minute because he needed to pee. So he went to the loo, came back into the bedroom and there she was waiting for him. He went over to the bed, but then he desperately needed to pee. And so on. It was frustrating, but not unpleasant.

However, the cycle was interrupted when crabs started nipping at his face and neck. Not the sexually transmitted kind of crab, the large, claw-wielding seafood-restaurant kind. They were joined by some lobsters, which seemed to know Richie's name.

He opened his eyes to see Clara glaring down at him. She was still in her nightdress, and looking angry. One hand was pinching the skin of his cheek, the other was holding a sheet of paper with blurred writing on it.

"Read this," she said. "It just came recorded delivery."

Richie freed his arms from under the duvet and held the paper still until his eyes had a chance to focus. The first thing he noticed was the coloured blob at the top of the page. It was the logo of a car-hire firm. Next he managed to read his name. This was interesting. He sat up to get a clearer view, and started reading what had to be a practical joke.

"Oh Christ. Oh shit. Oh bugger. Oh fuck," he said as he progressed from paragraph to paragraph down the page. He stopped reading and flopped back on to his pillow.

"You missed a few out there, but you're about right," Clara said. She was almost trembling with fury.

Richie was beyond fury. He felt like the man who has fallen into a twenty-storey lift shaft, and who, just when he gets to about two storeys above the point where he's going to smash to his death, notices that someone has left a bed of six-inch nails at the bottom of the shaft. And the nails are rusty.

The letter informed him that the car he'd hired at the airport had not been returned. He had the choice of returning it forthwith, and paying several hundred pounds in hire fees and penalties, or declaring it stolen and paying the insurance excess of a couple of grand, or (this wasn't in the letter but he assumed it was true) admitting that he'd stolen it and going to prison.

"I'll call Martin," he said. After all, it was Martin who'd driven it away, promising to return it to Heathrow.

"No, don't call him," Clara said. She picked something up off the carpet. She'd obviously prepared this interview well. "Go and wake him up."

In her hand she held a pair of nutcrackers.

Richie didn't have the keys to the flat above the shop, so, reverting to caveman mode for once, he shouldered the door open. It was surprisingly easy and satisfying, he thought. He ought to do it more often.

He walked straight into Martin's bedroom to be met by a pair of bare boobs. The breasts were attached, at a very attractive angle, to a beautiful girl, Indian-looking, with cropped black hair and dark eyes. She was young, 19 or 20, a clubber type. One of her nipples was pierced with a large gold ring. Instead of gasping and pulling the sheet up to cover her modesty, she simply widened her eyes as the enormous, shaven-headed man advanced towards her.

"Don't worry," Richie told her. "I'm his brother. This is his morning alarm call." He smiled and pointed towards Martin's sleeping head, next to the girl's pleasantly coffee-coloured outer thigh.

"Can I borrow your tea a minute?" The girl was drinking from a large Homer Simpson mug. She handed it to Richie.

He thought a moment about where to pour it, and took a sip to test the warmth. The mug was half-empty, the tea tepid, so Richie decided he wouldn't do any permanent damage by filling Martin's ear.

"Yafak!" It was certainly effective. Martin sat bolt upright, wide awake. "Fuckinell-yabast. Oh, hi," he said, smiling with pleasure as he noticed the girl. Their friendship was quite recent, it seemed.

"Where's the Beetle, Martin?" Richie asked.

The girl clenched her buttocks, apparently assuming that they were talking about a lost insect.

"The what?" Martin feigned sleepiness.

"I want the car keys and let's say, two thousand quid, now."

"Oh, grow up, Richie." he yawned and stretched. "You know I haven't got the car. I sold it. How do you think I paid you back for the hire so quickly?"

"What?" Once again, Martin's impossibly twisted "logic" had Richie on the defensive.

"Yeah, it's a good deal all round, though, isn't it?" Martin grinned at the girl, who was watching him with a slight smile on her face. Mr Cool was doing his trick again. "It'll only cost you the insurance, but I'll get five grand for it as soon Mr Big sells it on."

"And now I'm supposed to pay the insurance? What with? Blood?"

"No, my faithless brother. You are forgetting those bits of paper we found in the wood. Your half of the profits will easily be worth enough to pay for the car insurance. All you've got to do is come with me to see Mr Big and collect."

"No way." Richie turned away symbolically. "You're not getting me anywhere near that nutter again, or his bloody donkey. You go and get the money." The girl giggled. These brothers were fun, she thought.

"One last time."

"Every time's the last time with you, Martin."

"You've got to come or you don't get paid. Sorry, bro."

"Fuck!" Far from being the dawn assassin, Richie was the one who'd been blown away here. But it wasn't a fair fight. He respected Queensbury rules. Martin used the rule book as a blunt instrument.

The girl giggled again as Martin nuzzled her ear.

"Why the fuck didn't you tell me about the car before?" Richie asked.

"Because you'd have gone mad and screwed things up before I had the chance to negotiate this wonderful deal that will enable you to pay off the car-hire people." Martin shrugged. Obvious, wasn't it?

"I can't go to Mr Big's place now. I've got to go and start at the hotel," Richie said, saving at least a few shreds of dignity.

"Fine. I'll see you later. I've got plans for now anyway. I've got to get reacquainted with little Pam here."

"Param," the girl corrected him, rolling the "r".

"Like it," he said, bending to grip her nipple ring in his teeth. "Wham bam, thank you Param."

"A little advice, Param," Richie said, as the girl stroked the back of Martin's head. "When you leave here today, go straight to a jeweller and get that ring valued. He'll probably have done a switch."

"Yes," the girl said, but she was talking to Martin.

54. Qavan!

It had been a piece of trickery based on the fundamental principle of all magicians' acts – people's desire to see what they wanted to see. The first (American) pig was, poor thing, nuked in the teleporter. Even its ashes had been turned to ashes. The second (English) pig was made to appear by a lab technician with a small projector and a pre-edited film, prepared by Blender's team in Iowa, of a pig "materializing". In fact, when the technician had tripped the trapdoor to let the real English pig out of its soundproof hole in the floor, the animal had gone wild despite the sedatives in its veins.

Luckily, it had smashed the camera that was supposed to be filming the experiment. That, too, contained film of a pig materializing. But one thing they hadn't prepared was footage of a man being gored by an enraged porker.

Blender wasn't as pissed off as Jeb had expected. He had shaken Jeb's hand and said "good result". If it'd gone too smoothly, Blender said, people might have got suspicious. As it was, the observers had gone away chuckling but apparently impressed.

Predictably, Johnson began to whip up a campaign amongst the scientists to get on to human trials straight away.

Hamlet was stalling for time, but he had to get in touch with Blender, who'd gone into town to be with the politicos. Under the circumstances, Blender had said that no sensitive information should be communicated over the phone, even via a scrambled signal. But Jeb had to talk to him.

He was in the shower when he hit on an idea. Hit was the right word, he hoped – it was a real hit-or-miss concept.

Klingon. A snooper who didn't know the language would assume he was using a code based on English, and get nowhere. And anyone who understood it should be at least partly sympathetic to the cause.

Jeb had forgotten a lot, but he'd learnt the fictional Trekkie language in high school and later, at college, he'd spent countless nights hanging out in the Klingon-language chatrooms trying to get laid. It never worked. Klingons were only interested in fighting. Or at least the earthbound ones were.

So now Jeb sent an exploratory text message to Blender's cellphone: "qavan! pongwIj nuq?" (I salute you! What's your name?). If Blender didn't know the language, there was no point yet rooting about on the web for more elaborate vocabulary that would enable him to express his anxieties about Johnson. His memories of Klingon didn't stretch to "human trials" or "lost laser locator".

To his astonishment he received an almost immediate reply. Too quick to have got a translator in.

"Qavan!" Blender wrote, "nuqneH?" (What do you want?). And he signed off with "Qapla' ", a word for "goodbye" that literally meant "success". Blender certainly knew his Klingon.

55. Gunning for President

There are some things that a Stanford alumnus of my generation never forgets, Blender thought.

How to order Dim Sum in San Francisco's Chinatown. How to fall off a surfboard. And how to swear in Klingon.

He and his university friends figured that there had to be more to Klingon than what they heard on Star Trek. So they did their best to push it beyond its final frontier by inventing new words. Blender's favourite was Ovunq'O, the term he had coined to describe that smooth curve of a well-endowed woman's breast that protrudes from the side of her bikini top.

OK, so their females might not wear bikinis, but the Klingons were going to need words to describe what they saw if and when they eventually started vacationing in California.

Blender was sitting in an empty car-park, his phone and his laptop hooked up to a portable satellite dish. While he waited for Hamlet to compose a more explicit (though not too explicit, he hoped) Klingon message about whatever was bothering him, Blender clicked on the movie attachment to an email he'd received.

The picture quality was surprisingly good. It had been filmed from a great distance, across a rose garden and through a window made up of 12 small panes of glass, but it wasn't too jumpy. And even though the film had been made during the hours of darkness, the contrast had been very skilfully enhanced.

The only annoying thing was that there was no sound, so the dialogue was spoken by a lipreader. The conversation was often one-sided, and there were total silences when everyone turned their back.

This was a shame, because Blender would have liked to hear how the Prime Minister spoke to the President. Was she the humble ally, the young, inexperienced woman? Or did she turn on the coquettish irony? He'd have to wait until both leaders were at the summit to find out.

The film that had been sent to Blender was of the PM taking a call from the President. Blender knew why he was phoning – it was to announce his early arrival in the UK. Well, diplomatically speaking, it was to request the PM's permission to unleash his security preparations early, but they both knew she wasn't going to refuse. Mainly because the President was already on his way in Air Force One.

Whoever made the film (for security reasons, Blender didn't always know the source of the material he was sent) had spent a fair time lingering on the hem of the PM's skirt.

This was pleasurable enough to look at, but irritated Blender slightly. Was this habit of flashing her thighs totally innocent, Blender wondered. Or was she cultivating them? Practising the art of artless sexuality. Maybe her spin doctors thought the electorate would react well to "inadvertently" revealing photos. Perhaps they were even going to try the Princess Diana trick – a few "unauthorized" shots of the PM in the gym in clinging Lycra. Would sex win a British election, or would the silent majority turn away in shock? Blender didn't know them well enough to decide.

The only person that she was knowingly flashing her thighs to in the film was a male assistant. She was sitting in an armchair with her shoes off and her feet up on the chair. She was in a private lounge at Chequers, her red-bricked country residence. She'd been entertaining some of the foreign military there. Probably trying to sell them some British guns that only shoot people they haven't been introduced to.

She – or rather the male lipreader – was going through the pleasantries. What can I do for you, Mr President, that sort of thing. It was bizarre to hear the lipreader's toneless drone in place of the voice that he had listened to so often in the past few days.

She tilted her head, a look of curiosity on her face. Blender knew that the President was suggesting that they meet up the following evening, before the summit began, to discuss certain "security developments at the airbase" that Blender had reported to him.

Now the PM looked frankly suspicious. She sat up straight, feet on the carpet, knees locked together. The cameraman, deprived of his thigh-shot, zoomed tighter in on her head.

"What exactly do you mean by developments?" The concern on her face was not reflected in the flat voice-over.

The President wasn't going to explain over the phone, of course. Her concern turned to visible irritation, but she simply went though the farewell motions and hung up.

The lipreader provided snippets of the ensuing dialogue about the phone call.

"... some geiger counters down there," the PM said.

"The last thing we want ... serial killers materializing all over the place."

"... police around the boundaries?" the assistant asked.

They started to discuss where the President was going to land. This, Blender knew, was at "his" airbase.

"The runway didn't look long enough for Air Force One," the PM said.

Her assistant looked shocked. "Do you want me to make some enquiries?"

"No, don't bother. He'll find out soon enough if it's too short."

At this, even the lipreader, an American of course, allowed his voice to rise a tone.

Blender wasn't worried. This was just Brits having one of their jokes. That was sort of detail that would be checked and double-checked.

Hamlet's Klingon message came through, informing Blender that "the science officer whose title begins with MJ wishes to teleport the human hostages immediately," and requesting "an official order from Imperial Ambassador MB forbidding such action."

What should he reply to this, Blender wondered. He seemed to remember that there was a Klingon phrase along the lines of "stop shitting asteroids into my solar system."

A word of apology to everyone who'd like to see more superheroes in the book.

Sorry.

OK, more than a word, an explanation. The reason they aren't in here is that Batman, Spiderman, the Incredible Hulk, the X-Men et al haven't really inspired scientists. No one's invented a Bat Boomerang or a way of turning green when you get angry.

There's only one superhero I'm going to include – Superman. As a character he was a bit derivative, an Americanization of Nietzsche's Ubermensch and Hitler's Aryan ideal. But when Jerry Siegel and Joe Shuster created Superman in the 1930s, there was one way in which they were about 50 years ahead of their time.

The 1930s were a decade when underwear was baggy. Unless underpants were equipped with strong elastic, men's willies were doomed to dangle down their thigh (or in Errol Flynn's case, his calf). And after a quick dip in the pool or the sea, people's cotton swimming costumes went all floppy. Chafing was the norm.

Superman, though, and many of the heroes who came after him, had skintight suits that were totally unavailable to mere mortals. This seems to have set scientists dreaming, and in 1959 the Dupont chemicals company patented Lycra, the skin-hugging, butt-moulding material that, with the help of Jane Fonda's boobs and Olivia Newton John's rear end, would later help to turn boring old PE into sexy aerobics. Suddenly in the 1980s, gyms were full of supermen and superwomen. And when you look at those early aerobics photos, what do you see? Everyone is wearing their leotards or shorts outside *their Lycra leggings.*

Thanks a lot, Superman.

A Brief History of the Future, chapter 16 (extract)

56. A Room of One Zone

"I think I've got it," Richie said. "If a guest calls down and asks for a cheese sandwich, I take a cheese sandwich up to their room. But if they ask for two Martinis, I must under no circumstances take them a cheese sandwich. Right?"

"Come on old chap, don't make it hard for me," his trainer pleaded. This was Filipe, the head waiter, a tall 40-something Madeiran with a sing-song accent that was part Portuguese, part Oxford language tape. He'd worked at the hotel for ten years and never varied his briefing to new room-service waiters, whether they were reasonably bright 30-year-olds or brain-dead adolescents.

"Yeah, but don't forget my wife works at the hotel, so she has explained to me what a door is, and how you knock on it," Richie said.

"I know your wife works here, otherwise you'd already be fired for being cheeky to the head waiter."

"Sorry, Filipe, I've just had some bad news."

"Yeah, me too, and I'm stuck with you for the whole season."

"Have I got time to have a quick word with Clara before I start?"

"OK, we're not busy now. Come back in quarter of an hour?"

"Great, cheers, Filipe." Richie left the kitchen and Filipe turned to moan to his brother-in-law, the commis chef, about people who get jobs for their relatives.

Clara worked from a small office behind reception, just out of sight of the guests. There was no one at the front desk, so Richie leaned over the counter and tried to catch Clara's eye.

To Neil the manager, who had just come up from the basement swimming pool after his daily inspection, Richie looked like a naughty boy who'd been hoisted on to the counter for a good spanking. Not that that was the type of thing that Neil imagined very often.

"Dusting the front desk with your stomach isn't part of your duties, you know," he said, and Richie leapt upright.

"Sorry, Neil, er Mr er," Richie said sheepishly. This really was like going back to school.

"I'll get her for you," Neil said. He was glad of the chance to boss Clara's husband about, but a room-service waiter who couldn't remain dignified in public was bad news, especially if the guest requiring service was a world leader. Filipe would have to deal with the more important guests himself, Neil decided. Those that didn't have their private catering staff.

"Clara," Neil called as he walked into the back office. "You're going to have to break off reorganizing the room allocations for the President's premature arrival. Your husband wants a chat." His army career had provided him with almost limitless resources of irony.

"I'm sorry, I'll send him back down to the kitchen." Clara made a point of finishing off what she was doing before getting up, even though she was dying to go and hear a blow-by-blow of Martin's violent death.

"Make it quick, Richie. I've got the PM and the President turning up early. It's hell in there."

She pulled him across the lobby towards the staff staircase.

"The PM? When's she arriving?" Ideas began to hatch like maggots in Richie's fertile mind.

"Tomorrow. But never mind that – what about the car?"

"It's OK, Martin's going to pay." This good news did not have the soothing effect Richie had hoped. Clara's eyes flared.

"Where have I heard that before? What the hell did he do with the car?"

"He sold it."

Clara did a silent pirouette of distress, her hands gripping her hair. "He sold the hire car?" she hissed.

"Yes, and now he's going to pay for it." Richie tried to put his hands on her shoulders, but she shrugged him off.

"You're not going to take the blame for this, Richie. It's your name – our name – that'll go down on the debtors' list."

"No, no. I'm going to tell them I assumed Martin had driven it back to Heathrow and he assumed I had done. That's why we didn't notice it had been stolen."

For a moment, Clara was speechless. Just for a moment. "For Christ's sake. You think they're stupid? You think they'll believe that crap? And were you down as a second driver, anyway?"

"Shit." He hadn't thought of that. If people didn't want their cars crashed or stolen, Richie thought, why did they hire them out in the first place? "That doesn't matter, Clara," he said. "They don't have to believe it, they just have to be able to disprove it, which they can't."

Neil stuck his head out of the office and coughed theatrically.

"I think your country needs you," Richie said. He kissed Clara on top of the head and bounded down the stairs towards the kitchens and freedom.

Eight hours later, Filipe was relieved. Richie had delivered sandwiches, Martinis and more complex orders to the appropriate places, and had got some fairly impressive tips. This despite the fact that half the hotel was being cleared to make room for the political entourages that were on their way. Filipe didn't know that Richie had earned the tips by revealing inside information about the hotel's compensation thresholds.

"Refuse to pay your bill," he told one disgruntled guest. "Don't tell them I told you, but if you're mad enough about losing your room a day early, you won't have to pay a penny. Believe me, my wife's reservations manager." Enter one hefty tip into Richie's shirt pocket.

So Filipe let Richie off dead on time, and he was already phoning Martin as he jogged out of the hotel's back entrance.

"Just walk along the clifftop and I'll pick you up," Martin told him.

"What, towards the town centre?"

"No, other way. Fucking copmobiles everywhere. Makes me nervous."

Richie ambled, looking out over the flat silver sea towards the distant Purbeck Hills. He'd walked along the central ridge of those hills as a schoolkid. He smiled to himself as he remembered the outing. The class had started the hike on Studland Beach, a mile-long bar of gleaming white sand which had a notorious gay nudist beach in the middle. "Eyes front!" the geography teacher had bellowed as nude men came frolicking out of the dunes for a post-coital swim. Innocent days. Shit, even a week ago felt like innocent days now.

The Renault Espace pulled up alongside him and he hopped in. The teleporter was in the back, he noticed.

"You still got this car?" he asked Martin. "You sure it's a loan?"

Martin cackled. "Course it's a loan. You think I'd nick one of these?"

Martin and Richie wouldn't have been able to meet up in the town centre even if they'd wanted to.

Martin had seen vanloads of police driving in, and they were just the stragglers. During the night, the seafront had been the scene of the most frantic activity it had witnessed since the town had hosted the 1995 World Sandcastle Championships. Under a hundred floodlight moons, an army of blue-overalled workmen had begun to erect a ten-foot-high barricade around an exclusion corridor or, as it was being called, Zone.

When completed (target time: noon GMT), The Zone would run from the conference centre along the seafront road to the Prince of Wales Hotel. This would allow world leaders to be filmed taking an ecological morning stroll to their meetings instead of using their limos. Perhaps not all the way – it was almost half a mile, after all, some of it uphill.

The Zone was to extend about 400 metres inland, to the Winter Gardens in the West and the Pavilion Theatre in the east. The management of the Pavilion weren't too happy about this, because it meant that anyone wanting to attend the first-ever Bournemouth World Music Festival would be interrogated about whether they believed in globalization. Anybody with a hairdo that didn't fit into a high-street hairdresser's catalogue wasn't going to get in – including, probably, 90% of the musicians. A performance by the Iranian Army Choir had already been cancelled.

After much lobbying, it was agreed that The Zone would not include the prom and the pier (the town's tourist focal points) or the main shopping streets. So if protesters had really wanted to cause trouble, they'd only have had to go up to Debenham's fifth-floor coffee lounge and bombard the defenders of capitalism with cheese-salad baps.

By dawn, the workmen had completely fenced off the conference centre behind a double row of barricades. Each row consisted of round metal rods, coated with Teflon (impossible to get a grip on), and tapering at the top to spikes that were deadly but disinfected, in case a policeman somehow got himself propelled up there during the expected riots. The rods were set ten centimetres apart, with no horizontal bars to climb up apart from one at about knee height and another right near the top of the fence. Nothing larger than a mouse could have got past, except maybe a greased snake or an armour-plated gibbon. And according to the latest CIA intelligence, even the most extreme anti-globalization movements had not yet got round to training a hitsquad of armour-plated gibbons. Still, it was only a matter of time, and fence technology would have to keep ahead of them.

The barricades were to be guarded by the British police, some from the local force (to give the Dorset Chief Constable the chance to put on a bulletproof vest and feel like a real cop for once), but most from special riot-control units imported from upcountry.

That first morning, the Pleasure Gardens, which ran beside the old Bourne stream into the sea (or rather into a mysterious tunnel about 50 yards from the sea, never to appear again), looked like a Roman encampment, with tents of all sizes being put up on the lawns, and gangs of policemen (they were all male) trying on their gladiator gear.

They had the gladiatorial breastplates, full-face helmets, shields and even the shin-guards. Their batons looked a lot like Roman short swords. The only thing they didn't have was the skirts. And overall they were drabber than their ancient counterparts. Everything they wore was the same blue-black colour – Teflon colour, presumably so that nothing would stick to them, not even the insults of a militant mob.

Operating outside The Zone were discreet groups of SAS and secret-service personnel – male and female. The town was suddenly full of tourists who looked much more muscular than the usual breed of off-season visitor. Much more alert, too – never had the rhododendrons been gazed at with more rapt attention.

57. Laser Wotsit

"Ah, Richie the wrestler, glad you could be with us."

Mr Big greeted Richie as if this was a garden party and not a criminals' brainstorming. He draped a heavy arm across Richie's shoulder, and began to walk him around the patchy front lawn. The older man's shirt smelled of lemony deodorant.

"Yeah, well, thanks for inviting me," Richie said. "Nice day for it."

Mr Big laughed loudly. "That's why I like you Richie, son," he said. "You're a wrestler. Wrestlers know how to work an audience. Most of my boys do these fucking martial arts." He made it sound like some new sort of combat sodomy. "Wrestlers need more than calloused hands and silk pyjamas. They need to create a rapport." Mr Big hugged Richie tighter. "You created a rapport with me, and with my Rufus."

Richie saw his brother wink encouragingly to him as he walked into the house with the machine. "You think so?" Richie looked over towards Rufus, who was standing at his post, less than excited by the arrival of his new chum.

"Yeah, he didn't bite you, did he? He bites most people. That's why I've done you a little favour." Mr Big stopped guiding Richie in circles and turned to whisper in his ear. "I heard about your wager. So I've taken out some insurance for you."

"You have?"

"Yeah. I've bought up 80% of the stake. So if you lose, you'll only owe two grand to the bookies."

"Really?" This was incredible. Only two thousand to pay off? He could earn that in three months if the tips kept up.

Mr Big looked delighted at Richie's delight. "Yeah," Mr Big said, grinning. "The other eight grand you'll owe me." He gave Richie's shoulder another lemony squeeze.

"Ah. Right. Great." Richie guessed that owing eight grand to Mr Big was not good for one's health.

"Yeah. Keep it all amongst friends. Now, what have you boys got for me?" Martin came out into the garden and Mr Big waved him over to join the huddle. Martin was already pulling the laser locator from his pocket.

They did a test with the laser beam. First, Mr Big got them to transport a cheap wine glass over the road at the woman neighbour's door. When it materialized and smashed to the ground, Mr Big roared with laughter.

"Do it again," he said. Martin went to the kitchen to get a new glass and they did it again. And again, until Mr Big tired of laughing.

"Slag nearly died," he said. "Her old man called the police.

The *police*. On me. After I phoned the paramedics and saved her fucking life." Martin and Richie made incredulous noises. "Yeah, lucky for her," Mr Big went on, "she used to do shopping for Mother when I was away wrestling. I can't send my boys to sort out some of Mother's old friends."

The brothers didn't ask how Mr Big had dealt with the law. Presumably he had dealt with them, or he'd have been in a cell by now.

"Right, I want to do a few more tests before I part with my hard-earned cash. Now ..." Mr Big looked around his sitting room for inspiration. "Take this." He picked up a plate from his mantelpiece. It was a decorated dinner plate with a painting of the Virgin Mary riding a donkey. One of those Sunday-paper "limited edition" offers. "This is very precious," he warned them. Probably, Richie thought, because it symbolized his whole religion – the mother-saint-donkey transfiguration.

"You, take your laser wotsit and go down the garages at the end of the road," he told Martin. "My car's parked there – you got a phone?" Martin nodded and patted his jean pocket. "OK, I want you to shine the beam through the window at the back seat. Then you phone and give us the word and we'll beam this over. Clear?"

Martin agreed that it was, but said that he didn't think it was a good idea.

"What if the paint doesn't transport? We'll spoil the decoration."

"Shit." Mr Big put the plate back in its place and held his hand out to Richie. "We'll use your watch."

Richie sighed and put his watch in the machine. There were bound to be bits of it that wouldn't survive. Oh well, he thought, all it was doing was counting down the seconds to his financial ruin.

While they were waiting for Martin's call, Mr Big seemed happy, or at least not unhappy, to stand in silence, staring out the window at his bored donkey. Richie felt less comfortable.

"You know that time you beat Big Daddy?" he asked.

"Yeah." Mr Big gave a twitch of the nostril that was meant

to be discouraging, but this was a subject that really interested Richie.

"I was probably the only kid in England who was glad."

Bandit turned to stare at Richie for a moment. "You reckon?" he asked, and looked away.

"Yeah. People loved to hate the Bandit."

Bandit turned to his fan again. "No. You're wrong. I used to get sackfuls of mail. And only half of them contained dogshit. I had loads of real fans." He said this with no nostalgia in his voice.

"Then why –"

"Did I retire?" Mr Big's voice was mocking, as if he'd heard the question a million times. "Normally, son, anyone who asked me that question for the second time would be unconscious by now."

"But it's important to me. It's what made me give up wrestling myself."

"Then you're a soft-headed dipshit," Mr Big told him. "Where's that even softer brother of yours got to?"

They stood in silence again for another minute. This time it was Mr Big who spoke.

"Y'know, son. One thing I will tell you about my retirement is this: people can be evil bastards. Never trust them. Not one of them. You know where you are with donkeys."

I'm not a big Star Wars fan, but the movie and its sequels have made it into the book for two main reasons.

First, because in the 1980s Ronald Reagan's administration called their missile defence system Star Wars. I mean, what were they thinking – that they'd make nuclear arms escalation attractive to kids?

Secondly, because of the fanaticism of Star Wars freaks. Some of them tried to corrupt the most recent population censuses in New Zealand, Australia and Great Britain. They'd heard that you only needed about 10,000 people to declare themselves of a certain faith for that faith to become a recognized religion in the country. So, if enough people were mobilized, the governments of those countries would be powerless to stop one of its national religions being Jedi.

The dark forces of the Australian government responded with brutally repressive measures. Its Bureau of Statistics warned that anyone putting "Jedi" in the religion box would face a $1,000 fine (and, presumably, three blasts of a Deathstar ray). Trouble was, a lawyer pointed out, in order to impose the fine, the authorities would have to prove that the defendants didn't honestly believe they were Jedi.

Didn't believe? Of course they believed. Just look at the sheer immensity of the profits earned by the movies, more than 100 books, the duvet covers, fridge magnets, Monopoly sets, beach towels, light sabres, "limited edition" figurines and especially the clip-on pigtails (available in Anakin Skywalker or Obiwan Kenobi models).

Star Wars fans believe.

A Brief History of the Future, chapter 12 (extract)

58. Sacrificial Ham

A few minutes later, at the same time as Martin was reporting the successful arrival of Richie's watch (or most of it, anyway) in the back of Mr Big's car, Bournemouth's American scientists were in the flying-club bar at the aerodrome, holding an official pig-crisis meeting.

The English Yorkshire was dead, and they were running through the events that had led to its demise. Jeb was the only man in the room who knew exactly what had happened.

After breaking out of the hut, the enraged pig had run off across the tarmac of the landing strip, and tried to butt and chew its way through the perimeter fence. The lab technicians had fired a knockout dart into its flank and then carried it back to the pens. But by the time it got there, it had died, probably due to the massive doses of sedatives it had been given over the previous 12 hours.

The ten scientists had watched the videos of the experiment and were now sitting around a table over some bottles of USAF import Budweiser, while the pig lay in the kitchen cold store, waiting for a vet to do a post-mortem.

"My theory is," Jeb said to the world's assembled experts in the new (and already controversial) field of porcine teleportation, "that the living tissue, including the brain, can be re-materialized successfully. However, the psyche, the soul if you like, can't just be blown apart and re-assembled like that. If it has this effect on a pig, we can't risk it with humans." This was the only argument he could think of that might dissuade Johnson from lobbying even harder for human tests.

"That's amateur psychologist bullshit," Johnson objected, blowing a cloud of smoke up over the table. "The pig was just suffering from temporary trauma. It didn't understand how it came to materialize in a different place, and panicked. Pigs don't have a soul. And neither, from what I've read in their case notes, do most of our condemned men."

He got a laugh from everyone except Jeb.

"Jeb's right. We should get that pig's brain analysed by a veterinarian before proceeding." This was Walter Nusbaum.

"Slight correction. I say we get an animal behaviourist over here from the States," Jeb said. That would take a couple of days at least. "Then do one or two more pig tests. It seems to me that if there was a simple physiological explanation caused by the teleportation, the pig would have been paralysed, or deformed, or something. Physically, it looked in pretty good shape. It was running like an athlete. Until it dropped dead, of course."

"But what did we bring the prisoners for, if it wasn't to test theories like that?" Johnson puffed. "I get the feeling that you don't want to go ahead with human testing at all."

"Not prematurely, no," Jeb said.

"But who are you to decide? You have only a 10% vote here."

"We'd have to get the OK from Max. And I don't think we're ready to ask for it."

"And you're project director all of a sudden?"

Jeb saw that Johnson's vehemence was working against him. It was embarrassing or annoying the rest of the team. Jeb made sure his reply was calm and reasoned.

"No, the director is Dr Blender. And I don't think he'd want us to rush ahead without conducting –"

"We don't have time to get psychotherapy for our fucking pigs," Johnson interrupted him. "Besides, if it turned a docile pig insane, it might have the opposite effect on those psychos we brought with us."

"Wow, Mark, you're wasted being a scientist," Jeb said. "You should be a judge."

59. Effing Grand

Richie had a dilemma. The question was, how do you persuade your wife to call her sister and ask her to snoop around the Prime Minister's bathroom, without arousing said wife's suspicions? There are few, if any, reference books on the subject.

Working on the premise that honesty is the best policy, but only if you can't think up a good enough lie, Richie hit on The Compromise.

As soon as he got indoors, he strode into the kitchen and offered to make fried rice, with sloppy sauce of course. This got a roar of approval from under the table, where George and Ella had set up a dog-breeding kennels with their cuddly toys. They didn't have any dogs, so for the time being a Tyrannosaurus Rex was being courted by a bison. Now there's a hybrid that would take out a pitbull, Richie thought.

"Hey Clara."

She turned round from laying the table to see her husband holding up a thick roll of notes. This was his share of what Mr Big had paid for the locator plans. To be refunded if the plans turned out to be fake, but Martin had sworn that they were genuine. "Cross my heart and hope to be impotent," he'd said, his gravest oath.

"Your tips?" Clara asked.

"Two grand," Richie deadpanned. "To pay off the car-hire people."

Clara couldn't help smiling. "Martin paid up, eh? Wonders will never cease. Well, that is a load off my mind. I hate having debts like that hanging over us."

"Yeah. Talking of which." Richie began peeling vegetables in his most blasé way. Now was the time for The Compromise. "You think the PM will be getting her hair done before coming down for the conference?"

"Why?" Clara was back on full alert and holding a dangerous-looking plate.

"Well, I was wondering if you could ring Angie and ask her again about the PM being pregnant."

"She's not. I told you."

"She's trying though, isn't she? Otherwise why would she be getting tests and stuff?"

Clara put the plate down.

"What's this got to do with a debt hanging over us?" she asked.

Damn, Richie thought, why did I have to say "talking of which"? Sounds stupid at the best of times.

"Well, I had a little bet on it," he said, energetically peeling a mushroom for the second time.

"Little?"

"Well, large actually." It was not a good time for her to be opening the cutlery drawer, he thought. "A hundred quid."

"A hundred quid!?"A fistful of forks fell loudly back into the drawer.

Richie tried to imagine the effect if he'd told her the truth. The volume of her squawk would have been multiplied by – what was it? – a hundred.

"Well, fifty. Martin's down for half."

"Of course he is. Whose bright idea was this as if I didn't know?" Clara demanded, angrily scooping up dangerous metallic objects.

"Mine. I got 100-1 that she'd be pregnant within three months. That's ten grand if we win. I thought it was too good a chance to miss, what with getting inside information like that." He kept his back to her, bracing himself for the moment when the first fork would embed itself between his shoulder blades.

"God, Richie." Things went quiet for a few moments. As he peeled, Richie could hear the table being laid. Then she spoke again, grudgingly. "Well, it's probably a better bet than a year's worth of lottery tickets."

She continued laying the cutlery on the table. "So that's why you were so shocked when I told you she wasn't pregnant. And," she stopped placing forks and smiled at him, "that's what you were burbling about when you came back from the pub. Ten thousand pounds, you kept mumbling. Ten effing grand."

Richie thought that it was damn lucky he'd chosen to say the stake was a hundred. Dumb luck. He rode with it.

"Yeah, I thought that if you phoned Angie now, she might be able to tell us if the Prime Minister's said anything more about it. Or if there are any, you know, clues."

"Clues?"

"Yeah." Richie lowered his voice for the children's sake. "Pill packet in the bin. Subscription form for a year's supply of Pampers. You know what I mean – just find out if she's taking contraception. If she's not, it means we've got a real chance of winning. It'd be reassuring to know."

"Yeah," Clara said. "Ten thousand quid. It's worth a try. I'll go and call her now."

"Great."

Clara hurried off into the front room to phone. It had all gone so much better than Richie had expected. Much better than if he'd told the truth. But wasn't that always the case?

60. Cash on Delivery

If someone had invented an ambient anxiometer and installed it in The Huntsman, its needle would have been fluttering even before Johnson pulled into the car park in his white estate car.

Richie was in the pub, having just got the news via Angela

that there was no way she'd go ferreting about in the PM's bathroom, or anywhere else in Downing Street, even if she got the chance, because a piffling hundred-quid bet wasn't worth the trouble if she got caught. Richie couldn't of course, tell her how worthwhile it really was.

Angela also said she'd met the PM's hubby a few times on his rare visits to Downing Street (he was an international lawyer), and if she was any judge, the First Man was as straight as a bag of hair curlers. She had become suspicious of this whole pregnancy thing. She thought it might just be a PR smokescreen to counter rumours about the husband's gayness.

Clara had looked philosophical about the apparent loss of fifty pounds. But the phone call had sent Richie's anxiometer reading sky-high.

Dr Mark Johnson, meanwhile, was sweating profusely from both palms as he walked into the pub. He desperately needed to get the laser locator back tonight, in time for a visit by the full presidential party tomorrow. There were bound to be extra security checks.

Martin was sitting with Richie and a couple of mates at a corner table. Johnson saw them and hesitated, uncertain whether to barge in.

"I'm telling you," Martin was saying. "This one, she must have had the Kama fucking Sutra sewn into her knickers at puberty. My dick was begging for mercy in fucking Arabic."

"Indians don't talk Arabic do they, Richie?" one of the mates asked.

"Punjabi, probably," Richie said. "I know Martin's arse can fart in Punjabi, so I don't see why his dick can't talk it."

"No, bro. Must have been Arabic. That's why she didn't understand. She just kept on bouncing up and down on the poor thing."

Martin finally acknowledged Johnson's presence. "Hey, Markie Mark. We've been expecting you. Come through."

Martin and Richie stood up. Johnson's palms sweated some more as he followed them towards the games room.

When the door opened in front of him, his first instinct was to run. There was another Richie (this was Michael) playing pool in there, and an enormous, bloated old guy with a pony tail sitting in one corner fiddling with a laptop.

"This him?" Mr Big asked. Martin nodded. Michael stopped playing solo pool, and Johnson heard the door click shut behind him. He turned to Martin.

"I just need to take the –" he didn't know if he could mention the locator by name.

"Dr Johnson, right?" Mr Big said. "The same one that invented the baby lotion?" He laughed and Michael and Martin joined in. Johnson smiled uneasily. "KY Jelly, that's Johnson's an' all, isn't it?" Mr Big asked. Everyone shrugged. If anyone knew, they weren't telling. "Anyway, doc," Mr Big went on, "you seem a tad nervy. Sit down and relax."

Johnson looked around for a free chair. There wasn't one. He turned back to Mr Big, who was smiling as if he didn't realize there was a problem. It was a test of his nerve, Johnson decided.

"Sorry, uh, mate," he said to Michael, and perched on the corner of the pool table. It was uncomfortable – he was sitting right on top of a pocket – but his honour was intact, he felt.

"Now then," Mr Big said, "I've shown this to some Chinese friends of mine." Christ, thought Johnson, how many people have seen it? A fresh jolt of panic hit him in the diaphragm. "And they say that the basic components are pretty simple. In fact they can't believe it's that simple. Just like a bomb sight, they say."

"Yeah, but it's been upgraded," Martin interrupted, "made more accurate. And it's configured to talk to the teleporter."

Mr Big waved the interruption away. "Martin's biased." He gestured towards the computer and beckoned. Johnson extricated his testicles from the pool table and went to squint down at the screen. He recognized the plans for the locator. "My friends think these plans might be fakes," Mr Big said.

This hadn't occurred to Johnson. "I just took the plans out of a file, man. I'm a biologist. I don't know if they're fakes."

"Ah, but you must know a man who does. And we want you to ask him."

"I can't just ask –" Johnson was dumbstruck. He thought he'd be getting himself at least partly out of the shit tonight.

But it looked as if he was sinking deeper and deeper in.

"We need you to get us confirmation that these are the real plans. We'll give you the laser thingy back, as a sign of our faith in you, and to avoid causing you any problems when the President and his friends arrive tomorrow. We don't want the project getting stopped now."

"You *know* he's arriving early?" Johnson was horrified.

"Oh yeah, we have our sources," Mr Big grinned. The President's early arrival in Bournemouth had been announced on national TV, but Johnson hadn't been watching the BBC. "Now what you do is, when you've checked, you send an email to an address that Martin'll give you. If the plans are OK, you say 'you were right'. If they're not OK, 'you were wrong'. Keep it simple. Fair enough?"

Johnson nodded mutely.

His scientific mind was calculating fast. He'd taken enough risks just getting the plans. There was no way he could question anyone about their authenticity without dropping himself in it. But if he didn't come up with the confirmation, then these guys, who were obviously well-connected even if they did look and talk like hicks, were going to drop him in it. In short, he was doomed to be dropped in it right up to his neck. Unless ...

"Look, real or fake, and I'm pretty sure they're real, these plans are as good as I can get. If the fake plans are on our system, it's because the real ones are hidden, right?"

Mr Big nodded. The logic was unpalatable but convincing.

Johnson went on. "I'm getting pretty pissed off with the whole situation out at the aerodrome. The heads of the project are trying to keep all the credit for themselves. So I figure, fuck them. It's every man for himself." He paused, then took the plunge. He had no option. "What would you pay," he asked, "for the plans to a teleporter that's capable of transporting something the size of a car? And living creatures. Humans." A slight exaggeration, but pigs were biologically almost the same as humans, everyone knew that.

There was silence in the room except for Richie's intake of breath. His book had just suffered another attack of inbuilt obsolescence.

"No, not just the plans," Johnson corrected himself. He was pleased with the sensation he'd created. "As we've seen with the laser locator –" He held out his hand to Martin, who gave him the device. "It's better to get your hands on the real thing. I could tell you how to get hold of this new machine. And," he added in a flash of inspiration, "some human guinea pigs."

"Amazing," Richie said. "You're charging ahead in huge technological leaps. How did you –"

"Oy! No fraternizing." Mr Big cut off the question, but Richie's voice had faded anyway in response to Johnson's "who-is-this-amateur?" grimace.

Mr Big was thinking hard. He looked around the room. Martin's eyes were bright. Richie's were drilling into Johnson's head, as if trying to read all the secrets there.

"Er," Martin said, and came over to whisper in Mr Big's ear. Johnson shifted uncomfortably from foot to foot. He hadn't known Martin long, but already knew him well enough to fear his brainwaves.

After thirty seconds or so of fast-talking, Martin finally backed off. Mr Big turned to Johnson and said, "OK. We'll pass on the guinea pigs, ta all the same, but we'll take the machine off your hands. Cash on delivery OK?"

When the American had slunk away with his laser locator and his promise of large cash payments, and had been followed out of the car park by two military-looking men in a car identical to his own, Mr Big came and rested his log-like arm on Richie's shoulders.

"You're the one who started this whole gravy train rolling," he told Richie. It was meant to be gratitude, but Richie could imagine a prosecutor saying the same thing, with different intentions. "If you hadn't brought that machine back, we'd all be living in the past round here."

"Right, thanks." Richie tried to move away but the log held him back.

"Which is why I want you to come and work for me permanently. Be one of my boys."

"I've got a job," Richie said, perhaps too hastily.

"A waiter? Call that a job?"

"No, I'm a writer."

This took Mr Big by surprise. He withdrew his arm.

"What sort of writer?"

"I've written a book and I'm trying to sell it. Once it's published, I'll write a TV series based on the book and try to sell that." It sounded so simple and credible, even though Richie had that morning received his first rejection letter.

"What's this book about?"

Richie explained.

"So that's why you bought the machine?" Mr Big asked.

"Yeah."

Mr Big nodded slowly, as if confirming a deep-held suspicion.

"Got any ideas for other books?"

"No. Not really." This wasn't strictly true. Richie had been researching another book, but he didn't feel like sharing the idea with Mr Big.

"Think you could write a book about the mistreatment of donkeys?"

"Don't know," Richie said. How should he answer that without having his collar-bone broken? "I'm not sure I'd be the right person. Even though it is a subject I care a lot about."

Mr Big nodded and his arm went back on the shoulder.

He smiled at Richie, and breathed whisky vapour in in his face. "Don't lay it on too thick, son. I may have a soft spot for donkeys, but I ain't soft in the head."

"Sorry," Richie said, "you're right. It's always insulting when people don't tell you what they really think."

"Yeah," said Mr Big. "They flatter the pants off you then fuck you up the back passage the first chance they get. That's why if you lose your bet, I'll give the money you owe me to the sanctuary. It's a very good cause."

"Hmm," Richie said non-committally. As far as Richie was concerned, a roof over his head and saving his family life from disintegration were even better causes.

"Anyway, if you don't come and work for me, I'll have to ask for your stake money up front, and I'm not sure you could afford that."

Richie felt the arm pressing down on his shoulder.

"You wouldn't want your wife to find out how much you've bet, would you?" Mr Big increased the pressure still further. Bastard Martin, Richie thought, he's been talking too much. He resisted, holding himself up to his full height. "How's she going to react when she finds out you owe me eight grand?" Mr Big went on. Richie got another faceful of whisky breath and felt his shoulders give way.

"OK, I can give you a few hours when I'm off duty at the hotel. But any hard drug deals and I walk."

Mr Big patted him paternally on the cheek. "Richie, my son, don't say things that you might regret later."

Later, out in the car park, under the stars and The Huntsman's gently swinging sign, Martin was trying to lay his arm conspiratorially across Richie's shoulders as Mr Big had done. The difference in their height made this impossible, and Richie wasn't going to stoop for his brother. So Martin contented himself with a hand on Richie's bicep.

"When you've finished fondling me, can I go home?" Richie said.

"Yeah, yeah, bro. But listen. You know what Mr Big wants that new human transporter for, don't you?" Martin looked askance at his brother, like a schoolkid offering to tell where teacher hides the confiscated Game Boys.

"No."

"Immigrants," Martin said. "Can you imagine the money to be made? I mean instead of paying tens of thousands of quid to be crammed into lorries and leaky ships for three months, the illegals will just step into a machine in Asia or South America and reappear in Europe or the States or wherever."

"Holy shit. Is that what he said?"

"No, that's what I suggested to him. You feel like getting into that business? No, of course you don't," Martin went on, giving Richie no time for moral objections. "So you and him are heading for a major barney as soon as you refuse to cooperate. And that means you have two choices. Get the money to pay him your stake money, which he probably wouldn't accept anyway, seeing as how you're part of his new masterplan. Or ..."

Martin paused for dramatic effect. Richie looked up at the grinning Huntsman on the pub sign. Now he knew what a fox must feel like when a redcoat grins at it, however inanely. Hunted.

"Or you use this." Martin held up what looked strangely like the laser locator, even though it couldn't be, because Richie had just seen him give it back to Johnson. Richie's open mouth seemed to express all this, because Martin explained.

"I didn't give him the real one. I've got this mate who invents models for toy companies and he fixed me a fake. Said it was simple." He looked at it disparagingly. "Looked as if it was cobbled together out of a laser pointer anyway," he said.

"So that's the real one?" Richie asked.

"Yup."

An unpleasant thought occurred to Richie. "Does Mr Big know you've kept the real one?"

Martin hushed him. A bit late in the day for discretion, Richie thought.

"No. Fuck Mr Big," Martin whispered. "You've got to keep one step ahead of him. He's not above taking out a contract on the Prime Minister's ovaries to save paying up on the bet. And this is where the laser locator comes in."

Martin explained his plan. Richie's jaw dropped an inch with every sentence. At the end he stood back and let his eyes run over the full length of his brother's deranged anatomy, from stubbly head to trendy trainers and back again. He gazed up into the sky. Was that moving light an aeroplane or a spy satellite? If it was a US satellite, they'd be pissing themselves with laughter at the Pentagon right now.

"You're serious aren't you?" Richie said. "You're really serious."

"A million quid is serious money, bro. And anyway, you've got the easy part. You've just got to get into the Prime Minister's room. I'm the poor bastard who's got to blackmail friend Johnson to wank into his upgraded human transporter."

61. Porky and Pres

Air Force One overran the runway and burst a tyre on collision with an ancient English oak that had not been taken into account when the landing strip had been measured via satellite.

All the passengers had to slide down an emergency chute and dash across the aerodrome's lawns to safety. The President suffered two indignities. First, he was shoved down an inflated escape chute and ended up on his backside in the grass. Then, after being wrenched to his feet by two bodyguards, he was flattened again when some idiot had yelled "hit the decks!"

A minute or so passed before a Royal Air Force man (the nominal commander of the base, now only in charge of the landing strip) came strolling over and told the horizontal President that everything was in order. There were no terrorists in the vicinity, and the only damage to the plane was a puncture.

The President stood up, dusted the English grass off his suit and looked back at his aircraft, which appeared to be sniffing the old oak tree like a dog wondering whether to piss against it.

"Who the hell planted that there?" the President growled, unwittingly echoing a question that a certain Ella Fisher, age six, had asked a couple of days earlier.

"Henry the Eighth, I think, Sir," the RAF man said with one of those snooty English smiles.

"Well I wish he'd called my fucking pilot to warn him about it," the President said.

Word was, the President was now in the mood for a sacrifice. He was hungry, jet-lagged and pissed (in the American sense, as usual).

The British Prime Minister was on her way to join him for a teleportation crisis meeting at the airbase, and the President had ordered Max Blender to give him an immediate update on exactly how bad the crisis was. He was waiting in the base commander's office, going through his keynote speech for the summit.

Blender rounded up the scientists, his assistants, General Colt and a couple of soldiers and interrupted the President's reading.

The President looked up from his speech to scrutinize the array of people in front of him. His eyes blinked a greeting to Blender, scanned the gaggle of scruffy guys whom he correctly assumed to be the scientists, and lingered on Johnson, who was unshaven and panicky, standing crammed shoulder-to-elbow between two huge guards.

"OK, Max, what's the update?" the President asked. They hadn't had their golf game yet, but the invitation had gone out, so Blender had earned the right to be called by his first name.

"I asked you to come because things seem to have come to a head, Sir."

"What kind of head exactly?" the President asked.

"Well, anyone going off the base was naturally followed," Blender said. "And at first there were only minor irregularities such as small pieces of equipment going outside the perimeter." He raised an accusing eyebrow in the general direction of Hamlet and Johnson. "However, when one of those pieces of equipment – a laser locator – was stolen, things became far from minor." The President nodded. Go on, go on. "We have now retrieved the stolen property, but there's been a new development. Jeb, could you explain?"

"OK, well," Hamlet began, nervous at the prospect of addressing such an eminent audience.

"You are?" the President asked.

"Professor Jeb Hamlet, Sir, I'm the teleportation expert here. To beam or not to beam, as it were."

The President merely frowned.

"Professor Hamlet?" Blender prompted. Prompter was right. Hamlet's little announcement was to follow Blender's script. Things had gone slightly wrong, but the main thrust of Blender's plan was salvageable.

"Right, yes. OK, some outsiders, the same ones who had

temporary possession of the locator, have accessed the plans to the prototype. We know who gave them the access codes." Hamlet turned towards Johnson to stress his point, and to steer any guilt away from himself. "And our assessment is that if these locators are copied and get into the wrong hands, there are dangers. Theoretically, by extending the reception range of the laser, someone could beam anything anywhere. They could send over a perfectly innocent radio-controlled model aircraft and locate on us while someone on the other side of the world beamed in a nuclear device. No warning, nothing. Boom."

"You never told us about this risk," the President snapped at Blender.

"I didn't foresee it, Sir," Blender said. "Regardless of any theoretical dangers, we obviously didn't expect our own people to go around giving out military secrets like this." He gave Johnson a malevolent glare that made the scientist feel queasy.

"There is a solution, though," Hamlet added, and was pleased to see the anticipation on the President's face. "We can develop jammers to stop the teleportation beams coming in."

"How long will that take?" the President asked.

Hamlet shrugged and looked to his colleagues for help. They all made faces suggesting ignorance. "Weeks? Months? Years?" Hamlet estimated.

The President puffed his frustration.

"Yes, but it's going to take criminals and enemy powers that long to develop the transporters as weapons," Hamlet went on. "We can set up teleportation detectors and take out the machines as they're being tested. I honestly don't think that will be a major problem if we get to work on it straight away."

"Well why the fuck were we developing them if they're so easy to disable?" the President asked.

"Again, Sir," Blender replied. "We were supposed to be the only ones who even knew about the enlarged, improved transporters. Along with our British allies, of course."

"And you tested this enlarged machine on a pig?" the President asked.

"Yes," Hamlet replied. He blushed slightly. "It survived, but seemed to go insane somehow. And it died shortly afterwards. We decided not to try it on humans for the time being."

"Can I see this pig transporter at work?" the President asked.

"Ah, uh, well," Hamlet stuttered.

"That brings us to problem two," Blender said. "It was stolen this afternoon by a gang of armed men, apparently of Asian origin."

The President almost choked with disbelief.

"We have a very low-key military presence on site," Blender went on. "We didn't want to attract attention."

"Well that strategy didn't work out too well, did it?" the President scoffed. "How big was this thing?"

"As big as an average one-car garage," Hamlet said.

The President gave an involuntary laugh.

"We've alerted the police and the security services to look out for anyone carrying a suspicious garage," Hamlet said.

If the President's eyes had been fitted with machine guns, Hamlet's guts would have been splattered all over the wall. Here he was, just about to explain to the Prime Minister of England that his team had not only allowed major security breaches, they'd also screwed up their experiment and lost all their new equipment, and now this hairy little rugrat was making jokes?

The President had just reached full volume, and had almost used up his stock of expletives when his audience was relieved to hear a knock at the door.

"What the hell is it?" the President screamed, unable to effect a sudden decibel reduction.

A uniformed guard came timidly in, carrying a plate of amateurish-looking sandwiches.

"It's all I could find, Sir," he said.

"Never mind, at least one man here can obey instructions," the President replied. "What's your name, son?"

"Corporal Jerry Sticker, Sir." The young, blond-headed soldier saluted stiffly.

"Well thank you, Jerry." He picked up an inch-thick sandwich. "What's in it?"

"Ham, Sir," the corporal said. "Sorry if it's kind of doorsteppy. I had to slice the meat myself."

All the scientists' eyes followed the progress of the meat

from the plate to the President's mouth. Could it be? No. Where exactly *had* they left the body of the pig?

The President started to chew.

Now Johnson wasn't the only scientist in the room looking queasy.

62. Pressing the Flesh

Clara watched the presidential entourage arrive at the Prince of Wales, and wondered if the Leader of the Free World was always so grumpy. All the hotel staff were assembled in the lobby (or at least the presentable members were – a nose-pierced chambermaid and an explosively pregnant teenage kitchen assistant had failed Neil's inspection), but the President marched straight past them. He ignored the outstretched hands of the mayor, the mayoress, Neil and the chairwoman of the local Anglo-American ex-Servicemen's Wives Association, and stomped straight into the lift.

Once all the Americans except a couple of security guys had disappeared, Neil clapped his hands and told everyone to get back to their posts. Richie went downstairs as quick as he could, eager to carry on listening to the England-Portugal friendly on the radio. With the kitchen staff divided down the middle between Brits and Madeirans, it was a real derby game, and they'd had a sweepstake on which player would score the first goal. Luckily for Richie, they'd only put a pound each into the pot, because he had drawn the England goalkeeper, probably the second-least likely person on the pitch to score after the referee.

The President did have an extra excuse for being in such a bad mood as he entered the hotel. He was feeling bloated and sluggish, though his digestive system usually worked like a well-oiled machine.

In the lift, or elevator, as staff had been asked to call it in the President's honour, the advisors advised him that it might be politic to be more polite to the British people. Reporters would be looking for "what's he really like?" stories. It wouldn't look good if the answer was "an arrogant bastard".

In reply the President burped and winced.

When he arrived in his suite, he immediately demanded coffee.

"That was about the most indigestible piece of ham I ever ate. I feel like I'm going to fall asleep at any moment."

An aide said he'd call down to room service.

"No," the President said. "Let me do it. It'll give me a chance to interact with ordinary British people."

Richie had just asked the kitchen assistant the score (1-0 to England, though the goal hadn't been scored by the goalkeeper) when the room-service telephone rang.

"Oh, bollocks," Richie said. Filipe the head waiter wanted to serve anyone of international importance himself. But Filipe hadn't come back down yet, so Richie answered.

A man announced that he was the President of the USA and that he'd like some coffee. Normally Richie would have replied that he was the Sultan of Brunei and had no time to get refreshments for jokers, but in this case he suspected that the call might be genuine.

"You do know, Sir, that there are tea- and coffee-making facilities in every room?" he suggested helpfully.

There was a moment's silence, then the voice came back. "But I'd like you to bring some coffee up to my suite."

"I'd be happy to, Sir," Richie said, "but quite honestly it would be quicker and cheaper for you to use the facilities in the room. You simply fill the kettle at the tap in the bathroom and –"

"Listen, bloke," the President interrupted. "I am the President of the United States of America and I want to order some coffee from room service. You know that word over here? 'Service'?"

"Certainly, Sir. But you've already got the coffee in your room, in the paper sachets marked 'coffee'. Perhaps you'd like some more of those little plastic pots of milk? Some people like more than one in each cup, which tends to use them up prematurely."

The President gave up on diplomacy. "Bring me some goddam coffee right now," he snarled, "ready-made in a pot, on a tray, with cream and sugar and four cups, and yes I know I've got fucking cups in the suite but I want fresh fucking cups, OK?"

"Of course, Sir. What room number is it?"

"What fucking room number? How many fucking Presidents of the USA do you have staying in this fucking hotel?"

He slammed the phone down. There was an embarrassed silence in the presidential suite.

"Didn't sound British to me," the President said.

He was right. Richie had given his voice a very slight Portuguese lilt.

Filipe came in the kitchen door smelling of cigarette smoke. "Any more goals?" he asked.

"No," Richie said.

"Any calls?"

"Yeah. Coffee for four in the President's suite. You'll be wanting to take that up yourself, won't you?"

Once Filipe had gone and another room-service waiter had come down to the kitchen, Richie took the opportunity to work on his win-the-bet plan.

He'd rejected Martin's scheme, of course. The idea that Richie could have got into the PM's room at night, shone the laser locator between her legs, and then given the word to Johnson to deposit a fresh sperm sample into the teleporter that was capable of beaming living creatures, hadn't convinced even the desperate Richie. Besides, Martin conceded, Johnson seemed to have gone incommunicado all of a sudden.

Richie had come up with something much more practical. Well, less impractical, anyway.

The question was, how could an amateur like him break through the security arrangements protecting two world leaders?

In fact, the answer was simple.

There was only one problem with the American security arrangements for the Prince of Wales Hotel. They were American.

This is in no way to detract from the quality and motivation of US Government security agents. They had transformed the President's suite into a bug-proof, anthrax-proof, bomb-detecting, and yet still antique-windowed, fortress. But they should perhaps have allowed British security agents some input into the arrangements, instead of insisting on total US control.

When they had made their first preliminary visit to the hotel, the A Team (A Team 1, that is) had made the mistaken assumption that it was fundamentally like an American hotel. That is, based on one of two models: the motel model, ie reception area plus group(s) of rooms in separate building(s). Or the hotel model, ie central lobby plus several floors above.

However, the Prince of Wales was made up of two old buildings plus innumerable add-ons. Parts of it had been built (unlike 99% of buildings in America) before lifts were invented, so the liftshaft had been punched up through the floor from the lobby, which wasn't anywhere near the centre of the hotel. The lift and the main staircase were in the larger of the two buildings that made up the hotel, so that guests in the cheaper rooms often had to undertake a minor hike up and down small staircases from the lift to their door.

The floor system was chaotic. The "third floor", for example, was on two main levels. There was a group of rooms up a small staircase that were closer in walking terms to the fourth-floor lift – these should really have been labelled the third and a halfth floor. Room-service waiters always went to these rooms by going up to the fourth floor in the lift and then taking the small staircase down to the third and a halfth floor. They, or any intruder, could then continue on down to the third floor without passing a guard positioned by the third-floor lift or the main third-floor landing.

A Team 1 should really have walked every inch of stair and corridor themselves. Which they didn't. Or interviewed a room-service waiter about the short cuts between rooms and floors. Which they didn't.

FBI and CIA chiefs often complain these days that their agents are no longer true field operatives – they're office workers and computer geeks who've replaced nose-in-the-shit investigations with DNA comparisons, satellite photos and database searches.

It wasn't the fault of A Team 2, who implemented the security arrangements, that the 3-D graphics they were working from were inaccurate. After all, the graphics might have been based on faulty research, but they looked superb.

Of course, when the President and the Prime Minister were installed at the hotel, each had his or her own bodyguards, and the PM's personal policeman was constantly by her side. Plus, of course, the hotel, the car parks and surrounding buildings were swept day and night, by machines and men, for bombs and suspicious individuals. But Richie wasn't a suspicious individual, as was confirmed by the rock-star back-stage security pass hanging round his neck.

He'd prepared his strategy by making friends with the chambermaid who was to put the final touches to the PM's room. He'd given her twenty pounds in cash in return for a simple promise. All the chambermaid had to do was lend Richie her pass key for an evening after she went off duty, with the promise that it would be back in her pantry when she came in next morning. A simple plan. Trouble was, when she had come down to the kitchen earlier for a cup of tea, she had replied to Richie's smile with a shake of her head and a mouthed "no".

Richie walked innocently out of the fourth-floor lift.
"Hi," he said.
The guard put aside the book he was reading, a slim volume called Britspeak. "Where you going, uh, geezer?" he asked, inspecting Richie's pass.
"Just to have a word with the chambermaid. Maria." Richie let the merest hint of a suggestion of a suggestive grin flick suggestively across his face.
The guard, who was almost as tall as Richie, but had the JFK hairstyle that US military men adopt when they want to

try and fool people they're civilians, looked Richie in the eye. It was impossible to tell from his blank, well-shaven face what he thought of the idea of chasing after chambermaids, but the notion clearly computed somewhere. It was credible.

"OK," he said and nodded Richie past.

"Cheers," Richie said, leaving the guard invisibly but genuinely bemused. This wasn't in the book. Ever since he'd landed in the country, Englishmen kept saying cheers to him when they should have been saying thanks or see you. He wondered whether the British weren't such a nation of drunkards that they talked to everyone as if they had a beer in their hand.

Maria's trolley was outside her pantry by the staircase. Richie knocked on the door and went in.

As Richie was entering the pantry, a disgruntled Filipe was going down the stairs. He'd received a very undiplomatic reception in the President's suite. The President had just sat and glowered at him, and a security guard had bundled him out of the door, without a tip, when he'd begun to explain the practicalities of the room – trouser press, tea-making facilities, etc ... Filipe suspected that Richie might have had something to do with it. He would have to ask what exactly was said on the phone when the President placed his order.

So when he noticed Richie, who had no business being on the upper floors without a tray in his hands, going into the chambermaid's pantry, where he had no business going even with a tray in his hands, Filipe hurried to the nearest phone.

"Look, Maria," Richie said. "You won't get into any trouble. No one will check your pantry tonight."

"No," the girl said. "You want to go into the Prime Minister's room." It was the President's fault. His Mr Grumpy act had scared the shit out of her.

"No, I don't. Look, don't you want to earn the money?" Richie asked. "Just for helping me to play a little joke?"

"No. Here." She gave the twenty pounds back. "You want to poison her."

"Poison her? You think I'm nuts?"

The look in her eye told him the answer.

Richie tried to press the notes into her hand again, but she kept her fists clenched.

"Use someone's else's key."

"I can't. It's your floor."

"Ask your wife."

"I can't. Oh, come on, Maria."

"No." She was beginning to get a little frightened of this big man in her small pantry, and Richie knew that he didn't have much time to convince her before she panicked.

He fished around in his back pocket and held up five ten-pound notes. He fanned them out and wafted the scent of money in her face.

"You won't do it, even for all this?" he said, giving her his most reassuring smile.

It was at this point that Clara opened the door of the pantry.

She took in the scene: her husband, a pleading look, a large amount of money and a not unattractive young chambermaid in a confined space.

"How come you never offer to pay me for it, Richie?" she asked.

63. Fifty-fifty

Richie chased her down the stairs, smiling apologetically towards the JFK lookalike security guard as he passed. The guard did not smile back. He'd guessed what was going on when he saw the name on Clara's badge. It confirmed his view that the Brits were a fundamentally undisciplined race.

"Honestly, Clara, it's not what it seems," Richie said, knowing as he spoke the line that no one who says it is ever believed.

She ignored him and kept going. They were already down to the second floor. Two more flights of stairs and they'd be too close to the lobby to talk. He saw that there was no security guard in sight, and took a chance.

He accelerated as they crossed the landing, and hoisted Clara off her feet.

She still didn't speak. Instead she used the hand that wasn't squashed against his chest to slap him hard around the ear.

"You're going to listen to me," he told her, and opened the door to the second-floor chambermaid's pantry.

Filipe, who'd been hanging around in the staircase to enjoy the fun he'd set up, whistled to himself. First the chambermaid, then Clara, all in the space of five minutes. Who said British men were cold-blooded?

Richie deposited Clara in the pantry amongst the folded bed linen, the towels, complimentary biscuits and spare pots of tea-making milk, and stood blocking the door.

"Let me out, Richie."

"No," he said. "Listen to me."

"I'll scream."

"And lose both of us our jobs."

"What is it? You've got a hard-on and I'm second best?" Clara asked.

"I was trying to win my bet."

"Oh yeah? How?"

"By getting her to lend me her pass key so I can get into the Prime Minister's room."

"You were paying her – how much?"

"Fifty quid."

"Fifty quid, to help you win a fifty-quid bet? You're either lying through your teeth or you're even worse at maths than I thought." Clara looked justifiably dubious.

Richie realized his mistake and leaned back against the door, his eyes shut.

"So you *were* trying to fuck her?" Clara said.

"No." Richie decided he had no choice but to tell her. "I was trying to win the bet. It's a bit bigger than I told you."

"How big?"

Richie took a deep breath and dived in. "If I win, I'll get a million quid."

"A million?" Clara didn't believe him.

"Yes, a million. I bet ten thousand quid at 100-1."

Clara slumped on to a pile of clean sheets. She let herself sink down into the soft cotton.

"Ten?" She couldn't say the rest. "Richie ..."

"I know. I'm sorry. I thought I had inside information. Your sister's information."

"Don't try to put the blame on me or Angela."

"I'm not."

She shook her head. "You lied to me."

"I know. I've been trying to fix things so I wouldn't have to tell you. Until I brought home the million, that is."

Richie tried a smile, but it didn't work. Clara was using all her strength of mind to prevent herself from launching a verbal missile attack on Martin. Under the circumstances she knew it would be counter-productive.

"You bet ten thousand pounds? Where did you get it from?"

"I didn't. I've promised to pay it if I lose."

"Oh Jesus God." Clara was close to tears. Suddenly, the idea that Richie might have been trying to pay the chambermaid for sex did not seem the most tragic thing in the world. If he'd only admit it – yes, I fancied a quick fuck in the broom cupboard – everything would be all right.

"What do you need to get into the Prime Minister's room for?" she asked.

"To make sure she gets pregnant of course."

"You want to –" Clara bunched a fist. Richie enclosed it in his own hand, which was twice the size.

"No, Martin suggested that," he said. "That and even stupider things. My idea is much simpler."

"Go on, then. Try me."

Clara crossed her arms and challenged him to convince her. Somehow, even though she was lounging almost horizontally on a mound of sheets, she still managed to look combative. But Richie relaxed slightly. At least she was willing to listen.

"OK, I know two things for certain," he began. He held up his right thumb. "If her hubbie's gay and they don't shag, I'm fucked." He raised his forefinger to join the thumb. "If she's infertile, I'm fucked. But ..." He folded down both thumb and forefinger. "If they do shag and she's on the pill, or uses condoms –"

"Condoms? She's married. She won't use condoms."

"For a million quid I'm willing to cover all possibilities. If she uses the pill or condoms, I'm covered."

"Covered?" Clara's arms were more tightly folded than ever.

"With these, and these." Out of his pocket he pulled a foil-covered condom and a blister pack of pills.

Clara took the condom. "Richie, I think it's *less* contraceptives she needs, not more."

"Ah, yes, but that's got a hole in and these are made of baking powder." He let her guess which was which.

"A hole?" Clara examined the foil condom pack, which was still sealed, and showed no signs of having been tampered with.

Richie smiled with satisfaction. If Clara at her most sceptical couldn't see it, then no one in the impatient throes of lust would notice a thing. He had achieved his invisible condom sabotage by pricking the thinnest needle he could buy through the foil and then rubbing the pack so that the hole became practically invisible. It had taken three packets to perfect the technique, but eventually he had got to the state where he could have sold the patent to the Papal Anti-Birth-Control League.

Clara took the pills and examined the join between the transparent plastic and the metallic backing. This job he'd had to farm out to the friend of Martin's who made the dummy laser locator. The guy was a genius with a scalpel and plastic. A real plastic surgeon.

Clara threw the two small packets back at Richie. They bounced off him and on to the pantry floor.

"Won't work. What if she uses different brands?"

Richie retrieved his contraceptives. "I've made some up of all the most common brands of pills and condoms."

"And you want to sneak into her room with your pockets bulging? If they catch you they'll think you're a rapist with a conscience. Doesn't want to get his victims up the spout. You'll go down for years."

"No, no. I sneak in with the locator, do a recce, then phone

Martin and he *beams* in whatever brands I tell him to, to the coordinates I've sent him with the locator."

"How do you know you can beam condoms? No, don't answer that."

Clara rubbed her face vigorously in her two open hands, like someone trying to wake themselves up. Then she looked around the small pantry. It was, she realized, the first time she'd been in one. The second time, if you counted barging in on Maria. Unlike the rest of the corridor, the tiny room hadn't been redecorated, and the wallpaper, which had been battered by many seasons of mops, brooms and trolleys, was a vivid yellow embossed gorse-flower pattern that had probably been considered chic in the 1980s. It was horrible but comforting, a reminder of an age before teleportation, and a sure sign that she was in the real world and not some virtual-reality game that Martin and Richie had invented.

"You're right, Richie," she finally said. "That is so simple it's bloody stupid. What if she uses a diaphragm? What if she's got a coil?"

"Then I'm fucked. Can you lend me your pass key?"

64. Boldly Going

Even though Bournemouth wasn't quite the "Zeropolis" that Johnson had thought, it was a small pond.

And even though Mr Big was a big fish in that pond, he had to admit he was a flounder. (A freshwater flounder, of course, because you don't get seawater ponds.)

The ex-wrestler had underestimated his Chinese "friends". They and their associates in London had used their vast network of contacts, and the good old American-style capitalist skills that they'd honed in Hong Kong, San Francisco, Seattle and Singapore, to branch out on their own.

Richie was the first Brit to import one of the small transporter machines into the UK, but now the Chinese began to buy them using American ID and then smuggle them into Europe in bulk, along with the simple click-on locators like the one that Martin had had sent over to Mr Big. They'd also started to replicate the laser locators. And the large transporter that had been stolen from the aerodrome had totally disappeared. The FBI assumed it was already on a cargo ship bound for Asia.

Added to all this, someone had developed pirate software that allowed the microwave-sized transporters to teleport certain complex plastics and organic materials.

The results, both legal and illegal, were instantaneous.

Richie had passed through the barricades out of The Zone, and was walking away from the hotel along a fragrant, pine tree-lined street when his phone began to vibrate in his pocket.

"You got that key, bro?" It was Martin.

"No, but I will have."

"Great. When you win your bet, I've found a brilliant investment for you."

"Oh yeah?" Suddenly the street seemed less fragrant.

"Yeah. Know what I'd do if I had a million, or even ten thousand quid right now?"

"Gamble it away on a stupid bet?"

"No, invest it in terbium."

"What's that, a new designer drug?"

"No, a metal. The price is going through the roof. Used in the making of lasers, you see."

"Terbium? Never heard of it."

"Neither had I. Soft metal with a really high melting point. Named after the village in Sweden where it was discovered. Gitterby or something."

This rang a bell in Richie's mind. "Gitterby? It wasn't Ytterby, was it? Starts with a 'y'?"

"Think so. Why?"

"I mention it my book. Can't remember what for. Weird coincidence. Anyway, who's this chemist mate of yours?"

"Just a guy I know. Says terbium used to cost over two thousand dollars a pound, and the price doubled in the last week."

"Yeah, well it's a shame you didn't come up with a tip like that before you introduced me to your mate Terry."

"Couldn't. It's only just happened."

"What has?"

"These laser locators. Someone's gone into mass production and sent the price of terbium into orbit. It's like your mate Einstein said: times change with the speed of light."

"And it's like most of your mates end up saying to you – fuck you Martin."

Not for the first time recently, Richie cursed the gods that he wasn't rich. There were so many perfectly legal ways to make yourself richer.

On the less legal side, there was an instant boom in teleportation-related crime and anarchy all over the UK.

Stolen credit cards could be teleported and used almost immediately hundreds of miles away from their point of theft.

Not only designer drugs but plant-based drugs such as cocaine, heroin and cannabis started to move invisibly around the nation. Customs men stopped finding caches of narcotics overnight.

As this was invisible crime, it didn't cause much of a stir.

Much more newsworthy was the visible mischief.

Listeners to the normally sober news programmes of BBC Radio 4 heard surreal reports like this one:

"In Manchester this afternoon, a lorry crashed into a bus stop, killing six bystanders and injuring three others. A post-mortem on the driver revealed that a number of compact discs by the American entertainer Bing Crosby had been beamed, using a teleportation machine, into the man's brain, heart and lungs, killing him instantly. The discs still had their price tickets on, and police are currently interviewing staff of a chain of record shops in the hope of tracing someone who bought five Bing Crosby CDs. A police spokesman said that they are hopeful of getting a quick result."

Thanks to the chain of events that started with Richie buying his transporter in New York, Britain was boldly going where even America had never been before.

It was in 1968 that Stanley Kubrick brought HAL the talking computer to life in the film of Arthur C Clarke's 2001, A Space Odyssey.

Just eleven years later, Texas Instruments created the first computer chip capable of reproducing a human voice from digital signals. However, the rest of Clarke's technology didn't follow – instead of integrating their chip into a rocket sent to meet aliens, Texas Instruments used it to make a Speak & Spell toy.

Clarke overestimated the speed of the space race, but he got one thing dead right. With HAL, he showed how much mayhem can result when a computer malfunctions, and he seems to have given the makers of certain omnipresent software products some very bad ideas.

A Brief History of the Future, chapter 19 (extract)

65. End-of-Pier Show

"I'm not paying that! Thirty-five pee to go on my own bloody pier?"

Mr Big was giving the lad on the turnstile a hard time. This was a gap-year student who had so far spent a pleasurable few months sitting in his booth listening to CDs all day and giving out tickets to pensioners and families. He'd seen Mr Big and his friend from twenty yards away, and knew they were going to be trouble. You didn't often get two wardrobe-sized, mean-looking guys going on to the pier to buy candyfloss and ride on the roundabout. He wished he'd never asked for the money now.

"Do you know how many years I've paid rates in this town? I've probably paid for the whole fucking pier!"

The old guy with the pony tail was turning red in the face. His mate, all muscle, was cracking his knuckles. The student thought he recognized him. A bouncer at one of the clubs, he thought, sold E sometimes.

"We're not fucking tourists, sonny, we live here! You should fleece the fucking tourists. That's what they're for!"

The old guy was grating his teeth, and seemed to be working himself up towards some act of gratuitous violence, so, in a spirit of solidarity with the local community, the student decided to let it go.

"OK, Sir. You can go through the exit gate. I'll buzz it open for you."

The gate swung open and Mr Big and Michael marched through. The student was so relieved to see the back of them that he didn't even consult the rule book to see if donkeys were allowed on the pier.

When Martin and Richie arrived for their meeting with Mr Big, they were surprised to be waved through for free. The student had decided Richie looked too much like the bouncer to risk asking him for money.

"Cheers," Richie said to the kid in the booth. "Friend of yours, Martin?"

"No. He's probably heard about our money troubles and took pity on us. Every penny counts."

"Rub it in, why don't you?"

Martin cackled as they marched along the pier. It was almost empty except for a few dazed-looking oldies slumped in their deckchairs while they recovered from their morning hobble along the prom.

"Come on bro, you're just making it hard for yourself. Ballsing about with booby-trapped rubbers and fake pills. All you've got to do is take her up a bottle of champagne, on the house, ripple a few muscles at her and she'll be gagging for it."

"If you're so keen, Martin, you have a go."

"Nah, she looks a right ball-breaker. Think I'd rather fuck the President."

Martin's loud declaration of love for the Leader of the Free World made an old woman look up from her Daily Mail and say a silent prayer for Bournemouth's lost decorum.

"Hey, look, he's even brought the bloody donkey," Richie

said as they entered the end-of the-pier caff.

"Course he has," Martin said. "To see you. It pines when you're not there."

"Sit down, boys. Tea?" Mr Big asked.

"Er, yeah, great," Martin said.

"Well go and get it yourself, this is a self-service."

"Right. Any more for any more?" Martin asked, fishing in his pocket for cash.

Michael shook his head. Rufus lifted his and snuffled on the table.

"He wants another muesli bar," Mr Big said.

Martin went off to get the order from the anxious staff, who were standing behind the counters gaping at their unusual customers. The café manager was in his office, talking to the police, but having no luck. He didn't know that they turned a deaf ear to most complaints about bulky men with hooved companions. Especially when they were expecting the town to be overrun at any moment by anarchist hordes.

"Sit down, Richie. Say hello to Rufus."

"Morning, Rufie," Richie said as he joined them at the table. They were sitting as far away from the serving counters as possible, against the windows in the large semi-circular café. The only other customers were two middle-aged couples and a young family. The young parents were trying to stop their children pointing at the funny donkey men. Like the student on the gate, the parents were picking up definite trouble signals from the animal and its friends.

The three men and a donkey sat in silence for a minute. Uncharacteristically, it was Mr Big who spoke up.

"All these fucking cops everywhere. Scaring kids away from the clubs. I'm losing a fortune."

Richie nodded in sympathy. Oh dear, he thought, drug sales plummeting.

Martin returned with two mugs of tea and a muesli bar. He put them on the table, and Mr Big pushed the muesli bar towards Richie, who opened the packet and fed Rufus. The animal wolfed the bar down in one gulp.

"Told you, he likes you," Mr Big said. "He nearly had Michael's hand off."

"Nice to know you care, Rufus," Richie said. The donkey dribbled in reply.

"Right, I wanted us to get together here because it's not safe to talk at the house any more," Mr Big said.

"Police trouble?" Martin asked.

"Don't be a dick," Mr Big grunted. "It's these pirates. They're getting on my fucking tits. You know what they did? They beamed a fucking Chinese takeaway on to my sitting-room table. Four fucking portions of chicken chow mein popped up while I was having my doormen's roundup last night."

"Might have been a goodwill gesture," Richie suggested.

"Yeah, right. Piss-take more like. There was a little note inside saying 'this is all you're getting'."

"Cheeky," Martin said.

"It's fucking piracy!" Mr Big wailed. "We never said they could start making these laser wotsits without us. Especially not without paying."

Richie found it hard to sympathize when it was stolen goods that had been stolen. All part of the game, wasn't it?

"So what do you want with us, then?" he asked. Some big unarmed combat showdown on the pier, probably, he thought. Ninjas against the bouncers. Bollocks to that.

"There's only one way to make money out of the situation now, boys." Mr Big leaned closer to Martin and Richie and lowered his voice. "We're going wholesale. I want you two to take the machine to Amsterdam and start beaming."

"Beaming what exactly?" Richie asked.

"Fucking tulips, of course. What do you think?" Mr Big stared at Richie for a moment. "All you two have to do is check the gear for purity. Then you beam it over and forget all about it. You don't need to know where the merchandise is going, do you, son?"

"I told you, Mr Biggs, no drugs," Richie said.

"You'd only be along for the ride. Martin here'll be doing the checking."

"What does he know about checking drugs for purity?"

Mr Big ignored the question. "You'd pay off your debt in a few weeks."

"This sounds like the kind of business that involves guns. Not interested. I've got kids, you know," Richie said.

Mr Big drew in a long, exasperated breath. "What you got against drugs, Richie?"

"Nothing. Like I haven't got anything against piranhas. I just don't fancy sharing my bath with them in case I get my balls chewed off."

"You're talking shite, son. Getting out of your tree is a perfectly natural thing to do. In fact it's the first thing men did as soon as they climbed down out of the trees. That's probably why they call it getting out of your tree. Every country's got their own ways of getting pissed and stoned. Cocaine and heroin are just more foreign than whisky and wine, that's why people are prejudiced against them."

"Yeah, judges are especially prejudiced against them, so they can land you a bloody long stretch in prison. And get your assets confiscated."

"What fucking assets? All you've got is debts."

Richie didn't have time to answer, because there was a glassy clink, and a small bullet materialized on the plate that Martin had brought with the muesli bar. Instinctively, everyone at the table except Rufus ducked down and looked around to see where the bullet had come from. There was no one in sight outside the café. No one inside the café looked in the least bit Chinese.

Very cautiously, they sat back upright again.

"You want me to go and have a look outside?" Martin asked.

"No point," Mr Big said. "I intend to take the hint. I'll tell them I won't be expecting any payment for those plans."

Mr Big picked the bullet up and rolled it between his fingers. "Half the world's police loafing about a hundred yards away and they still can't fucking stop this lot."

Richie looked at the inch-long cartridge and knew what he had to do. He stood up.

"I'm off," he said. "Coming, Martin?"

"Can't afford to, bro," Martin replied.

"Neither can you," Mr Big said as Richie walked away. "I want paying. Now. You owe me eight grand." His voice grew louder as Richie got nearer the door. Richie was conscious that people were staring at him. He walked out of the café and took a double lungful of sea air. It tasted somehow of freedom.

Whoever had used the laser locator to beam in the bullet was long gone, of course. He walked slowly back along the pier, looking down through the planks of the walkway at the slopping green waves below, and running his fingertips over the warm key in his pocket. Tonight he would have to use it.

66. Last Night on the Prom

It was almost seven in the evening, and Richie was sitting by the phone in the room-service office. He was engrossed in an old wrestling mag that he'd dug out of a box in the wardrobe, from under 30 or so pairs of Clara's "I'm sure I'll wear these again one day" shoes.

The magazine was an Ace Bandit special, with the evil monster himself on the cover, baring his teeth at the camera as he gouged the eyes of a suffering opponent. When he was a kid, Richie had been convinced that this was a real action shot taken in the heat of combat. But now he found it hard to believe that he'd been taken in. The referee was behind Bandit, his eyebrows raised in an expression of complete ignorance about the foul Bandit was committing. The bikini'd assistants were hovering in the background like two she-devils at a martyrdom. If the photo wasn't posed, the girls had chosen exactly the same hundredth of a second to pout and thrust their boobs at the photographer. Even now, Richie could feel the gut-deep urge to *be* Ace Bandit, up there in that world of sweat and noise and sex. For some reason he still couldn't bring himself to hate the stupid old bastard. Our teenage heroes never die, he thought.

Clara came down the stairs into the muggy kitchen.

"You can knock off now, can't you?" she asked.

"Got to wait for the Generalissimo. I'm playing secretary for him. I take the orders on the phone, he goes and gets the tips."

"Let someone else take over."

"If the reservations manager gives me her permission," Richie said. He put the magazine on a shelf. "You want to play call centres, Bob?" he asked the washer-up. "Take any room-service calls and give them to Filipe? He'll be down in a minute. Tell him I'll be back at eleven."

"Sure," the washer-up said, wiping his bleached and wrinkled hands. Richie and Clara were out in the fresh air twenty seconds later.

"What's the hurry?" Richie asked. "You've left your mum with the littl'uns, haven't you?"

"Yeah," said Clara. "I've asked her to do a full evening shift."

They didn't talk again until they'd gone through the Zone checkpoint. Walking those hundred yards, even with your pass dangling prominently from your neck, was an unnerving experience. There was no one in the street except riot police, no vehicles except marked squad cars and official-looking vans. You knew that eyes, both human and electronic, were on you as you walked. As were cameras and microphones, no doubt. Not conducive to lively conversation.

They badged their way through two sets of gates, guarded by two sets of machine-gun-toting police and then, at the final checkpoint, one local bobby.

"Night, folks," he said cheerfully, as if he was waving them out of a village fete carpark.

They walked out into unoccupied territory. As soon as she felt at ease again, Clara took Richie's arm.

"You want to take the condemned man for his last supper, is that it?" Richie asked.

"Richie." She took her arm away, then slid it back and gripped tighter. They strolled on towards the pink sun as it got ready to take its evening dip in Poole Harbour.

They sat in a pub and talked.

"I just had a visit from the neighbour's sister," Clara said.

"Invasion of the Tribbles? God help us."

"She wanted to know how he was coping."

"Coping? What, with being a moron?"

No, Clara explained, he wasn't a moron, or a Tribble. His name was Johnny and he was suffering from Asperger's Syndrome, a mild form of autism that makes sufferers unable to pick up social signals of any kind. Facial expressions are alien to them, the sister said. If someone yells at them, they just think that the person is speaking loudly, and take the words at face value. Once, Johnny had been told by an unsympathetic employer to "get out of my sight". He'd hidden under the table.

"So when I give him my most meaningful glare because he's taking up too much parking space, it's totally meaningless," Clara said.

"He smiles, though," Richie said.

"Yeah, he went to some school where they teach them how to interact with people. How to smile, what muscles to use and when to do it. And she says if we're scared of his dog, we should just tell him straight, 'Please keep it chained up. I don't want it to jump over the fence and attack my children'."

"What if we said 'please sell your dog and buy a goldfish'?"

"No, he loves his dog. Mind you, he loves you almost as much. Thinks you're some kind of chief Trekkie because you've written a book on the subject."

"He told me he didn't like the book," Ricky said. "He came round at one o'clock in the bloody morning to let me know all the chapters were back to front. He'd put them back in the right order, the bastard."

"Well, he's a fan, anyway. Do anything for you apart from pull his dog's teeth out."

"Reckon he'd lend us ten thousand quid?"

The talk naturally turned to Martin. Clara had a lengthy dig at him, but a rational one. She'd been thinking hard about The Martin Problem.

"I don't hate him," she said. "I just hate what he does to us. He's so destructive. Sometimes I feel as if you put your brother above me and the kids."

"No," Richie reassured her. "If it came to the crunch, of course I'd choose you. He's my rival for head of the flock. You and me are the bloodline."

"Talk about excessive testosterone. You've been drinking the stuff."

Richie was relieved that she was able to joke again, because the previous night had been a toughie.

Clara was already asleep when he went to bed, or so he thought. After a minute or so lying in the darkness, he realized she was silently crying.

What do I do, he thought. Pretend I didn't notice? No, he decided, this was one of those women's traps. "So what if I was being silent, you should have heard," she'd say. So he rolled over and snuggled up. She didn't acknowledge his presence, but at least she didn't backheel him in the shins.

He knew all too well what she was crying about, and he felt totally helpless. With kids, there's usually a simple solution – you'll see your friends tomorrow, we'll buy another one, of course Daddy doesn't love your brother more than you. But in this case, things weren't so simple. You couldn't spirit the trouble away with one short sentence. You couldn't beam it away.

They chose a seafood restaurant and splashed out on sea bass and white burgundy, followed by two espressos for Richie.

"Got to keep my energy levels up," he said.

"You have indeed," she said.

They walked down along the prom. It was dark now, and the police were milling around the seafront in their gladiator outfits, as if expecting an invasion of giant lobsters.

Clara and Richie headed away from the pier and the densest concentration of uniforms. They could see the ornamental lamp-posts – coloured lightbulb outlines of butterflies, birds, boats, fish – curving away along the prom for literally miles in both directions. The wind was ruffling the tops of small, Guinness-coloured waves. They went down a set of sand-encrusted steps on to the beach, which was empty except for a dogwalker and a couple of deckchairs that the stackers had missed. The moist sand felt good under the soles of their shoes. Hard, but yielding. Restful.

"Come on," Clara said after they'd walked a hundred yards or so, and pulled Richie away from the sea.

"Come on where?"

She tugged him up on to the prom. "The beach huts, of course." She smiled.

He could feel the hard-on growing as they slipped behind the nearest row of beach huts into the two-feet of privacy that has long been one of Bournemouth's twilight groping zones. She undid his trousers, and he felt the cool evening breeze exploring his buttocks. Clara pulled her knickers off and stuffed them in his pocket.

"You may want to sniff them for comfort in the cells," she said.

Afterwards, they emerged giggling, just as a teenaged couple passed by. The two youngsters looked at each other and grinned.

"I can recommend this one," Richie told them. "Air-conditioned."

"No," the boy replied. "People can see you from up top."

Clara shrieked and swivelled to look up at the clifftop. Two twenty-something men were leaning over the wooden railing a hundred feet above. One of them pointed to his watch and gave a thumbs-up. Clara shrieked again. Richie pulled her knickers out of his pocket and waved a farewell as he and his wife continued their sedate evening stroll along the prom.

Half an hour later, they went their separate ways. Clara home, Richie back to the hotel. He could see that Clara wanted a fond farewell, but he broke off their goodbye kiss before tongues got involved. After all, if everything went well, he'd be home in the morning.

As usual, he entered by the rear entrance of the hotel, which had been fitted with a badge reader at the request of the security people. There was an American guard outside the door armed with a gun and a dangerous-looking moustache which was bristly enough to poke your eye out if you tried to get past him uninvited.

Richie gave his name, swiped his badge and went in.

The dark passageway was lined with cooking-oil cans and trays of tinned tomatoes. By now the kitchen should be empty except for the night chefs and a room-service waiter or two, possibly including Filipe.

Richie stopped and listened for voices. He didn't really care about being seen by anyone except Filipe. The others wouldn't ask questions about what he was going to do.

From behind the double fire doors, all he could hear was a radio. He pushed on a door. There were only two chefs in the kitchen. He nodded hello and went into the small room-service office. Here, he performed a speeded-up version of his settling-in ritual – he poured himself a mug of coffee (extra-strong this time, with a dash of whisky from Filipe's "secret" bottle, to keep his senses buzzing and his upper lip stiff). He opened the local newspaper and lay it across the table.

Then, departing slightly from his normal routine, he took a new bottle of the PM's favourite mineral water (one that "significantly reduced water retention" ie made her piss a lot) from a fridge and put the bottle on the least dented tray he could find. Next, after taking a gulp of the scalding coffee, he did a brief equipment check. One pass key – check. One teleportation beam locator (non-laser) – check.

He donned his least terrorist-like expression and left the kitchen.

At the top of the kitchen stairs, he stopped and listened. He could hear voices coming from the bar. Loud voices. Of course, the rooms that weren't taken up by politicians and their cronies were full of journalists. A raucous mix.

Richie slid out of the staircase, round the corner (the receptionist was sitting down at her computer and looking the other way), and pressed the button for the service lift. It wasn't there. It was up on another floor. He heard the lift react, but knew it would be several seconds until it arrived. He stood facing the lift door, waiting for the moment when Filipe would tap him on the shoulder.

Why, Filipe would ask, was Richie taking a bottle of mineral water up to the PM's room? That was Filipe's job.

Ah, Richie would tell him, she didn't actually order it. But, he would quickly add, trying to talk Filipe out of that "are you crazy?" frown, a Prime Minister needs her mineral water, especially if she suffers from water retention.

I don't even think she's here this evening, Filipe would reply, so how are you going to get into her room?

Ah ...

The lift doors finally opened. Richie pressed four, keeping his back to the lobby, and the lift began to move upwards.

When he got to the fourth floor, he was about to peep out when he realized that only an intruder would do that. The security man would jump on him straight away.

He marched out of the lift and turned to face the guard sitting on a straight-backed chair to the right of the doors.

"Hi," Richie said.

"Uh, wotcha," the guard said, and checked Richie's badge. He motioned Richie on with a lazy nod. This was not a secure VIP floor, so the guard didn't ask any questions.

Forcing himself to walk with a room-service waiter's calm haste, Richie headed along the corridor towards the mini-staircase that would take him down to the three-and-a-halfth floor without going past the guard at the lift door.

He was just one corner away from the PM's door when he stopped by a large storage cupboard and used his pass key to unlock it.

This was a sort of annex to the chambermaid's pantry, used for stocking cleaning products and fill-ups for the tea-making trays. Inside, he turned the light on and breathed deeply, psyching himself up for crunch time. What if there was a security guy outside her room? Give the water to me, he'd say, I'll see she gets it. Shit. He needed something else. I've also brought her an extra – he looked around in the cupboard for inspiration – Toilet Duck? No, the little milk cartons. Perfect. He grabbed a handful. Much too fiddly for the security guy to deal with. OK, it was a shitty cover, but it might work.

Well, no, it wouldn't work at all, but like a blunt knife in a jungle full of vampire bats, it was better than nothing.

Three more deep breaths and Richie was out of the storage cupboard and in front of her door. No security outside. Great. There was a chair beside the door. Security guy gone for a pee maybe? Or he and the rest of the security team were out with the PM herself, more like, and thought the floor was sealed off by the guys at the lift and the main staircase.

Richie didn't care – he was inside the room within seconds and insulting himself.

What a dickhead. What if someone had been inside? He hadn't even bothered to listen at the door.

But the room was dark and empty, and he had to get on with the job.

He was in a sitting room. Of course, it was a suite.

The curtains were open, and the street lights and passing cars were throwing shadows on the ceiling. Keeping away from the window, he edged his way through the sitting room to the bedroom door.

The curtains here were drawn, and it was dark. Fuck, didn't even bring a torch. What a shite criminal, he thought. Do you get a shorter prison sentence if you're shite?

With the sitting-room door open, he could see just enough to move around.

There in front of him was the prime ministerial bed, the source of all Richie's hopes. It was looking very prim and proper, with its tight folded-down sheet offering no room for sexual gymnastics.

He put down his bottle of water on the bedside table, next to the opened bottle that was already there, and crossed the bedroom towards the faint light coming out of the bathroom.

The bathroom faced the back of the hotel, so the street lights were further away, but there were no curtains and he could see enough to operate through the frosted window.

He put his trayload of milk cartons on the floor – damn, he thought, mustn't forget to put those with the tea-making facilities on the way out.

There was a toilet bag near the washbasin. He rummaged inside it, but it was hopeless. A mass of bottles, tubes, combs and stuff. Shit. He crouched down and lifted the contents gently out, item by item, on to the white tiled floor. Bugger. Balls. Bum. He swore every time he hit a blank.

There were pills, but nothing that looked like the pill. It'd be fun, he thought, to take some of these tablets away to get them analysed. How else do politicians keep up with their 20-hour days? No condoms in there, either. Bollocks. Arse. Cock. Loads of make-up. No diaphragm or Femidoms or anything. Fuck. No luck.

He replaced everything as carefully as he could, then opened the bathroom cabinet. Empty of everything except the hotel freebies. Soaps, shower caps and the like. Hey, maybe she used the shower cap as contraception. It'd work. One look at a woman in a shower cap was enough to give any man the floppies.

Shit, he thought. Nothing I can do. Better get out of here.

Then two things occurred to him. One, bedside table drawer. She might keep her contraceptives in there. And two, fingerprints. He hadn't worn gloves or anything. If someone got curious, they'd find his prints all over everything in her toilet bag. He'd have to get all her stuff out and wipe every item. Christ. What idiot had thought up this plan?

He froze.

Voices.

A key.

More voices, closer but hushed.

Holy shit, they were in the bedroom.

A man and a woman. Probably the PM with her bodyguard. What was the next thing the guard would do? Check the bathroom for intruders.

Oh well, Richie thought, if he was going to shit himself, he was in the right place.

There was a little squeal, then a murmur. A long mmmm. Like you make when you're snogging. So it wasn't the bodyguard, it was the hubby. He'd arrived early, and he swung both ways.

But now Richie was going to screw up their reunion shag. Hubby was bound to come in for a preliminary pee. No way would she feel like it after an intruder had been found in her bathroom. Talk about shooting yourself in the foot.

What could he do? Emerge innocently from the bathroom with his tray and say "room service – I thought you might like some extra milk cartons in the bathroom. Very good for your complexion"? No, perhaps not.

Climb out the window? He tiptoed over and looked out. There was a wide ledge just below the window frame. If there was a balcony further round, maybe ...

He stopped and listened. Funny, he thought, the PM's hubby isn't supposed to be American.

"It's OK," he heard her say.

"Are you sure?" the American voice said.

Richie was intrigued. He recognized the voice from somewhere. Could the Prime Minister and the President be cementing the transatlantic alliance? Was this what was meant by the special relationship?

Curiosity finally won out, and Richie tiptoed back towards the closed bathroom door to listen in.

"Come on," the PM said, sounding a lot like Clara a short time before. The sea air certainly gave the gals an appetite.

"But what about your husband?" the man said.

She laughed. "Didn't you know? My husband's as gay as a drag queens' ballet troupe. You look a lot like him, actually."

"I look gay?"

"No, you look like his heterosexual big brother."

"So I get to play his clone? A clone dildo?" the man asked, though he didn't sound too unhappy about it.

"Yes, just be an unprotected dildo, please," Richie begged silently.

There was some unzipping and a bit more slurping, then the PM spoke again.

"Mmm. You see, it's a power thing. All men get turned on by the idea of fucking a powerful woman. Except my husband, that is. I have to blackmail him."

She laughed, and Richie had had enough.

There was something gruesome about hearing your Prime Minister getting horny. Though he had to be thankful that it wasn't Maggie Thatcher on the other side of that door. Just imagine *her* at it.

No. He had to get out of there. Better to plummet to his death from a hotel window than keep that image in his head.

He opened the bathroom window and received a cool blast of night air. Not exactly the right weather for shirtsleeve mountaineering, but he had no choice.

He looked down into the staff car park, which was empty by order of the security people. The back entrance was on the opposite corner of the building. Richie could just make out the guard's silhouette. If he didn't make too much noise (ie by splatting on to the tarmac below), he should be OK.

He climbed up on to the toilet seat, then manoeuvred himself outside. It was a difficult manoeuvre – the window hadn't been designed for the well-built intruder, particularly one who had his trouser pockets full of milk cartons and a tray stuffed down his shirtfront. He eased himself gradually down until his feet touched the ledge.

Now for the big moment. He let the ledge take his weight. It felt solid enough. But what would happen when he let go of the window frame? Would he plummet forty feet backwards? Wasn't it wiser to give up trying to play James Bond, go back in, apologize and be sure of surviving, albeit in a prison cell?

Yes, he decided. That was wiser. But this was no time for wisdom – they might be winning a million pounds for him at that very moment.

He let go and gripped the brickwork as best he could with his finger tips. The ledge held. It seemed OK, even if it was only about two feet wide and a sickeningly long way from the all-too-solid-looking ground. He felt the heat of his breath against the wall. He was practically kissing the bricks. Shit, he thought, why didn't I hide in the bathroom until they fell asleep? Or wait until the guy orgasmed, then run for the door? There's no way he'd have come galloping down the corridor with his receding boner. They must have given the security guy the night off, surely. Yeah, I should have made a run for it, with a towel over my head. They'd be looking for a Palestinian, not me.

But he was forgetting the danger of the preliminary pee. The guy might go into the bathroom and wonder why the window was open. Better get a move on. He began to slide his feet sidewards.

After one minute and several thousand heartbeats, his fingers reached a corner, and curled around the brickwork. He edged nearer and felt a drainpipe. Yes. The gods were smiling on him. As long as it wasn't the smile of someone watching a man walk towards a banana skin. In this case, the banana skin could be an FBI marksman, taking aim with his infra-red night sight and radioing for permission to put a hole in the intruder. Shit, he thought, should have put the tray down the back of my shirt. Here he was, in the centre of probably the most heavily-policed square mile on the planet, acting just like a terrorist assassin. It would be a serious security screw-up if he *didn't* get shot. He could almost see the teardrops of sweat oozing from his fingers.

He inched sideways and gripped the drainpipe as if his life depended on it, which, it occurred to him, it did.

He was above the hotel garden and could hear loud voices. He looked gingerly down. The patio doors from the bar were open. Because of the chilly night breeze, there were no drinkers in the garden, and there didn't seem to be any guards roaming around, either. No time to worry about being seen now, though. He had to get down into the garden. At least down there, if he was shot, he could fall over without bursting his skull open on impact with the ground.

He gave the drainpipe a few tugs to make sure it was strong enough, and started to edge down. He scuffed his shoes and scraped the skin off his knuckles, and then almost died of a heart attack when he lost control and began to skid groundwards. His hands and toecaps squealed sickeningly against the metal of the drainpipe, but he couldn't brake. One hand slipped free, and he knew he was going to fall. Then his feet slammed onto the second-floor ledge and the squealing noise stopped and he gripped the drainpipe harder than he'd ever gripped anything in his life.

He took a few seconds to calm his breathing and count his fingers (all present, surprisingly), and then risked a quick glance down to where he'd almost done his backward somersault.

No one had come out from the bar to see who was trying to play tunes on the drainpipe.

Just below him he saw a cluster of downward-pointing metal prongs designed to stop people climbing up the drainpipe. He used them as a step, then eased his body past the points, which prodded up under the tray into his stomach like accusing fingers. Or threatening gun barrels. Fortunately, they had been painted so often that they were rounded. If the FBI had had them sharpened, he would probably have decorated the drainpipe with his entrails.

He shook himself free of the prongs, losing only a shirt button in the process, and climbed down to the first-floor ledge. If a guard was going to spot him, it was now or never. He was about ten feet diagonally above the bar doors. Smoke and conversation were billowing out. He slid nimbly down the last length of drainpipe and ended up crouching on the lawn.

"Damn."

He'd forgotten the milk cartons in his pocket. A cool white wetness started to dribble into his crotch. With a bit of luck, he thought, something similar but warmer was just happening to the Prime Minister.

Normally he would have felt self-conscious about walking through a bar looking as if he had wet himself, but tonight he didn't care. If what Clara said about pre-conference parties was true, there would be quite a few pairs of trousers getting peed or ejaculated in before the night's drinking was over.

One of the best non-scientific authors who has crept into the Top Twenty Club is Ian Fleming. Not for Q's gadgets – the literary Bond (as opposed to the film Bond) relies more on guts than gadgets.

Fleming is in here because he more or less invented product placement. As we all know, in movies these days, everything a hero eats, drinks, wears and drives is sponsored. The producers of the Bond movies were at it right from the start – the best known example being that Sean Connery would never have driven an Aston Martin if Jaguar hadn't been too stupid to give Bond an E-type.

But Fleming had turned 007 into a brand addict long before Bond made it onto the screen. In the early novels we knew his favourite champagne (Taittinger), car (an old 1930s Bentley), gin, golf balls, cigarettes, even his shampoo (Pinaud).

Mind you, secret agent 007, licensed to kill, the free world's last line of defence against a psycho with a dozen nuclear missiles and a persecution complex, worried about getting the right shampoo?

Maybe it's best the studios didn't use all of Fleming's ideas.

A Brief History of the Future, chapter 13 (extract)

67. Get off the Bus, Forget about Us

By the end of his shift, Richie's nerves were frazzled.

He had been able to take a little time out to dry his trousers under the toilet hand-drier and sew on a new shirt button. He'd made cryptic calls to Clara and Martin. But half an hour after climbing out of the window of the room where the country's leader was indulging in adulterous (and possibly treasonable) sex, he was back saying "here's one pint of lager, Sir," to a bored man in baggy grey underwear who gave him a one-pound tip for being brave enough to come up from the kitchen in the lift.

There had been a close call when the PM rang down, but fortunately it was just to order a bottle of champagne.

"Hmm, the conference must be going well," Filipe said.

"I think they call it congress, not conference," Richie said.

As the hours passed and the light through the windows got stronger, Richie thought that the likelihood of a security man bursting into the room-service office and flattening him against the wall was getting smaller.

But it was one hell of a relief to get out of the hotel and into the dawn air. The breeze was tangy. The waves were crashing in as if they'd had a good night's rest to get back their energy. Richie headed out of The Zone and down the hill towards the town centre bus stops, which had been displaced 200 yards inland, presumably, Richie thought, to stop anti-globalization demonstrators from getting a ride right up to the barricades. Make the buggers walk.

He only saw one other civilian, a posh-looking dog-walker who had turned her back to a Cocker Spaniel so she couldn't see that it was crapping on the pavement. There were a pair of armed cops standing on the street corner watching her. Why don't they shoot the mutt, Richie wondered, that turd might be booby-trapped.

Richie hauled himself up the stairs to the top deck of the bus and slumped down on to one of the front seats.

He was in a half-slumber, his head leaning against the cool window, when the American closed in.

"Hi."

Richie opened his eyes and saw someone smiling at him across the aisle. Someone much more awake than he was. It was a face he knew. He studied it blearily, trying to remember where from. Then he remembered.

"Hi," he said. "You find one?"

"Find one?" The American looked confused for a moment. "Oh. Yeah. Yeah, I found one."

"Really? Here?" Richie studied the man again. There was something not quite right. He recognized the voice and the face, but separately. It looked like the guy who came into the shop asking for a teleporter, the one Richie told to try Army Surplus. But Richie knew his voice from somewhere else.

The bus began to roll forward from its terminus, and the engine grunted as it swung the bus up the hill passed the rows of closed shops.

"You're Richard, aren't you?" the American said.

"Richie, yeah."

The American held his hand out. Richie shook it.

"I'm Max."

Max? Max the dildo? Richie was suddenly wide awake. Shit, they'd come to get him. They'd just waited till he was out of range of the hotel to create less of a scandal. "You're the one who was –" he searched for a polite verb and didn't find one – "with the Prime Minister last night."

Max seemed taken aback. "How do you know that?" he asked.

Richie didn't understand. Wasn't that why Max was here? The bus swung violently left and right through the back streets, avoiding the pedestrian precinct as it headed for the main road. Max let himself be jogged sideways and continued to stare at Richie.

"I'm a room-service waiter. We know everything," Richie said.

"Ah, the champagne?" Max said. He thought back to when it had been delivered. He hadn't seen the waiter who brought it. Had the guy looked through the crack in the door? Had Ann called his name before coming back into the bedroom?

"Right," Richie said. The bus was powering up the hill past Martin's shop, which was locked and shuttered in his absence. Richie prayed towards the "Martin's ames" sign for some help with his bullshitting. "We room-service waiters know everything, but tell nothing," he said.

Max laughed and relaxed. "I know some stuff about you, too. It seems that our destinies are linked."

"They are?"

"Yeah." Max tutted to himself. "I should have mentioned. I'm Mark Johnson's boss."

"Ah." Richie looked over his shoulder to see whether this was the cue for the FBI or CIA or Klingon guys to jump on him. All he saw was a teenage girl in a pale-blue nylon overall, her ears bunged with a pair of Walkman headphones. Presumably a cleaner on her way home.

"You're Martin's brother, aren't you?"

"Martin?"

Blender smiled. "It's OK, I knew about Martin before Johnson started giving him all my secrets. Your teleporter was used from his address."

"Ah. Yeah. He's left the country."

"Yeah, so has Mark." Max laughed. He seemed to be taking the whole industrial sabotage thing very lightly, considering.

"I didn't, we didn't know ..." Richie began, and stopped when Max laid a hand on his arm.

"Don't worry about it," he said, then grimaced as the bus accelerated around a roundabout to get in front of a car coming in from the right. "Christ, all these fucking roundabouts. Doesn't it screw up your suspension? I've never turned the steering wheel as much in my life. And I spent my honeymoon on a motor tour of the fucking Sierra Nevada."

Richie looked at him, this American spy or cop or whatever, this shagger of world leaders, capable of getting mad at a Bournemouth bus, and they both laughed together.

"They're really incredible machines," Richie said. "The teleporters, I mean, not these buses."

"Thanks. I wasn't particularly bothered about Johnson giving you that stuff, you know. I wanted to see what you'd do with the teleporter."

"Not much, I'm afraid," Richie said, modestly ignoring the teleportation of mints, cocaine, watches, condoms, fake contraceptive pills, a veggieburger and one unhappy rodent.

"No, I meant you as a people, the Brits. I wanted to see where you'd take teleportation. And it only took you a matter of days to start using the locator, teleport new drug compounds, and distribute the plans to our new laser device all over the world. Spectacular." Max's eyes looked almost warm for once.

"You really don't care?" Richie couldn't get his head round this.

Max's hand gripped his arm again, but only for protection, as the bus bounced down a hill into a hollow where some flower-bedded gardens led towards the rhododendron thickets and the beach. Hell, Max thought, the idea of meeting on buses sounds great in theory, but those IRA guys must have had damn solid butts. Or Irish buses must give a much smoother ride than anywhere else in the world.

"Normally it goes slower," Richie said. "But the roads are much quieter with the town centre barricaded off."

Max nodded in acknowledgement of Richie's apology on behalf of his country's transportation technology. "I've read your book. Or the last chapter of it, anyway," Max said.

"My book? How?"

"Copied it off the PC in your brother's shop."

"Ah."

"And I see why you're so frustrated. We have been pretty secretive these past few years. We had to get a good head start. But now I've decided to give the technology its head. I want to know how it survives in the wild. You see what I mean?"

"No," Richie said. "You mean you're giving away your secrets?"

"Not all of them."

"What about the machines capable of teleporting humans?"

Blender looked surprised. "Humans? Johnson tell you that?"

"Yeah."

"Well, it breaks my heart to admit it, but it's not true. We haven't even tried human teleportation yet. Shit." He gave Richie a friendly punch on the arm. "You're making me talk too much."

"Sorry."

"No, it's not your fault. It's mine." Max looked at him paternally. "See, I get the feeling from your book that you really care."

"Yeah, I suppose I do," Richie said. "Watch out, left turn."

The two men leaned left like a pair of bob-sleighers as the bus skirted behind a shopping precinct and shuddered to a halt outside a multi-storey car park to pick up passengers.

A couple more people came up on to the top deck. None of them looked like US secret-service agents. There was a twenty-something guy in a sports anorak and baseball cap, a walking ad for just doing it. He went and sat at the back, his legs splayed to give the whole aisle a view of his crotch. One of the first to enjoy it was a middle-aged man in a plaster-flecked sweatshirt, who pulled a rolled-up newspaper out of his shoulder bag and started to read the sports pages. He was about five rows behind Max and Richie, out of earshot.

The bus pulled away, and took a right and a left on to the main road again.

Max lowered his voice. "I know you have to get off in a minute. I just wanted to tell you before I leave England that everything is cool."

"Everything's cool?"

"Yeah. It's all in hand. The Johnson stuff. The plans, the stolen locator and all. You and your brother can forget about it."

Richie thought about things for a couple of hundred yards. He must have been under surveillance ever since he filled out that form in New York. The Americans had been into Martin's shop, they'd tracked the teleporter. They'd even let Martin carry on dealing drugs just to see how the machines would perform. It must be one hell of a top-priority project, and he was sitting with the guy who seemed to be running the show. It was the equivalent of having a chat with Bill Gates or Captain Kirk.

"I've been reading up about all the other technology, too," Richie said. "The gas syringes, phaser-type guns and stuff. It's like that film, Galaxy Quest, you know? When the aliens have made all of Star Trek's technology come true?"

Blender laughed as if remembering a joke. "Galaxy Quest. Yes, camouflage."

"Camouflage?"

"Yeah. Double bluff. You make an absurd sci-fi comedy on the subject. Who's going to believe someone's really doing it?"

"You mean that your people made ...?"

"Not 'my people' exactly. But friends of mine, yes." Blender held up a hand. He was saying no more.

"Can't I just ask you a few more questions for my book?" Richie asked. "I don't absolutely have to get off yet."

"No, sorry. I really can't tell you anything else. It'd look as if you had inside info, and that doesn't suit my purposes."

"Shit." Richie was going to miss out on an unrepeatable chance to make his book publishable. "Well, can I just ask you one thing about the Prime Minister?"

Max looked faintly amused, as if Richie was flattering his ego. "You can *ask*," he said.

Richie leaned in close across the aisle. "OK. Don't take this the wrong way. But did you use a condom?"

Max laughed. "What kind of a question is *that*?"

"I mean, is she trying to get pregnant?"

Max whistled. "This is your stop, isn't it?" he said as they crossed the railway bridge.

Richie gave a "doesn't matter" wave of the hand. "Is she? I really need to know."

Max stared at him for a few seconds before answering. "OK, maybe I shouldn't tell you this, but I owe you a favour," he said. "If you let on to the media or anyone, I'll have you arrested for espionage and drug dealing, OK?"

"Fine." Richie accepted gladly.

Max grinned and looked around conspiratorially. "Let's just say I'm going to be doing my damnedest, at every available opportunity before I go home, to help you win your bet."

"My ...?" Richie was dumbfounded. "You knew?"

Max was pleased with the effect he'd achieved. "Richard, next time you think to yourself, Max can't possibly know this, think, yes, he probably does. You can tell that to your brother as well."

"Bloody hell," Richie said. Like the President before him, he could feel the tentacles of technology reaching through walls to enfold him. Was there nowhere you could hide these days? Christ, he probably even had a video of Richie and Clara doing it behind the beach huts.

Then it hit him.

Up until now, the only person helping him to win the bet was Martin, with all the treachery, inefficiency and downright stupidity that that implied. Now he had an altogether different team-mate, someone who really made things happen. If this guy's sperm was up to it – and he looked a very healthy 45 years old – and the PM's ova were as feisty as the rest of her, then the bet was as good as won. He closed his eyes and clenched his fists for a silent grin.

"When're you going home?" he asked.

"In a few days."

"Right." Richie hoped it was ovulation time. "Well, good luck, for all of our sakes."

"Yeah," Max agreed. "It's in her interests too. She thinks a baby will help her chances of re-election."

Richie thought about this and nodded. "Probably right. People think she's a bit un-natural. She needs a baby to give her the human touch."

"Yeah, she is a little hypernatural. But that's what's so good. She and I are going to make such a good ... such a promising ..." Max searched for the right word.

"Partnership?" Richie suggested.

"Gene mix."

Richie didn't recognize the distant look on Max's face. But then it was the first time he'd seen a man picturing a line of his own descendants stretching across time and space towards 23rd-century Iowa.

68. Yes We Have No

The politicians didn't know whether to feel insulted or relieved.

Against all expectations, and after millions of pounds (and dollars) had been spent on precautions, the massive anti-globalization demonstration hadn't happened.

The agitators had stayed at home, and the evening news reports had been totally devoid of any footage of police getting bottled or stoned (in the lapidation sense, of course) or impaled on railings by young people, or of young people getting clubbed, shot or impaled on railings by the police.

This should have been good news for the politicians (as it was for the police and young people who would have got bottled, stoned, clubbed, shot or impaled on railings), but it wasn't.

Because to make up for their lack of riot footage, the TV networks had commissioned their jokiest reporters to file ironic comment pieces on Boring Boringmouth. The journalists had all found the predictable old lady in her windblown deckchair and persuaded her to say "conference? what conference?". And they'd all poured their wittiest scorn on the political non-event of the decade, the conference that no one cared about, the speeches that were just public sessions of people talking to themselves while being translated into a dozen exotic languages.

"Bro, it's me."

"Hi, Martin, what's the weather like over there?"

"Scorching. Indian summer, man."

"But that's in autumn. This is May."

"No, I mean really Indian."

"Oh, right."

"She's hot, bro. I think it's love."

Richie laughed. "I know you. You'll get fed up with curry."

"No, mate. Indians eat nothing else for their whole lifetime, and now I understand why. There's like, so many variations, you know what I mean?"

"Hang on. Are we talking about food or sex here?"

"Both, man, both, that's the joy of it. Shag kebab, aloo shag, it's heaven."

Richie laughed again. He'd never heard Martin talk about a woman like this before. Not after the first week, anyway. She'd obviously got it right – the way to man's heart is through his stomach, via the thing that dangles below it.

"You are stoned, I hope, Martin?"

"Course I'm fucking stoned. This is A'dam."

"Good, because peace and love and eternal happiness isn't usually your thing."

"I'm a changed man, man. Another few weeks here and I'll have earned enough to pay off all my tax debts and lend you what you need."

Richie's expression darkened. "Just make what you need for yourself and get out of there, Martin. That's danger money you're earning."

He didn't tell Martin that he hoped he wouldn't be needing any loans. There would almost certainly be no Prime Ministerial period this month. Almost certainly.

"Don't fret," Martin said. "I'm going to come home with enough money to start up again. A new shop – security, alarms, privacy software, snooping stuff. All legal. You know there's this software that you can put on someone's computer that records every keystroke they make? Passwords, everything."

"Great. One of your first clients should be yourself."

"Uh?"

Richie began to explain about Blender breaking into the shop, but Martin interrupted him.

"Shit, I don't know what the fuck you're talking about, bro. Who the fuck's Blender?"

"Oh, never mind."

"Shit. This fucking dope."

"What is it? Ash burnt your trousers?"

"No," Martin said. "I keep forgetting why I called you. It's Mr Big. Watch out for him."

"Don't worry." Richie had had a couple of calls from the man, saying he wanted his money, threatening "retrieval action". Richie had just told him to be patient. Somehow he felt that Mr Big, or at the least the Ace Bandit part of him, wouldn't harm him. Richie seemed to have been adopted as an honorary donkey.

"He's been ranting about you on the phone," Martin said. "You've got no respect. People don't owe him money, they pay him money. Stuff like that."

"It's OK, I can handle it."

"Watch your back, that's all," Martin said.

"I don't think he fancies me."

"I'm not joking, bro. Hey, shit, yeah, that's another thing, watch the President on the TV tonight."

"That dickhead? I've already seen him in the flesh. I don't need to see him again."

"No, watch him, bro, watch him."

So that evening, after a dinner of fish and rice and tomato salad and chocolate ice cream and just a bit more chocolate ice cream please Mummy, the Fisher family sat in a row on their settee and watched the President. There was a calmness about them that there hadn't been since before their involvement with teleportation. Richie and Clara held hands. George and Ella held cuddly toys.

"Can't we have a cartoon, Daddy?" Ella asked.

"This is a cartoon, pumpkin. That's Daffy Duck in a suit."

The President had tried to liven proceedings up a bit by having an anchorman flown out from the States so that they could engage in a heated "debate" in front of a live audience (of rigorously frisked and vetted pro-globalizers).

The anchorman was a widely-respected and very famous TV personality. The kind of journalist who asks probing, provocative, career-threatening questions, but only if the autocue is working properly.

So the two of them went up on the stage of Bournemouth's conference centre in front of millions to get as mean as only two men who've played golf together once a month for 20 years can get.

First, given that there was supposed to be an eco-summit on, they spent a few minutes discussing the future of the planet.

The anchorman pushed the President hard – isn't it a tough reality to be faced with that you can't halt the great onward march of progress, he asked, and don't the developed industrial nations, after all, feed more people than they pollute?

"Yes," the President agreed, and the anchorman nodded in admiration at this insight as he waited for the next question to be reeled up and a fifteen-second ad to run on US TV.

As soon as they were off camera, the anchorman have the President a discreet thumbs-up. But the President wasn't happy. He didn't have many lines in this script. He knew the Brits thought that most Americans were basically retarded. He wasn't sure that short answers like "yes" would convince them otherwise. Why hadn't his people given him some longer words?

George wasn't happy with the script, either. "Snot a cartoon," he said.

"It's not very funny," Ella said.

"No, it's not, it's tragic," Clara agreed.

"Yes, but Uncle Martin told us we had to watch it," Richie said.

"Really?" Ella's eyes widened. Anything to do with Martin meant potential fun.

The two men turned to the teleportation question. The anchorman wondered whether the President regretted that what had started out as a humanitarian project – finding a means to beam aid into famine-afflicted areas – had been hijacked by criminal elements.

"Yes," the President replied. "Of course," he improvised.

After the anchorman had inquired exactly how much personal pain the President had felt when he realized that his research teams hadn't been able to follow through with their noble-spirited teleportation experiments using food parcels, Richie offered to go and fetch sickbags.

"Sshh, Daddy," Ella told him.

The anchorman asked a heartfelt question about the chaos caused by the pirates who had hijacked teleportation technology. The President opened his mouth to reply and stopped. The watching masses (or mass, anyway) didn't know it, but he had hit a problem. The autocue had gone off. Other world leaders might have frozen, or insisted they go to an ad break, but the President soldiered on. He kept his composure and began to improvise. He'd give the Brits a few long words to chew on.

"We will not bow our heads in the face of this epidemic of anarchialism that threatens to disgulf society as we know it," he said. "I, alongside with the Prime Minister of the United Kingdom of England and the other world leaders present here, have pledged to work together to stamp out this outwageous rave of techno-crime. We will illegalize certain types of teleporter and give the police unlimitless powers to cross borders and glob!"

The Fishers, like those fortunate few who hadn't given in to the almost overwhelming temptation to change channels, stared in silence. A banana had appeared in the President's mouth.

Then the President's head jerked left and right as what

looked like two small twigs materialized one after the other in each nostril.

The Fishers burst out in a family laugh.

There was one Fisher who wasn't laughing. He was whooping. Over in Amsterdam, Martin was sitting by a Beam-Me-Up machine, a packet of pretzel sticks in one hand, a phone in the other.

"Now shine it at the reporter guy. In his mouth. You got it?"

He hit the keyboard of his laptop and whooped again.

Next to him in bed, a dark naked girl was bouncing with laughter.

"Agh kak!" the anchorman spat, his first and last unscripted words of the night.

There was now a production assistant on the stage, pointing at the audience. The cameras swung to focus on the thousand invited guests, who were beginning to stampede towards the exits.

Later, when they analysed the films, the FBI would see a man wearing what looked like a pair of ultraviolet glasses. He was stashing some kind of pen or torch in his pocket and talking into a tiny microphone. His wig looked ridiculously false.

"That was a funny film, Daddy. Did Uncle Martin make it?" Ella asked.

"Yes, pumpkin, I think he did."

If George Orwell had only been remembered for the invention of terms like doublethink, I wouldn't have put him so high in my futurists list. What clinched Orwell's number three spot in the Top Twenty was the invention in Holland of the reality TV game show, Big Brother.

This wasn't like having a film version of a book made, this was proof that the world had turned Orwellian. The concept of the show, where people live like Winston Smith, knowing that their every move is filmed, was explicitly Orwellian, of course.

*But beyond that, the show had a very Orwellian irony about it —
how many people who watched the show and its offshoots all over the
world knew where the title came from? Without being snobbish about
it, most of them had probably never heard of Orwell. They were TV
proles.*

A Brief History of the Future, chapter 3 (extract)

69. The Late Great

Fortunately for the President and the anchorman, it was not
a busy time at Bournemouth's main hospital. Had it been a
Saturday night, they might have been forced to wait their turn
on a trolley while doctors dealt with injuries more serious
than a badly transplanted banana.

But the two Americans were whisked straight into surgery,
and a couple of hours later all their breathing passages were
clear. The President had only minor damage to his nostrils
and palate, largely thanks to the accuracy of Martin's friend's
aim and the ripeness of the banana.

As soon as he'd been swabbed and stitched up, the President
refused a sedative and summoned Max Blender from the A&E
waiting room, which had been full of an unusual mix of snoring
drunks, wailing children, twitching journalists and armed FBI
agents.

Unusually for him, Blender was slightly nervous as he walked
along the corridor to the President's ward. It's not every day that
you're indirectly blamed for an assassination attempt (if that's
what it was) on your head of state. Blender could, after all, be
accused of providing the weapon (the teleporter rather than
the banana, of course). His people were already tracing the
origin of the beam and the phone call to the man with the wig.

He'd need results fast. Now was not a good time to lose
government funding, if there ever was such a time.

People were constantly asking him how his team had got so far so fast. There was even a rumour going around that amongst Gene Roddenberry's papers, his family had found a set of blueprints for a real, working teleporter. If that was true, people asked, where had the plans come from? The future? Aliens? Blender scoffed at this suggestion. If such plans existed, he said, he'd never seen them. And he had no idea where they could have come from.

He did know where the rumour came from, though. He'd started it, to take attention away from the real secret of his success.

Because he'd got this far without any help from aliens. He'd done things the good old American way, using vast amounts of money to get the best people, the best equipment and the maximum amount of freedom for his project. That's how the US had built the first H-bomb, that's how they'd won the race to the Moon. Anyone who didn't realize it was plain stupid. And he'd raised extra funding by releasing the general-public teleporter on to the market.

Apart from his desire to "set the technology free", he needed the cash because his allies in the Pentagon were only willing to let him duplicate so many diamonds, and so many tons of gold, uranium, dilithium, titanium and other valuable elements. They didn't want world prices to drop. They'd even told him to stop duplicating terbium, which he hadn't been selling – he'd been manufacturing it for use in his own lasers.

The President represented a stream of federal dollars, and Blender had to keep the stream flowing.

He ran his not-guilty plea through his mind. It had been tough working out how much he wanted to tell the President. It had taken him quite a while to unravel the deceptions into explainable form, and he'd planned most of them himself.

Blender found his head of state in a small, guarded, one-bed private room decorated with a framed sea-view print and a damp patch. The President was sitting up in bed in a white surgical robe, with one nostril bunged full of cotton wool.

It was surely no coincidence, Blender thought, that interrogators do not usually choose such a costume. You don't intimidate a man into talking by threatening to lift up your surgical robe.

"How are you feeling, Sir?" Blender asked. He stood by the bed, his hands clasped in front of his slightly tender crotch. The PM was proving quite a handful, or pantful.

"Even worse than I look," the President said in a slightly lisping, muffled voice. "I'm wondering why the hell I shouldn't blame you."

"Me?"

"Yeah. You people were the ones who wanted the whole conference to be about teleportation." The President looked Blender in the eyes.

Blender looked back unflinchingly. He'd often been told that his eyes gave nothing away, that people felt as if they were looking into an iceberg – they didn't know how deep in they were seeing.

"No, Sir. We just wanted to latch our tests on the back of it. All of this is a terrible, unforeseen consequence of teleportation."

"I'm not just some pawn in your game to get your technology on top of the budget line?"

"No, Sir."

It was, Blender realized, very easy to lie to a President, if you were well-prepared enough and had enough backing. And especially if the man seemed to fall so short of his title. You couldn't "preside" from a hospital bed. The world "invalid" described not only the man but his questions.

When the President tried some veiled threats about "sending his people digging for the truth where it hurts", Blender simply did his best to look regretful, as if he'd just realized that it was time to make a clean breast of things, and began to confess the "truth".

"We can teleport machines," he began, "including weapons, especially those made of certain types of plastic. We have had some success with mammals, but only if they're dead. Well, those that weren't dead before teleportation were afterwards. And that was back on the base in Iowa, where we have our biggest teleporter and our most powerful software. So far, we've never tried them on humans, and have no intention of doing so yet."

Blender omitted to mention the ethical problem of replication that would have arisen if human tests had started. No need to complicate things.

"What about that test with a pig?" the President asked.

"A fake. We can't teleport mammals with a machine that size. We brought over some dummy machines and put on a magic show."

"Christ."

"It was convincing, though, Sir, you have to admit." Blender couldn't help smiling. "It was all a smokescreen for our enemies and competitors. They had to see with their own eyes that we're theoretically capable of transporting humans. That way, they're going to divert massive sums from their conventional weapons budgets to try and copy our technology. And we had to lie to you so that you couldn't be accused of lying to the world. I'm very sorry, Sir. But I can assure you that no one else will ever know what has gone on here in England."

"Not even the Brits?" the President asked.

"No, Sir." It was true. He'd told the Prime Minister lots of intimate things recently, but nothing so intimate as the true state of his teleportation work.

"So this techno-crime business was not part of your plan?"

"No, Sir." That was less true.

"But what will happen when the Chinese test that machine they stole?"

"It was a dummy, so the first unfortunate animals or people anyone puts in there will be frazzled."

"Christ. So how come your scientists were so keen to put those prisoners in there?"

"Some knew about the fake test, some didn't. We never had any real intention of letting the human trials go ahead in England."

Blender saw the President trying to figure everything out. He thought that, if it weren't for the pretzels and the bananas, the President probably wouldn't give a damn about all this. There had to be lots of stuff he was never told about, lots of speeches he made without knowing all the background. The thing was not to shove his ignorance in his face, literally or metaphorically. Don't piss him off with newspaper articles and don't humiliate him by beaming savoury snacks up his nose.

"Tell me Max," the President finally asked. "Am I a great man?"

"Wow, Sir," Blender began. "What a question." If you had to ask the question, the answer was obvious. And a man sitting there in some kind of medical lingerie with a comedy nose and a lisp was not the man to ask it, even if Churchill had had two out of three of those.

"It seems to me, Sir," Blender finally ventured, "that there's only one thing that all truly great men have in common. Men like Washington, Einstein, Roddenberry or Churchill, for example."

"What's that?"

"They're all dead."

70. Good News, Bad News

Public interest in the eco-conference was already almost zero, but without its star speaker, it was in danger of fizzling out completely.

The British Prime Minister won worldwide plaudits from the less cynical green groups for her determination to stick it out to the end. Blender promised the President that he, too, would stay on in Bournemouth to make sure all the loose ends were tied up, and to interface with the PM about America's willingness to share its technology. Anglo-American contacts were, he reported, open, frequent and very workmanlike. He hoped they would bear fruit.

Five days later, the politicians finally went away, having

achieved nothing tangible except an increase in Bournemouth's CO_2 levels.

Blender flew to Washington, his team flew to Iowa, and the death-row prisoners went back to prison, their sentences commuted to life imprisonment.

Martin came home from Amsterdam. He had less money than he'd hoped, but was due to go back and earn more very soon. Meantime, he said he wanted to lay low for a while, and went to stay at Param's flat. The young lovers didn't seem to mind much being stuck indoors. They found stuff to do.

Richie alternated between shifts at the hotel and trying to sell his book. He fiddled about with his conclusion, updating the ending with examples of "techno-crime", and trying to give hints about what the Americans were up to without incurring Blender's transatlantic wrath.

Mr Big didn't phone.

Then, one summer Saturday morning, the Prime Minister was on TV in front of 10 Downing Street, waving to cameras and gushing at a barrage of microphones. Her husband stood by her side, looking calm but slightly surprised.

"It's true," the PM said. "I, we," she took her husband's hand, "are proud to announce that we are going to be a mother."

The assembled reporters laughed. One of them called out the obvious question:

"How will this affect your duties as Prime Minister?"

"I really don't know," the PM said. Her spin doctors had told her that it would look good if she appeared slightly overwhelmed by the whole business. "I'll have to see. We might have to cut a semi-circle out of the Cabinet table." She mimed a bulging belly and again she got a big laugh from the reporters. Even the hardened political hacks had to admit she was good. "But you know, there are working mums doing a lot harder jobs than mine. I'm privileged compared to some women out there."

She allowed a moment's empathy to flit across her face and the flashbulbs sparkled, capturing an image that would earn her millions of votes, she was sure of that. The only question was when to call the election. She wouldn't be able to campaign once she got massive. Blotchy elephantine women weren't good election candidates, except perhaps in parts of rural Alabama. Should she wait till the baby was there to look cuddly on the posters? No, better wait till she'd got her figure back so that *she* wouldn't look too cuddly on the posters.

Richie switched off the TV. Clara was at work on the early shift. Her mum was already at the house because Richie was due to start his shift at ten. He called a taxi and went straight to the hotel, leaving the kids playing in the front garden, watched over by their gran. He didn't explain anything to his mother-in-law. He had to go and tell Clara first.

In the taxi, he wondered about calling Martin. No, things had been very peaceful since Martin had been keeping out of his finances.

He left the driver a huge tip and went into reception.

"Can you get Clara for me, please?" he asked the receptionist.

"Well, I think she's –" the girl began to object.

"It's OK, I'll get her," he said. He lifted the flap and walked through.

Clara only just had time to recognize him before he stooped down, planted a kiss on her lips and whispered something in her ear.

She stood up, took Richie's hand and followed him past the receptionist.

"If Neil comes in, tell him I've gone to shout and dance about outside with my husband," Clara told her.

The receptionist watched as Clara and Richie ran down the front steps into the car park and did as promised. They held each other and pogoed around, shrieking with joy. Guests looked out of their windows, and passing drivers slowed down. Everyone smiled to themselves, as people do when they see real happiness. Some wondered if they weren't perhaps relatives of the Prime Minister.

"What shall we do?" Clara asked when she couldn't leap any more.

"I'll go down the bookies first."

"I want to come with you."

So they walked together, carried along by a mild southerly breeze, and Clara felt no pangs of conscience about leaving all the following week's room allocations unchecked. Neil could do them on his own. Pressure and stress seemed to have been beamed away.

They started to discuss what they were going to do with the money, and Clara was full of plans. Richie wasn't so sure that they'd get Mr Big to pay up everything he owed, but he didn't want to dampen her enthusiasm. So he let her fantasize about buying a small hotel in the Seychelles, and fantasized with her, though part of him was only glad that the ten-grand debt had been wiped out, and the status quo returned to him intact.

"Shit, it's shut," they said together when they got to the bookie's shop in the town centre. Richie didn't know whether this was normal practice or because Terry the bookie had been watching the same news report as he had.

"Never mind, I'll come back later," Richie said. With Martin, he decided. Time for him to return some debt-collecting favours.

In any case, he wasn't too disappointed about the shop being shut. If it had been open, he would have had to explain to Clara that most of the bet had been laid off with the town's best-known gangster. That might have worried her a little.

They were just debating what to do next when Richie's phone rang in his pocket.

"Hello? Yes, she's with me. What is it?"

Clara began to feel uneasy. Richie was pulling a strange face, blocking one ear to hear properly. The voice on the other end sounded loud and incoherent. This definitely wasn't Neil using his sarcasm to ask whether Clara was intending to come and drink her coffee before it got cold.

"You sure? Call the police. No, just call the *police*. We're on our way."

Richie rang off, grabbed Clara's hand and strode out into the road in search of a taxi.

"The kids, she's lost the kids," he said.

71. Taxi Driver

There are lots of stories about people who cross the Atlantic to see a sick parent, only to arrive minutes after the parent died. The plane journey must be hell. You look out of the window, willing the clouds to go by faster, willing your parent to die slower. You can't watch the inflight movie, can't read, can't take your mind off the time – it seems to be dawdling for you, speeding for your parent.

Crossing Bournemouth in a taxi is equally stressful sometimes. There are traffic lights, Sunday drivers, pedestrian crossings. You wish you could beam yourself home.

"Fast as you can, please," Richie told the driver. Clara was sitting beside him, every muscle apparently knotted.

"Got your lunch in the microwave or something?" the driver asked.

He looked back in the mirror at Richie and saw that the joke was misplaced.

"Oh, problems?" he asked.

"Yeah. With the kiddies. They've gone missing." It was physically difficult to say.

"Right." The driver swung left down a one-way street and accelerated. Suddenly the clouds were going by much faster.

"Thanks mate," Richie said.

"You live just the other side of the park, then?" the driver asked.

"Yeah."

"OK, we'll cross it, see if they aren't there."

"You can't," Clara said, "they've blocked the road off."

"Don't worry about that."

The taxi sped along a mile of dual carriageway then squealed round a roundabout before hitting the park. At this end there was the football stadium and the field where the circuses set up the big top in summer. There were few cars about, so the driver kept the speed up until he came to where the council had blocked the road by grassing over two or three hundred yards of tarmac to prevent cars doing exactly what the taxi was doing – using the park as a shortcut.

Richie and Clara were scanning the stadium car park and the lawns, looking for wandering kids. It was possible that George and Ella had gone off to the playground for a lark and got lost.

The taxi mounted the kerb, slalomed between two concrete posts and began to skid across the lawns. There were a few boys having a kickabout, and they stopped to watch the taxi as it steered a course only twenty yards or so from them. Richie opened the window and yelled out.

"Oy, lads, you seen a couple of small kids – four and six?"

They shook their heads blankly.

"Let's just get home," Clara said.

The taxi stopped outside the house. Clara ran indoors. Richie got out his phone.

"Martin, it's me."

"Hey, bro, how's it hanging?" He hadn't heard about the Prime Minister, then.

"Not good. It's George and Ella. They've gone missing."

"Shitting hell. Where are you?"

"Home."

"I'll be over straight away."

"Can you look out for them on the main road? Go past Dave's?"

"Sure. Be there in ten minutes."

The front door was open. Inside, the driver was watching, embarrassed, as Clara consoled her weeping mother. Sometimes, being a granny isn't fun.

"They were playing on their own in the front garden," Clara said.

"On their own?" Richie asked.

"Mum had to go for a you-know-what."

"Bloody neighbour's fault," Richie said. He still couldn't bring himself to say "Johnny", not about someone with a murderous dog. "The kids should be able to play out the back."

Granny's crying increased in volume.

"It's not your fault, Mum," Clara said, rubbing the back of her mother's head as if she was a child.

"Police coming?" Richie asked.

"Yeah, Mum called them."

"Martin's on his way. He's going to make sure they're not down on the main road."

"You want me to take one of you round, see if they're not just wandering about the streets here somewhere?" the driver asked. "Meter's off."

"Yeah, good idea," Richie said. "Cheers."

"Can I come in?" Everyone stopped what they were doing (worrying or crying or both) and looked at the new presence in the front room. It was a tall, smartly-dressed muscular man with a shaven head. Michael.

"If you're after money, you can bugger off and tell your boss it's him that owes me now," Richie said.

"No, no, you don't understand." Michael's smile was absurdly out of place. "I've come to put your mind at rest."

"You can, by buggering off out the door again," Richie told him, and turned back to the taxi driver.

"The children are quite all right. There's no need to panic."

Now Michael had everyone's attention. Richie moved threateningly towards him, but Michael was too well trained in martial arts to show fear.

"Mr Biggs left me here to give you the message when you got home. The children are safe, and will be returned in, er, return for a simple guarantee."

Clara gasped.

"I'll give you a guarantee," Richie said. "You won't get out of this house alive until those kids come back here safe."

Michael smiled again. Richie was itching to hit him, but knew he couldn't without endangering the kids. Michael knew he knew, and this made his smile all the wider.

"No, I've got to go and deliver the guarantee in person, and then your children will be returned. Safe and sound."

"Who's Mr Biggs?" Clara wanted to know. "What's this guarantee?"

Michael smiled again. "That's more like it. At least someone here's showing some sense."

"Who's this Biggs?" Clara repeated.

"A guy we've been doing some work for. He bought up part of my bet," Richie said.

"What?" This was all happening too fast for Clara.

"That's right," Michael said. "Mr Biggs took over some of Richie's bet. In a way he's been protecting you all."

God, Richie thought, that smirk of his wants wiping off with someone's fist.

His body language must have given him away, because he noticed that Michael was giving him a tut-tut-don't-be-a-silly-boy look.

"Richie!" Clara screamed.

It was the first forearm smash he'd delivered since his teens. It was the only time he'd hit anything animate since he kicked the haunches of a horse while taking his first (and, he hoped, last) riding lesson in the Forest several summers ago.

He had years of pacifism balled up inside him, and he'd put it all into one blow. Saving his negative energies till he really needed them.

Michael took the forearm on the side of the chin and collapsed like a stack of baked-bean tins.

"Richie, you heard what he said," Clara said.

Richie's body was flooded with adrenalin. He was running on excess testosterone. He stood over the dazed man, waiting for the slightest excuse to hit him again. This was the head of the flock protecting his own.

"Richie, he's got to deliver this guarantee."

Michael moved an arm. Richie grabbed his hand, straightened the arm up and twisted it so that Michael was forced over on to his stomach. Richie put a foot on his neck. He was immobilized.

"No," Richie said. "Mr Big doesn't give a shit about this tosser. He hates people. If it had been a donkey I wouldn't have hit it. But this." He jerked the man's hand and got a satifsying grunt out of him. "Where are my kids?" he asked.

"Dunno."

Richie twisted the arm some more. "I'll break it. Mr Big won't give a fuck. Sorry." He glanced apologetically over at his mother-in-law. He didn't usually say that word in front of her. But she was too busy weeping to care about swear words. He turned his attention back to Michael, renewing his grip on the arm. "He'll just fire you. Not many one-armed bouncers in town, are there?"

The man grimaced and sweated. "You're wrong, he'll –"

"Where are they?" Richie twisted even further, stretching tendons and ligaments to breaking point.

Michael gritted his teeth. "I dunno. He took 'em."

"What's this guarantee then?"

"Listen. If I don't call him, something bad's going to happen."

"Call him, then. Tell him what a wanker you are."

"Richie." Clara was getting scared. Physical violence made her ill. And violence bred violence. She just wanted her kids back. Then *she'd* break Michael's arm.

Richie bent Michael's hand over until the ball of his thumb was almost touching the inside of the wrist. The man's eyes popped. Richie increased the pressure on his neck. He was going to have to do something. If Michael got his energy back, he'd be a dangerous opponent. He'd just been too cocksure when he came in.

"Right," Richie said and braced himself to break the arm.

"No!" Michael yelped. "It's the money. Don't claim the money."

"What?"

"If you don't claim your winnings, it'll all be OK."

"Fucking hell." Choosing between your children and a million pounds is a very easy decision for most sane people. You just don't expect to get the opportunity to choose.

Richie shifted his weight and began to bend the man's arm back. There was a squeal, from both Clara and Michael, but a second later, Michael was flat on his face, with his unbroken arms behind his back and most of Richie's weight crushing his ribcage.

"Clara, can you get some gaffer tape, please."

Clara went into the kitchen.

"And can you sit on his legs?" Richie asked the taxi driver.

The driver nodded and flopped down with unnecessary violence on to Michael's calves.

"Bastard," Michael hissed through gritted teeth.

"Sorry, chum." The driver winked at Clara's mum, who looked as if she was sinking into shock.

Clara returned and they used almost a whole roll of gaffer tape trussing up the bouncer on the floor. His arms behind his back, ankles together. Richie hesitated, then wound a length or two around the man's eyes.

"You're going to have shaven eyebrows, but it's better than a broken arm," Richie told him.

"You'll fucking –" Michael began to make a threat.

Richie put his hand over the man's mouth. "To quote your boss, don't say anything you might regret," he told him. Michael shut up. "And don't think it, either," Richie said. "There's a pitbull out the back, and if I even thought you were considering harming my kids, I'd take you out there and rub raw meat on your goolies."

"Christ." Martin was standing in the doorway. When he recognized Michael, he thought he understood. "Mr Big wants his stake money?" He flicked his eyes at Clara, thinking she might not know about the full extent of the bet.

"No." Richie explained the basics of what had happened since he'd heard about the PM's pregnancy.

"You bastard. Fucking pay up." Martin landed a savage kick on Michael's knee. The man suppressed a groan of pain.

"Leave it, Martin, we've done all that," Richie said. "We've got to get him out of here before the police come."

"Why?" Clara said, aghast. "He can't just kidnap our kids and get away with it."

Richie shook his head. "You don't know Biggs. We've got to sort this out ourselves. The police won't be any use."

"No," Clara said. "We're not bloody gangsters. We get the police on to it."

"I don't think he'll hurt the kids, Clara, we've just got to talk to him." He hoped it was true.

"No, let the police talk to him. In the cells, preferably. Using truncheons."

"You got your car, Martin?" Richie asked.

"Yeah."

"Right, we'll take Michael here over to Mr Big's house. Clara, you stay with your mum and tell the police where we've gone."

"No, we're all staying here," she said.

"Please trust me," Richie said, sensing that time was running out.

Clara looked hard at her husband. His face as slightly flushed, but he was breathing calmly. He looked in control, especially with his human parcel lying gift-wrapped at his feet.

"OK," she said, "but I'm coming with you."

"I'll stay with the lady," the taxi driver offered.

"Brilliant," Richie said. He started to reach for his wallet.

"No, leave it. Get going," the man said.

"Right. You leave us your phone number, OK?" Richie said, starting to lift Michael to his feet. "If I get my winnings you're in for a major tip."

The driver nodded.

"Mum, call Dad. Get him over here," Clara said.

The Espace was double-parked in front of the house.

Richie and Martin lifted Michael into the central row of seats and they left with Martin driving, Clara in the front passenger seat.

Richie sat next to Michael. He nudged him in the ribs.

"What's Biggs's mobile number?"

Michael told him and he dialled.

"Mr Biggs. It's Richie. I want to talk to my kids."

"Where's Michael?"

"He's here. He said I should call you, work things out."

"What do you mean? Put him on."

"He wouldn't be able to hold the phone. His hands are taped up behind his back."

"Useless prick. I told him what to do."

"Let me talk to the kids." Richie kept his voice calm. Clara turned to watch him.

"No, not yet."

"There's some things the police won't overlook, you know."

"Bollocks."

Richie listened to the background noise. "You driving?"

"No."

"Sounds like you're in a car."

"I'm not driving it. Don't want to get pulled over by the police for using a mobile, do I?"

"Are the kids in the car? Where are you taking them?"

"Look, son. You know what I want."

"You want me to choose between my kids and my winnings."

"Yeah. Trouble is, you get your kids back and you'll be free to go round telling everyone I welshed on a bet."

"You mean you can't pay?"

"Who do you know that's got eight hundred fucking grand? I'm not Tom fucking Cruise."

"Fuck the money. Just give me the kids."

Mr Big tutted. "Won't work. People would know I'd welshed."

"I won't tell them, will I? I swear it. On my kids' heads."

"Not good enough."

Richie didn't know what to say. The man had flipped. How could Richie make a believable promise? It was like the man who'd seen too much saying "I promise I won't tell."

"But I thought this was what you wanted? My guarantee?"

"Yeah, but I'm not sure that's enough."

"Look. I don't need your money. I'll have Terry's two hundred grand." Richie said.

"Just get off the fucking phone, will you. I can't think with you jabbering on at me."

"Let me talk to the kids first."

"Look, bugger off and leave me alone, can't you," Mr Big grumbled, as if he was the victim here. He switched off his phone.

Perhaps he'd realized that he'd got himself in too deep, Richie thought. Beating up lowlifes and doing shady deals is one thing. Kidnapping children is another. Especially if you're a single man with lots of photos of your mum on your wall. People have prejudices these days.

Richie hit the red button.

"No!" It was Clara. Her whole body began to tremble.

Richie elbowed Michael. "Where's he taking them?"

"You should have listened to me," Michael said. "Take this tape off me now if you –"

Richie interrupted him by gripping his throat. "Are there child locks on this thing?" he asked Martin.

"Dunno. You want to go for a little spin along the dual carriageway and try them out?"

Richie tightened his grip on the throat. Michael pressed himself back against the seat, but there was no escape. It would be so easy, Richie thought, to carry on pressing, and pressing.

"The sanctuary," Michael hissed.

"Sanctuary?" Richie asked.

"Donkey sanctuary."

Richie let go of his throat.

"Of course," Richie said. "He's taking the kids to see his mum."

72. End of a Career

The sanctuary was out on the edge of the Forest. It was just a few wooden stables on a scruffy smallholding. The Espace pulled into the driveway past a sign saying "Badger Farm Donkey Sanctuary." An arrow and an amateur painter's silhouette of a donkey pointed the way for less literate visitors. Donkeys in search of a home, perhaps.

There was a dark Mercedes parked on a rectangle of tarmac outside a brick bungalow.

They pulled up and jumped out of the car, shutting Michael in. He started to struggle as soon as he was alone, but Richie thought it was too late for him to do any damage now.

Clara was the first to run around the corner of the bungalow towards the stables. She saw a giant standing by the stable door and stopped. She knew who he was immediately. The shabby bulk of the man, the lank hair and sagging eyelids said child abductor.

"Where are my kids?" she yelled. Mr Big ignored her. He looked tired, almost mournful.

Richie and Martin arrived alongside her.

"Come on, Bandit, this is me," Richie said. "Your biggest fan. Don't do this to me. I thought we had a rapport."

"Where are they?" Clara repeated. "George! Ella!" she shouted.

Still Mr Big ignored her. Richie refused to believe the worst.

"Don't forget Ace Bandit was a nasty piece of work. You think it was all faked?" Mr Big asked.

"What have you done to them?" Clara begged him. "Ella! George!"

"You haven't thought this through, Bandit," Richie pleaded. "No one will respect you for stealing kids."

"No, but it'll scare the shit out of them."

"But these are my kids," Richie said.

"I told you, humans are bastards, son. Including me."

Clara sobbed. They were dead, she knew it.

"You wouldn't," Richie said. "Not for money."

"It's not just about money, Richie. That's the problem. That's why I had to do this to you. People would think I've lost it. First that business with the laser wotsits. Then this bet. I'd be screwed. It's all down to how scared people are of you. It happened to Bandit. Now it's happening to Mr Big."

"Hit him, Richie. Kill him!" It was Clara.

But Richie's adrenalin was spent. Violence had seemed worth it when there was something to be achieved. Now ...

Mr Big started to grin. He was looking over Richie's shoulder. Richie turned, and saw Michael hopping along, his feet still bound. He'd clearly been guiding himself by the voices, because now, with everyone silent for a moment, he lost his bearings and crashed into a wall, knocking himself off his feet. Mr Big roared with laughter.

Richie didn't know where he was any more. He'd been beamed to a parallel, schizophrenic, universe. He and Martin looked at each other, and at the chortling kidnapper. They were lost for words or reactions. Not so Clara. She let out a primal yell and ran for Mr Big. When she was two yards from him, she hesitated as if wondering where to hit him, then swerved and rushed past him.

"Come and see the donkeys!"

It couldn't be. Richie looked over and saw Clara running towards Ella, who had come out of the stable and was beckoning to her mum.

"Where's George?" Clara asked, trying to speak calmly so as not to spook the girl.

"He's feeding Rufus."

"George!" Richie shouted as he ran towards the barn. George came out leading Rufus. There was a middle-aged woman in a green padded waistcoat behind him – the owner of the sanctuary – and a bouncer bringing up the rear.

"I fed Rufus, Daddy," George said proudly. "You've got to keep your hand flat, like this." He demonstrated. The woman smiled.

Clara was crouching down, face to face with Ella.

"We thought we'd lost you. Granny's ever so worried." Clara was fighting back the urge to bawl Ella out. How many times had they given her and George the "nasty strangers" talk?

Ella looked guilty.

"You shouldn't have gone anywhere without telling Granny," Richie said.

"But he said he's your friend," Ella said, and started to cry.

Richie turned to look at Mr Big.

"You shouldn't leave kids unattended in a front garden," the big man said. "Dangerous."

"Thanks for the advice." Richie patted Rufus and talked quietly to George, explaining what had gone wrong without scaring the boy too much.

He went and hugged Ella and said it was OK, he knew that she wouldn't do it again. Everything was all right now.

Except that it wasn't. Mr Big was still standing there, dispassionately watching the cosy family scene that he could disturb again any time he wanted, unless something was done.

Richie looked the man in the eye. "OK, here's the deal," he said. "You help us get the two hundred grand off the bookie. We'll forget the rest. And we won't bring charges."

"No," Clara said. "He doesn't get off that easily. I want him put away."

Mr Big puffed an aborted laugh. "She's a pushy lady."

"No, I'm an angry lady." Clara's relief was wearing off and being replaced by a rising fury. She started marching back towards Mr Big.

Martin, who had been strangely silent until now, stepped in.

"Clara." He held up his hands in a peacemaking gesture. There was still big money to be made working for Mr Big.

"And you. This is all your fault," Clara told him, and kept on walking. "You opened Richie's parcel. You took his machine."

"Bought his machine," Martin corrected her.

"Never paid for it," Clara went on. "Got him embroiled in this bet ..."

"Which is going to make him rich," Martin said, and took a step back.

"And which nearly lost him his kids," Clara concluded.

She was standing right in front of Martin now. He moved back again. Or at least his head and torso did. His feet stayed where they were until his centre of gravity caused them to lift off the ground. Clara began to moan and shake her hand. She'd punched Martin as hard as she'd hit anything since taking an axe to those rhododendrons on Brownsea Island. The punch had hurt both of them equally, in different places.

Martin sat on the ground rubbing his left cheekbone.

Mr Big applauded.

"Brilliant," he said. "I can use you at the clubs, breaking up the catfights in the ladies' loos. You'd do better than that prat over there." He pointed over at Michael, who was on his knees, still struggling to right himself.

"I'm not working for you and neither is Richie," Clara said. "The only people you'll have working for you are prison warders." She was flexing her sore hand as if preparing to punch someone else.

Mr Big watched her, the small woman who had screamed at her husband to kill their aggressor and who had punched out Martin, quite a muscular lad despite his small size. She was, it occurred to him, the opposite of his own mother. Saints don't usually defend themselves well. That's why they become saints.

He smiled almost wistfully. "Your kids are lucky. Not everyone has parents who'll fight for them like that."

"And we haven't finished yet," Clara said.

"Yeah. Here's what I'll do, Richie. I'll make sure you get your two hundred grand. But you're going to have to earn the rest."

"No way," Richie said. "I've had my fill of paying off debts."

"But that doesn't solve my problem, Richie. People have got to respect me. And you're going to make them, by working for me."

Stalemate. And a draw wasn't good enough in this bout.

Richie saw that all eyes were upon him. It was like being back in the wrestling ring. The rubber ropes had been replaced by the plank enclosures of the donkey sanctuary. The arena was now a clearing in the woods. The crowd was small, but impatient for action.

Why couldn't Mr Big fuck off with the dogs, the drugs, the debts and all the other things standing between Richie and a peaceful life?

And Clara was usually good at suggesting solutions to their problems – why was she staring at him so expectantly now?

But she was right to stare, he realized. He'd let things get this far. It was up to him to end it.

Richie did have one final card to play, though he hadn't expected to use it under these circumstances.

"OK," he told Mr Big, "there's something different I can do for you."

"What's that?"

"I'll make everyone respect you. Not just here. All over the country."

"How?"

"I'll write your story. Ace Bandit's story."

"Fuck off."

Now it was Clara who thought she'd been beamed to another universe. Instead of attacking or setting the police on this monster, Richie was negotiating a book deal.

"You know how many websites there are on Bandit?" Richie asked. "Hundreds. Half of them with crackpot theories about why you retired."

"What sort of theories?" Bandit asked guardedly.

"Crap theories. You tested positive for cocaine. MI5 ruined you because you wouldn't become a spy. Thatcher wanted to shag you and you turned her down. Your hair was a wig and you were scared it would slip."

"Bollocks!"

"They'd buy the real story," Richie said.

"You tell that story and I'll fucking kill you," Mr Big spat.

"No, times have changed, Bandit. You know you're a gay icon?"

Martin, who was still sitting on the ground, flinched, expecting Mr Big to lash out. But the blow didn't come. Clara saw what was happening. Richie was using the same voice he used on the kids when they were fighting or having a temper tantrum. Soothing, evoking the possibility of better things, better times.

"Bollocks!" the big man said.

"They'd buy the story, I'm telling you."

"No one's ever been interested in the real story, only the rumours and the fucking dirt."

"Times have changed. The real story will blow them away."

"You don't even know the real story. You're just bullshitting."

"I think I do," Richie said, his voice even softer now. From his magazines, from what he'd seen at the house, from some of the rumours on the web, Richie was pretty sure he'd pieced the story together. "A man blackmailed by – who was it – your manager? The promoters?" Richie asked.

"Manager. Cunt." The memory was still raw.

"A top professional sportsman, a *star*, blackmailed by his own manager for being gay. Wasn't the done thing back then. Manager said give me a massive increase in my percentage or you're finished. Threatened to tell the promoters. And they'd have cancelled all your fights, right?"

Mr Big nodded mutely.

"The public might have forced the promoters to back down, but you couldn't take that chance. So, disgusted with the whole business, the whole of mankind, one of the country's biggest sports stars gave up his career so that his mother wouldn't hear the truth about her only son. Your father was already dead by then, wasn't he? But I expect he was pretty homophobic while he was alive."

Mr Big's "huh" suggested that Richie had not exaggerated.

"And you were afraid your mother might be the same."

Mr Big was silent, staring down at his feet.

"It needs to be told," Richie said.

For the first time in his life, Martin thought his brother was a genius. Minutes after they'd been begging for the safety of the kids, Richie was putting his arm around the town's biggest psycho to console him as his shoulders heaved and the tears gushed down his face.

"People are bastards," Bandit sobbed.

"Yeah, but now it's payback time," Richie said. "You can screw the people who screwed you. Blow the whistle on them. We can both get rich. Legally. You keep on doing those transporter drug deals and the Yanks'll come and get you. They're a little bit peeved about what happened to their President, you know. We've all got to stop playing with those machines."

"Hey, wait a minute," Martin said, seeing a large chunk of his future livelihood sinking in an Amsterdam canal.

"You shut your cakehole," Clara told him, miming a kick to his head.

"I don't know," Mr Big was saying through his tears. "How much you reckon we could make?"

"Depends. Look what happened when George Michael and Elton John went public. Careers took off like a bloody space shuttle. Plus you've got the whole reformed gangster angle. People'll love it."

Richie could already see the first red-topped page of the tabloid serialization.

"And there's the donkeys, of course," he said. "George and Elton never had donkeys."

"Don't take the piss." Mr Big was sounding happier already.

"Sorry."

"Mind you – reckon you could get me a guest spot on Animal Hospital?"

"Why did you hit Uncle Martin, Mummy?" Ella asked.

"Because he promised you a present and he never gave you one, did he?"

"No! He didn't!" Ella was shocked. Uncle Martin had broken his promise. "Can I have a donkey?"

"No, I've got a better idea," Clara said. "He could give you that lovely gold chain of his. Couldn't you, Martin?"

"Yeah, yeah," Martin said, getting resignedly to his feet.

Ella bounded up and kissed him.

He smiled, accepting defeat for once. Things hadn't gone too badly considering, he thought. In all the confusion, his IOU to Richie seemed to have been forgotten. So he was coming out of the deal two grand or so in credit. More, if Richie could be persuaded to lend him some of his jackpot.

The Fishers got into the car and drove slowly, safely, home to reassure the waiting police that they weren't needed after all, thank you.

73. Blender Twigs

It was after one a.m. Richie was lying full length on the sofa reading one of his old wrestling mags when someone started tapping on the front-room window with a white mop.

Strange, he thought. Window-cleaners on night shift.

Then he realized what was happening. "Shit." He got up and went to the door to tell Johnny the mop-headed neighbour to stop banging on his window. Why did he always pick such anti-social times for his social calls?

"I didn't want to wake the kids," the neighbour said. "You shouldn't ring the doorbell after ten o'clock."

"You're right, Johnny, but I've seen The Trouble with Tribbles at least five times, and that's enough for me," Richie said, adopting the new policy of perfect frankness.

He'd already told his neighbour that he thought the dog was at least partly to blame for George and Ella's abduction. Johnny had started to cry expressionlessly, and had gone to add two feet of wire to the garden fence. Richie had officially, if not sincerely, forgiven him.

"That's not why I've come. I've got something else to show you."

Richie felt that if the neighbour had been able to express excitement, he would have done so. One of his fists was clenched. The other hand was tugging at the sleeve of his red Captain Picard t-shirt as if it was trying to pull his body away somewhere.

"What is it?" Richie asked. "The Trouble with Tribbles - The Director's Cut? Raiders of the The Lost Tribble?"

"No. It's my birthday and my sister sent me a present. I've just finished setting it up."

This was not the time of day (or night) for guessing games. And Richie had no desire to go and feign enthusiasm for a cardboard cutout of some minor character from Deep Space Nine.

"Sorry, mate, but I'm just not moving unless you tell me what it is."

"It's a teleporter. You were right. They do exist."

"A teleporter? Where did she get it?" Richie couldn't believe this. Soon every home would have one.

"On the internet. It's got loads of stuff you didn't talk about in your book. I thought you might like to see it. Look."

The neighbour opened his fist to reveal a black pen-like object.

"A laser locator," Richie said.

"Yeah. You know about them?" the neighbour asked in his usual matter-of-fact way.

"It came with a laser locator?" Richie asked, pointlessly. Obviously it did, he thought, unless the neighbour's sister had had the same idea as Martin and started blackmailing American scientists.

"Yeah, and other stuff as well. You want to see?"

"There are no dangerous animals in here, are there?" Richie asked as he stepped gingerly inside the house next door. It was symmetrically identical to his own. You stepped left instead of right into the lounge, and the stairs went up the right-hand wall of the house. But the styles of decor couldn't have been more different. Richie's lounge was a carpeted jumble of furniture, toys, magazines and hi-fi equipment, with four remotes (TV, video, DVD, hi-fi) lying on a pile of kids' films at the foot of the television stand. The neighbour's house had scrubbed, uncluttered lino, a black sofa and armchair at perfect right angles, and cases of videos, DVDs and CDs with letters of the alphabet stuck at intervals on the shelves. There was a large TV in front of the fireplace with a VCR and a DVD player underneath it, each remote on top of the relevant piece of equipment. The only decorations on the white walls were a signed photo of a Klingon (an actor presumably) and a soft-focus poster of a "cute" pitbull puppy. The whole place reeked of anal retention.

Standing on a table next to the TV was a teleporter, hooked up to a PC. The machine had the same microwave design as Richie's (or Martin's), but the instruction leaflet had evolved radically. Richie's floppy 16-page booklet had been upgraded into a real cardboard-covered three-colour manual. Richie opened it at the contents page. It even had an FAQ page. FAQ? How frequently had people been asking questions like "what should I do if someone is trying to send me a mouse?", he wondered. And there was a whole section on how to use your laser locator, with a page showing a cross-section of it.

"In my day, we had to teach ourselves how to use these things," he said.

"It's easy," the neighbour said. "Look, I can water my rhodendrons without leaving the house."

"Isn't technology wonderful."

"Beaming water's one of the tests they tell you to do. Watch."

Richie sat on the arm of the sofa and watched as the neighbour went into the kitchen. He returned with a glass of water, opened the door of the teleporter, and poured a small pool of liquid on to the floor of the machine before closing the door again. Then he looked over at Richie and hesitated.

"I'll water the front hedge, so you don't have to get up," he said.

"Cheers."

He pointed his laser locator out into the garden, which was bathed in orange light by a streetlamp. Richie saw the red dot appear on the silhouette of the hedge.

"Now I click on the memory button and the co-ordinates are set. I hit return, and ..." He pushed the key and there was the whirring sound that Richie knew so well. It brought back unhappy memories of veggieburgers, ecstasy and donkeys. "There. Gone." The neighbour had opened the teleporter door and the pool of water had indeed been beamed elsewhere. "Course you'd have to beam water lots of times to water your rhododendrons. And you can't see the water that's on the hedge because it's too dark, but I did it before and ..."

"I believe you," Richie said. "Just don't beam anything over to us, will you? We're trying to give up teleporting."

"There's other stuff as well, look."

"Can't we do this tomorrow, or –?"

"There's a directory of all the teleporters where you can beam stuff to, and this little transmitter that you can –"

"A what? A directory?" Richie went over to the computer. "Show me."

The neighbour clicked on an icon in the shape of an open telephone book and called up the directory's contents page. It offered a click-on alphabet, a list of countries and a simple search.

"May I?" Richie took over at the keyboard and typed "Ri" before stopping. If he was listed, it would open up a whole realm of tedious questioning from the neighbour. He erased the "Ri" and typed "Martin Fisher" into the search box. An instant later, the computer gave him a name, address and a link to the coordinates. This Martin Fisher, though, wasn't in Bournemouth or Amsterdam. He was based in Portland, Oregon. That confirmed it, Richie was still listed. He typed in "Blender". He was simultaneously surprised and not surprised at all when the computer offered him an Iowa address.

"Let's send something," he said. He calculated that it must be about seven or eight in the evening out there.

"Is this a friend of yours?"

"Yeah. He kind of helped me write my book."

"What do you want to send him?"

This was a good question. What should he send Max? He wanted it to be an in-joke. A small pile of Bournemouth sand, maybe? Or a photo of the PM? A bit too personal. Don't want to provoke the man. No, there was a better idea.

"When you beam something, can you send a message with it?" Richie asked. He realized that he personally had never beamed anything during his teleportation career, except for one accidental veggieburger. "You know, like, this grilled mouse comes courtesy of the Acme grilled mouse company or something?"

"You can't send mice."

"No, you know what I mean, though. If you send a present, you want to send a card with it. Can you send it electronically at the same time as you beam stuff?"

"I don't know."

They hunted in the manual and on screen.

Richie now felt wide awake. It took him only a few minutes to find the relevant section on the computer.

"Yes. Here it is. When you OK the coordinates where you're sending to, you have a message box. Great."

The neighbour nodded at the screen. "What do you want to send?"

"Got any bananas?"

The neighbour didn't seem to think this a strange choice of gift, but he said no anyway. "Will an apple do? Or I've got some tinned peaches."

"Don't suppose you've got any pretzels?"

"What are they?"

Another good question. How do you explain a pretzel? "They're brown and shiny. Some are curly, and – "

"Like dog turds?"

"Yeah, but you eat them. And some are long. Pretzel sticks. They're salty. About this long." Richie held up his two forefingers four inches apart.

The neighbour stared blankly at them.

"They're snacks, like thin bread sticks –" Richie said.

"Twiglets?"

"Yes. Yes, brilliant. Twiglets. English pretzels." Richie laughed. "You got any Twiglets?"

"Yeah."

"Can I have two?"

The neighbour went into the kitchen on his Twiglet errand. Richie opened Blender's page in the directory again, clicked on his coordinates, and typed his message in the box.

When his new assistant returned, Richie arranged the Twiglets in the machine at a roughly nostril-entry angle, and hit return. The machine whirred again, and a few seconds later the computer played a celebratory chord and flashed a smiley to acknowledge the fact that Blender's teleporter had received the two pretzel-style snacks and the message: "Yes, we have no bananas. RF."

"I've got some beer," the neighbour said. "You want some? To drink, not to teleport."

Richie didn't usually start his drinking at two a.m., but this sounded like a good idea.

"Yeah. Why don't we watch a video?" he said.

James T Kirk was just realizing the potential threat posed by the furry little Tribbles when the computer screen flashed and said "uh-oh". They put the Tribbles' reproduction on temporary hold and went to look.

On screen was a "recipient message". It said: "I tried these when I was in England. But I didn't inhale. MB."

74. The Beginning

It took a few months, but they got everything sorted. The Fishers were on their island, near a clean beach and a good school, a few minutes' boat ride from some chic shopping opportunities.

The two hundred thousand pounds were in the bank. They still couldn't believe it – they had *two hundred grand* in interest-earning cash. Terry the bookie had been persuaded not to deduct betting tax. The only dent in their treasure chest was a little "loan" to Martin that Richie never expected to see again.

The house was rented out and paying off its own mortgage. They'd met a lot of prospective tenants, and finally found the ideal one. He was a DJ with a very large, sleek black van, and two only slightly smaller and less sleek black Rottweilers. Clara said it was cruel to Johnny the neighbour – his dog was always chained up now. Richie said, bollocks, if he likes big dogs he can have them, and there was no way they could rent the house to a family – too dangerous for the kids. In the end, Clara gave in, but only on the condition that the tenant returfed the gardens when he left the house. Rottweiler poop was not her idea of the ideal lawn food.

Martin confessed that he had set Richie up for the bet that night, to cover a poker debt to Terry. He'd heard that the Prime Minister's husband was gay, and persuaded Terry that the ten grand was as good as in the bank. Martin being Martin, he didn't worry about what would happen to Richie if he lost, or how mad Terry would be if Richie won. That was the future, that was tomorrow's problem. Richie was the futurologist, not Martin.

Just as he'd always done, Richie forgave his brother. But only because he feared for Martin's life if Clara got wind of the story.

Terry, of course, was somewhat miffed about losing, especially because he'd been forced to sell his BMW. He was not consoled by Martin's comment that he wouldn't miss the car because he wasn't allowed to drive it anyway.

Martin used Richie's loan to pay off the tax people, and spent the money he'd brought back from Amsterdam on some new stock. This was the security equipment he'd talked about – everything from mace sprays, mugger alarms, tazers and graffiti-proof paint to hidden cameras and privacy software.

He also acquired a large consignment of "jammer watches". These were brand-new gadgets that created anti-molecular force fields and blocked the signals from teleporter machines. They were selling very well. He was finding it much more profitable to help people to protect themselves than he had trying to cheat them. People's fear of crime seemed to pay better than the crimes themselves – at Martin's level, anyway.

He lost his driving licence in the court case involving his crashed car, but he now had a new business partner who could drive him about, and who was still helping him to discover new varieties of curry.

Things were less peaceful over on the other side of the Atlantic. As soon as the President got out of his hospital bed, he started yelling for revenge on every non-American teleporter. The CIA were immediately diverted from burning coca plants in South America to hunting down the sources of unlicensed teleportation beams throughout the world. It was only thanks to Blender's fondness for the Fisher family that no one ever traced the machine that had attacked the President.

Neither did the American security services ever find the enlarged teleporter that had been stolen from the Bournemouth airbase, despite leads that sent them jetting to various ports, truckstops, airports and storage yards all over the world. This was because Blender's team of "thieves" had dropped it from a plane into mid-Atlantic on the day it disappeared, to avoid anyone getting too close a look at it.

Jeb Hamlet got an uncomfortable debriefing from some CIA men who as good as accused him of being Chinese.

Blender had to lose three rounds of golf before he persuaded the President to leave his star researcher alone.

The other scientists, believing their project in disgrace, had resigned themselves to disappearing back to their universities and research institutes. Except Johnson, who was preparing himself for prison.

However, Blender told Hamlet and the others that they knew too much to be left in peace like that. So their salaries were doubled and everyone was told what had really been going on in Bournemouth, or a less edited version of it.

The banana and pretzels had convinced the President to rubber-stamp a massive budget for teleportation research that would keep the USA ahead of the pack. So Hamlet and the other scientists found themselves on a plane back to Iowa, a long way from the dangerous pubs of Bournemouth. There, they were introduced to a new team of Australian scientists whom Blender had recruited to work on photon torpedoes. By the entrance to the photon research lab was a sign saying "This way to the 23rd century". Competition was in the air.

To limit the risk of leaks, Blender announced that from now on all official communications were to be made in Klingon. He gave instructions to his young Brooklyn-based team to develop a code along the lines of an encryption system used by the US Marines in World War Two. The Marines' code was never cracked because it depended on a knowledge of colloquial Navajo. The only difficulty was that the Native-American Marines who wrote that code had to invent words to describe things that weren't part of their traditional culture – you don't get many submarines in the Arizona desert, for example. We have an advantage over Navajo, Blender said – Klingon already contains the words for photon torpedoes and teleportation.

Strangely, some months after the teleportation team's return to Iowa, a local farm worker claimed to have seen two warthogs suddenly materialize by the highway and go careering off, bucking like rodeo horses, into the trees. The FBI declined to comment, even when it was reported that the body of a soldier had been found nearby, having apparently been gored to death by a hooved, tusked animal.

A Bournemouth publishing house called Sea-Fi Sci-Fi was surprised to see that sales of one of its more obscure titles inexplicably began to take off. Amongst the buyers was Richie Fisher, who was considering adding a number twenty-one to his Top Twenty in honour of the author of "The Killer Warthogs of Iowa". The man was clearly a visionary.

Richie was still trying to sell his science book. He was thinking of including a batch of blank pages at the end for people to fill in the teleportation updates. The trouble with writing a science book was that science seemed to be evolving too fast for the printed page to keep up.

He was also getting ahead with his second book. Every so often he went and sat with Bandit and asked him questions. On Richie's advice, Mr Big was steering clear of drug deals, and had refocussed his business on safer activities such as the supply of dodgy cars. He and Michael were now living openly as a couple, much to the distaste of their neighbours. When Richie went to the house to talk about the book, Michael was civil enough, despite the fact that his eyebrows were now unpleasantly gappy.

Rufus, who was living full time out at the sanctuary, was not replaced. Richie's interpretation of this was that Mr Big had finally come to terms with the fact that his mother was dead. Or that Michael had refused to go on nurse-maiding aging donkeys.

And the Fishers' island retreat? The Caribbean, The Seychelles, Polynesia, they'd considered them all and settled for Poole Harbour. Clara had got the job of managing the tourist facilities at the nature reserve on Brownsea Island, where she used to go rhodie-bashing. It was something she still enjoyed doing at weekends. She hadn't been sad to see the back of her hotel. She'd even let Neil the manager take his turn at giving her a goodbye hug. It was all he was getting.

The children went to the island's tiny school and spent every free moment dashing about in the fresh air. Ella learned to swim and sail in the calmer corners of the huge natural harbour. George regressed a few million years and began climbing trees like an apeman. A dangerous dog, a speeding commuter or a deranged gangster would have had to brave the currents of the ten-fathom sea channel to get at them.

The Fishers were happy on their island. They invited friends over to stay. When they missed the town they went back to Bournemouth. They always wore their jammer watches just in case. You never knew what was going to materialize where these days. They didn't beam themselves to town, of course, because the technology didn't yet exist. But they had no ambition to do so, anyway. The boat was much more fun.

Richie even consented to join Clara in the occasional shoe shop. And he found the experience much less painful than it had been in New York. That was the best thing about the island, he thought. It was much too muddy for posh shoes.

As for the Prime Minister, she was looking increasingly pregnant, and her support in the polls was growing in exact proportion to her tummy. Her husband was content that his physical services would no longer be called upon, and that his share of the deal to publish the maternity-hospital photos was worth several years' salary.

The growing baby's real father watched its progress on TV from the USA, and got a running commentary about the horrors of pregnancy from the mother via a secure (very secure) phone line.

He gave the PM one more term of office. Then she'd get fed up with politics and he'd go over there and ask her to divorce. He was going to build a house on his plot of land in Riverside. Thanks to the influx of scientists in the area, the town was on the up. It'd be a good place to raise a kid. And the father had high hopes for the child. A world leader and a top scientist would give him or her an excellent genetic start in life. Could be the start of something special.

The bookies, Terry included, were taking heavy bets on the sex and name of the baby. Amongst the possible boys' names, alongside the obvious ones like William and Harry, was a surprise candidate. A mystery punter had placed a large bet on the unlikely name of Maxwell. He'd got odds of 100-1. This time, he'd placed the bet with one of the national chains of bookmakers, and he'd told his wife about it first.

Richie had high hopes of winning because he'd got inside information. In return, he'd promised to invest a share of his winnings in a research lab in California that was working on warp drive engines.

Why is teleportation technology advancing so quickly?

Basically, it's because the kids who grew up on the original Star Trek are now in positions of power and influence. They want to make the world as much like Star Trek as possible.

No, they want to make Star Trek come true.

And they have the money and political connections to make it happen.

A Brief History of the Future, chapter 1 (extract)

END

Also available from Red Garage Books

WHO KILLED BEANO?
A genetically-modified murder mystery
by Chris Kent

Coma is a company that is doing sterling work privatizing the poor old NHS. Coma will find you organs ("For sale: human kidney, one careful owner"). They'll find you a surgeon (he won't speak English, but you'll be under anaesthetic so you won't notice). And now, as a deadly flu-like virus marches westwards from Asia, the government needs Coma's help …

The politicians have to act fast if they are to protect their populations, and line their pockets by making deals with the pharmaceuticals multinational that has developed a vaccine against the bug. The British government leaps into action via the shady "Ministry of Development".

Unfortunately for Britain and the world, the man at the Ministry makes a fatal error – he gives the key role in the anti-virus campaign to Coma's Bernie Bridges, the, er, hero of this comedy thriller.

Coincidentally (or maybe not), the call from the government comes at exactly the same time as Bernie's colleagues and rivals start to get killed.

Bernie turns for support (and, he hopes, sex) to Claudine, a French supermodel clad in the shortest leather miniskirt known to man. But he obviously didn't listen during biology lessons at school. What was that about the black widow spider?

"A female Ben Elton."

Tragically, Chris Kent herself was killed shortly after completing this, her first and only novel.

Read a short excerpt from the novel on page 313 of this book.

Who Killed Beano? ISBN 2-9521638-2-0
Read more, and order the book, in paper or electronic form, on our website at **www.redgaragebooks.com**

Also available from Red Garage Books

A YEAR IN THE MERDE
The antidote to "A Year in Provence"
by Paul West

"There are lots of French people who are *not at all* hypocritical, inefficient, treacherous, intolerant, adulterous or incredibly sexy. They just didn't make it into this book …"

Paul West describes the French as they really are.

They're not "cheese-eating surrender monkeys", but they do eat a lot of cheese, some of which smells like pigs' droppings. In general, they do not wash their armpits with garlic soap. Going on strike really is the second most popular participation sport in France after pétanque. And they really do use suppositories.

An "almost true" autobiography in which young Englishman Paul West gives a laugh-out-loud account of the pleasures and perils of being a Brit in France. Less quaint than *A Year in Provence*, less chocolatey than *Chocolat*, this book will tell you how to get the best of the grumpiest Parisian waiter, how to make perfect vinaigrette every time, and how *not* to buy a house in the French countryside.

A few of the chapter headings …

God save the cuisine
Liberté, égalité, get out of my way
Make amour, not war
The joy of suppositories

Read a short excerpt from the novel on page 319 of this book.

A Year in the Merde, ISBN 2-9521638-1-2

Read more, and order the book, in paper or electronic form, on our website at **www.redgaragebooks.com**

WHO KILLED BEANO?

A genetically-modified murder mystery

by Chris Kent

A taster ...

1. COMA?

I have Beano's keys, so I let myself into his building and tiptoed up the stairs to his front door. I was going to go straight in, but somehow the idea of sneaking into his bedroom and waking him up seemed too sexual. Can a man wake his best friend up without it having some kind of homoerotic threat element? I don't know.

I rang his doorbell for about two minutes solid, then stopped to listen.

Beano's antennae were retracted deep this morning. There was no tumble from the bed, no slashing back of the curtains, no obscenities through the door.

I rang again – sixty seconds, timed by my new watch, accurate to within a millionth of a second per light year or whatever. It cost about the same as a small four-wheel-drive car, but you've got to treat yourself occasionally.

Nothing, except a few predictable complaints about noise pollution from the ground-floor neighbour. Well, it was before seven on a Monday morning. And Beano's bell is very loud. More of a heavy-metal bell solo than a polite dingdong. And if he didn't react to a whole minute of that racket, there was nothing for it but to go in.

The intruder alarm was off, which was no surprise: carefree

Beano often forgets to switch it on. Especially when he's unconscious.

The apartment smelt like an alligator's larder, but then Beano is something of an alligator, always dragging things down, leaving them to fester then coming back for another chew. It means his refrigerator is always disgusting and his ideas wonderfully twisted, like a well-aimed punch in the kidneys. When I first met him, he'd just set up a website called "Horrorburgers". This was a load of gross facts about what goes into fast food. It was back in the days when people thought dotcommers were digging a goldmine rather than a bottomless pit, and he made a fortune from the out-of-court agreement to shut the site down. Well, it seemed like a fortune then. Nothing compared to what we're all going to get now.

I trampled on a laptop, I kicked DVDs off a pile of plates, I scattered a few quarter-full coffee cups but made it to the window without collapsing in the stinking chaos on the bedroom floor. No Beano. I opened the window and took a few bodyfuls of air before trying for the bathroom. After one of his weekend benders he often spends a day or two in a coma on his bathroom floor. It's cool, white, and easy for someone else to mop.

At last, there he was. Surrounded by dried pools of unmarketable colours – dishwasher-outflow grey, run-over-squirrel's-innards purple, past-sell-by-date-mozzarella green. His blond head under the sink, a crust of gunk on his chin, there was Beano, in crumpled sweatshirt and stained white shorts.

"Beano, it's Bernie, come to scoop you up!"

Nothing.

"Beano, you rich bastard, on your feet!"

I nudged him. His lips dribbled apart. I just got the bathroom window open in time.

I once saw a French movie called *Madame Bovary*. She really was quite a Madame. A doctor's wife in the 1800s who drinks a corrosive poison that takes ages to burn her entrails out and kill her. There was more to it – a botched operation, sex in a horse-drawn carriage – but that's what stuck in my mind. Black vomit. This, apparently, is what the French were into before they invented Chanel handbags.

Anyway, I used Madame's death-bed scene on my "See Models Die" website. The site is (honestly) not as gross as its name suggests. You click – gently – on the model's face and suddenly you're standing at the foot of a brass bed. You see a naked-shouldered girl, asleep – dark swept-back hair, dark lips, long body under the white silken sheet. Then you swoop down and hover along the beautiful bumps of her, and just as you reach her face, she grunts awake and her lips start oozing black gunk and she dies. Caption: "Sulphuric acid – for Christ's sake don't drink it."

OK, it is a bit sick, but I was a student at the time. And the site was for medical students, who tended to have a pretty high morbidity threshold. After all, what other degree course involves hacking dead human bodies about? None. Except maybe contemporary art.

It was one of the first websites I put together, and even though it hasn't been updated for years I still get e-mails asking for details (phone number, availability for stalkers, etc) about the "dying" model. Her name is Claudine – she's French – ten feet tall, perfect skin, like a Lara Croft that didn't need to be surgically or digitally enhanced. Yes, Claudine's 100% organic.

And soon I guess she won't belong to me any more, because somebody wants to buy all our company shares. Don't ask me *why* they want to buy us out. Perhaps they're just too lazy to set up a business themselves.

And talking of laziness, what about Beano? He should be up by now, and yelling at me for kicking him when he's down. Beano, my inspiration. The Claudine scene was inspired by a movie, yes, but mainly by Beano's Monday-morning dribbles.

His bathroom was no worse than usual. Except that this time Beano turned out to be dead. As in not breathing. With two wicked blue bruises on his bloated gullet. I touched his temple – he was still warm, hot even, clammy from the fight, yet somehow cold. His eyeballs were puffed out like great poisonous mushrooms. The killer was probably in the kitchen getting a cool drink after the exertion.

I parked my breakfast on the floor and ran. I got down the stairs as silently as an exploding bottle bank. Beano's ground-floor neighbour jumped out of her apartment wielding a fat-encrusted frying pan at me. I tried to explain, but it only convinced her to take a terrified swing at my head. I ducked, belly-flopped across the hall, and finally managed to crawl to my car while the deranged neighbour woke the whole street, shrieking for someone, anyone, to save her from this dawn killer with a penchant for noise pollution.

In the old-fashioned world I might have been failing to get away unnoticed.

*
* *

For sale: VACCINES. Flu, smallpox, anthrax, all varieties of plague. Others on request. Fast delivery for batches from ten to ten million. *Vaccines guaranteed to be latest strains.*

For sale: one KIDNEY, blood type O+, hardly used, one careful owner. US$20,000 ono.
Buyer collects.

*
* *

2. QUESTIONS, QUESTIONS

Pigeon instinct took me straight to Coma, the office. In normal times, a labyrinth of bright corridors, revealing at every corner its clusters of screens and its wide-angle views across the bay.

I stumbled through the doors and collapsed on the first chair I saw.

If you didn't know us, you'd probably never guess what went on here. Headhunting? PR? International arms sales?

No, we're tapping into the motherlode of modern life (I hope): health.

We're a double-edged sword of a company. First, there's the doctors' internet service provider. The docs get free e-mail, they can set up their own websites, give on-line advice about embarrassing diseases, receive truckloads of freebies from the drug companies, advertise their skills at tummy-tucking and liposucking, all sorts of stuff.

That's been ticking over nicely for a while now, so we've gone international. Our advertising blurb says we've invented a new economic sector. We are, amongst other things, doctors' agents. An Argentinian footballer arriving in England needs help negotiating his multi-million-pound transfer fee. So does a Bulgarian doctor. If a hospital has a ten-year waiting list for cataract operations, we'll find them a specialist within 24 hours. He or she might not speak English, but the patients will all be unconscious, so a capacity for chit-chat is not a priority, right?

And it works both ways of course. There's a huge market for foreign hospitals selling their services to Brits who are browned off with being on waiting lists. You type in your illness on our search engine, we'll find you the cheapest, fastest treatment deal. I guess we're a sort of e-sickBay.

… Read more, and order the book, in paper or electronic form, on our website at **www.redgaragebooks.com**

A YEAR IN THE MERDE
The antidote to A Year in Provence

by Paul West

A taster ...

Septembre
Never the deux shall meet

The year does not begin in January. Every French person knows that. Only awkward English-speakers think it starts in January.

The year really begins on the first Monday of September.

This is when Parisians get back to their desks after their month-long holiday and begin working out where they'll go for the mid-term break in November.

It's also when every French project, from a new hairdo to a nuclear power station, gets under way, which is why, at 9am on the first Monday of September, I was standing a hundred yards from the Champs-Élysées watching people kissing.

My good friend Chris told me not to come to France. Great lifestyle, he said, great food, and totally un-politically correct women with great underwear.

But, he warned me, the French are hell to live with. He worked in the London office of a French bank for three years.

"They made all us Brits redundant the day after the French football team got knocked out of the World Cup. No way was that a coincidence," he told me.

His theory was that the French are like the woman scorned. Back in 1940 they tried to tell us they loved us, but we just laughed at their accents and their big-nosed Général de Gaulle, and ever since we've done nothing but poison them with our disgusting food and try to wipe the French language off the face of the Earth. That's why they built refugee camps yards from the Eurotunnel entrance and refuse to eat our beef years after it was declared safe. It's permanent payback time, he said. Don't go there.

Sorry, I told him, I've got to go and check out that underwear.

Normally, I suppose you would be heading for disaster if the main motivation for your job mobility was the local lingerie, but my one-year contract started very promisingly.

I found my new employer's offices – a grand-looking 19th-century building sculpted out of milky-gold stone – and walked straight into an orgy.

There were people kissing while waiting for the lift. People kissing in front of a drinks machine. Even the receptionist was leaning across her counter to smooch with someone – a woman, too – who'd entered the building just ahead of me.

Wow, I thought, if there's ever a serious epidemic of facial herpes, they'll have to get condoms for their heads.

Of course I knew the French went in for cheek-kissing, but not on this scale. I wondered if it wasn't company policy to get a neckload of Ecstasy before coming into work on a Monday.

I edged closer to the reception desk where the two women had stopped kissing and were now exchanging news. The company obviously didn't believe in glamorous front-office girls, because the receptionist had a masculine face that seemed much more suited to scowling than smiling. She was complaining about something I didn't understand.

I beamed my keenest new-boy smile at her. No acknowledgement. I stood in the "yes, I'm here and I wouldn't mind being asked the purpose of my visit" zone for a full minute. Zilch. So I stepped forward and spouted out the password I'd memorized: "bonjour, je suis Paul West. Je viens voir Monsieur Martin."

The two women gabbled on about having "déjeuner", which I knew was lunch, and they made at least half-a-dozen I'll-phone-you gestures before the receptionist finally turned to me.

"Monsieur?" No apology. They might kiss each other, but I could kiss off.

I repeated my password. Or tried to.

"Bonjour, je ..." No, my head was full of suppressed anger and linguistic spaghetti. "Paul West," I said. "Monsieur Martin." Who needs verbs? I managed another willing smile.

The receptionist – name badge: Marianne, personality: Hannibal Lecter – tutted in reply. I could almost hear her thinking, "Can't speak any French. Probably thinks De Gaulle had a big nose. Bastard."

"I'll call his assistant," she said, probably. She picked up the phone and punched in a number, all the while giving me a tip-to-toe inspection as if she didn't think I was of the required standard to meet the boss.

Do I really look that bad?, I wondered. I'd made an effort to be as chic as a Brit in Paris should be. My best grey-black Paul Smith suit (my only Paul Smith suit). A shirt so white that it looked as if it'd been made from silk worms fed on bleach, and an electrically zingy Hermès tie that could have powered the whole Paris metro if I'd plugged it in. I'd even worn my black silk boxers to give my self-esteem an invisible boost. French women aren't the only ones who can do underwear.

No way did I deserve such a withering look, especially not in comparison to most of the people I'd seen entering the building – guys looking like Dilbert, women in drab catalogue skirts, lots of excessively comfortable shoes.

"Christine? J'ai un Monsieur – ?" Marianne the receptionist squinted over at me.

This was my cue to do something, but what?

"Votre nom?" Marianne asked, rolling her eyes upwards and turning the last word into a huff of despair at my slug-like stupidity.

"Paul West."

"Pol Wess," Marianne said, "a visitor for Monsieur Martin." She hung up. "Sit over there," she said in slow, talking-to-Alzheimer-sufferer French.

The boss evidently kept the glamorous ones in his office, because Christine, the assistant who took me up to the fifth floor, was a tall brunette with poise and a dark-lipped smile that would have melted a man's trousers at twenty paces. I was standing mere inches away from her in the lift, looking deep down into her eyes, breathing in her perfume. Slightly cinnamon. She smelt edible.

It was one of those occasions when you think, come on lift, conk out now. Get jammed between two floors. I've had a pee, I can take the wait. Just give me an hour or two to work my charm with a captive audience.

Trouble is, I would have had to teach her English first. When I tried to chat her up, she just smiled stunningly and apologized in French for not understanding a bloody word. Still, here at least was one Parisienne who didn't seem to hate me.

We emerged in a corridor that was like a collision between a gothic mansion and a double-glazing lorry. A long oriental-looking carpet covered all but the narrow margins of creaky, polished floorboards. The ceiling and walls of the corridor were decorated with great swirls of antique moulded plasterwork, but the original doors had been ripped off their hinges and replaced with 70s-style tinted glass. As if to cover up the clash of styles, the corridor was lined with enough green-leaved plants to host a jungle war.

Christine knocked on a glass door and a male voice called "Entrez!"

I went in and there he was, set against a background of the Eiffel Tower poking its finger into the cloudy sky.

My new boss stood up and walked around his desk to greet me.

"Monsieur Martin," I said, holding out a hand for him to shake. "Pleased to see you again."

"You must call me Jean-Marie," he replied in his slightly

accented but excellent English. He took my hand and used it to pull me so close I thought we were about to do the cheek-rubbing thing. But no, he only wanted to pat my shoulder. "Welcome to France," he said.

Bloody hell, I thought. Now two of them like me.

... Read more, and order the book, in paper or electronic form, on our website at **www.redgaragebooks.com**

accented but excellent English. He took my hand and used it to pull me so close I thought we were about to do the cheek-rubbing thing. But no, he only wanted to pat my shoulder. "Welcome to France," he said.

Bloody hell, I thought. Now two of them like me.

… Read more, and order the book, in paper or electronic form, on our website at **www.redgaragebooks.com**

RED GARAGE BOOKS

The word was that since Harry Potter and Bridget Jones, people were reading books again.

But a lot of publishers didn't seem to understand why Harry and Bridget were so popular. Instead of looking for rollicking good stories, they were opting for celeb autobiographies, politicians' diaries and children's books written by people too famous to change their own kids' nappies.

Meanwhile, new novelists had to be cute, hip and preferably under 21.

We thought that some readers might still be more interested in novelists' words than their publicity photos. So we started looking round for good stories, without asking for authors' mugshots.

We chose three novels and decided to publish them immediately.

They're all comedies, because the world needs a laugh. But they're comedies with a message, rollicking good stories that will make readers laugh, think, and want to read more.

We don't want readers to lose faith in novels because of all the media-driven word candy taking up so much space on booksellers' shelves.

We're small, we don't have massive marketing budgets, and our authors aren't famous enough to create publicity by dating a pop star. We'd ask them to trash a restaurant or two, but we can't afford the insurance.

We'd like people to buy the stories because they're good stories.

Pathetically naive, we know.

On pages 313 and 319 of this book you'll find excerpts from the other two novels we're publishing. Please give them a quick read.

For more info, and to order books in paper or downloadable form, go to our website at **www.redgaragebooks.com**